WOMEN'S W

How mothers manage fl
in careers and family life

Zoe Young

BRISTOL
UNIVERSITY
PRESS

First published in Great Britain in 2018 by

Bristol University Press
1-9 Old Park Hill
Bristol
BS2 8BB
UK
t: +44 (0)117 954 5940
www.bristoluniversitypress.co.uk

North America office:
c/o The University of Chicago Press
1427 East 60th Street
Chicago, IL 60637, USA
t: +1 773 702 7700
f: +1 773-702-9756
sales@press.uchicago.edu
www.press.uchicago.edu

British Library Cataloguing in Publication Data
A catalogue record for this book is available from the British Library

Library of Congress Cataloging-in-Publication Data
A catalog record for this book has been requested

ISBN 978-1-5292-0203-8 paperback
ISBN 978-1-5292-0202-1 hardcover
ISBN 978-1-5292-0206-9 ePub
ISBN 978-1-5292-0207-6 Mobi
ISBN 978-1-5292-0204-5 ePdf

Cover design by blu inc, Bristol
Front cover image: istock
Printed and bound in Great Britain by CMP, Poole
Bristol University Press uses environmentally responsible print partners

For Kevin, Freddie and Maisie. Thank
you for our own stresses and successes.
This is for you with all my love.

Contents

Preface

The preface to my yellowing and rather fragile copy of Ann Oakley's (1974) text *Housewife* opens with a punchy statement:

> First of all this is a book about *women*. It is not a book about marriage or the family, and it does not aim to look at the situations of men and women equally …

When Oakley wrote *Housewife*, women's lives and labours had traditionally received very little sociological or historical attention. She wanted to redress the balance and give scholarly focus to women's unpaid labour in the home. Oakley was writing in the 1970s, the decade of my birth, and at that time the feminine ideal that women seek fulfilment through heterosexual marriage, motherhood and housewifery dominated modern industrialised societies. Men worked. Housework was not considered work and therefore was largely invisible. Today few women would describe their primary occupation as housewife. Although the job title might have changed, plenty of evidence points to stubborn resistances to the housewife role being anything other than feminised, private and undervalued. Women today work inside *and* outside the home, as indeed they have throughout history. We just study them a little more and talk about them a lot more today.

Inspired by Oakley this too is a book about women, women who are mothers *and* professionals in the second decade of the 21st century. Women who work. Women's work. The research that informs it draws on the lives and experiences of 30 women who might be referred to as 'working mothers' or 'career women'. Just as the housewife moniker feels a little dated today, the alternative descriptors for the lives and experiences in focus in this book feel almost as awkward and ill-fitting. 'Working mothers' manages to dissociate paid work from the significant domestic, emotional, mental and physical work of motherhood; 'career women' somehow narrows women's multiple identifications and minimises the maternal. I have settled on **professional mothers** to refer, not to women's approaches to their mothering, but to their dual roles and to their occupational positioning. All these labels sound a bit odd because it would not occur to us to differentiate categories of men in the same way and talk about 'career men', 'working fathers' or 'professional fathers'. The clunky discourse serves to highlight the enduring inequalities.

This is not a personal book in the autobiographical sense, but the research that informs it formed out of my own experience and from conversations with other women: conversations with colleagues in snatched moments in the office and with other mothers at the school gates. On rare and warmly welcomed evenings out with friends we would chronicle our personal quests for work–life balance and the ups and the downs of putting our lives and selves together as mothers, as partners, as daughters and sisters, *and* professionals. As well as supporting each other we were forming, informing and justifying our own approaches through our talk. Women worry about being good enough as workers and as mothers. My hope is that this book and the insight it gives into other women's lives offers some context and perspective to those concerns.

Work–life balance, and flexible working as means to achieve it, were not around when Oakley was researching and writing about housewives. The experience shared by the mothers in focus in this book is their move into part-time work, into job-shares, to compress and adjust their schedules, and to work from home and other places. These are ways of doing and being both a professional and a mother. To look at the freedoms women have to choose the way they combine motherhood with professional work implies a necessary focus on gender, on power and on equality both inside the family and inside the workplace. In sociological terms this is a study of social change viewed from the 'inside out' by studying individuals *in* change through a year in their lives and from their point of view.

Today more and more women and men work flexibly in a range of ways, so why do I focus on mothers? Because it is overwhelmingly women who continue to be positioned as responsible for children and family care, and who achieve different, less advantageous labour market outcomes because of it. Mothers of young children dominate part-time work, which tends to be clustered at the lower, less well-rewarded occupational levels, and women are missing in representative numbers from the top well-paid tiers of organisational and political life. These are urgent social and economic problems in search of solutions that must not rely on the effort of women alone.

Thirty women who shared their stories with me made this study. It was a pleasure to meet you and I am indebted to you all for giving your precious time over such a long time and for being so open about your experiences. Grateful thanks go to Tamsin Hinton-Smith and Lizzie Seal for guidance and supervision of the PhD thesis upon which this book is based. Kate Conway and Catherine Wolthuizen provided vital friendship during the sleep-deprived buggy-pushing years, when

I formed the idea that I might do this research. Thank you to Uzma Hamid-Dizier for experimenting with job-sharing, and to Melanie Richards for opening doors for me to take this research into industry. Grateful thanks to Jill Armstrong, Katherine Rake and Sarah Richards for reading and commenting on various drafts of this work, and to you all for cheering me on! Huge and heartfelt thanks to Holly Fitch on whom I depended to love and care for my children while I researched and wrote about how other women love and care for their children and do their work.

I promised my father that I would turn my research into a book. He didn't live to see it in print, but here it is Dad, wherever you are.

My mother, Jill Young, continues to support my own work–life combinations in all sorts of ways. Your support gave me the courage to make the leap into a new career and the energy to sustain it this far. Lots of love and thanks.

Zoe Young
March 2018

Women in the Middle

Emma's story

Emma progressed quickly during the first ten years of her career, faster than her husband had in the same profession, but right now she feels that her career has plateaued and his is taking off. They both work full-time and always have. They have three children aged 2, 6 and 8 and depend on a combination of school, after-school clubs, a nursery and her recently retired mother's support to make time available for their work. Emma is about to cut her paid working hours and work from home a little more, and it is this employment adjustment that is the focus of the research explored in this book. Emma talks about why she is transitioning to a flexible working arrangement, and what she sees as having influenced her decision. She talks about how her role in the family and her relationship with her husband influence her career opportunities and choices, and what it feels like to combine a professional job with motherhood on a daily basis. Extracts from the first of three interviews with Emma in one year illustrate the central themes of this book:

> "It's not that I want one or the other [family or work], I want both … If it was just me making decisions about me, on my own, it would be so much simpler, but my decisions to make about my career come in the context of this incredibly complex network of logistical, emotional, practical, lifestyle and ideological issues for each one of us."

> "Having three small people's lives in my head all the time is mentally taxing. The day-to-day grind of family life, you know? … It was like someone had let the air out of the balloon. I very much felt it happen to me consciously I thought 'I can't do this any more'. The momentum just wasn't there. Something had to give."

> "My career has been plateauing anyway. I mean, I do what I need to but I can't do more, and doing more is how

you develop your career … in a way this flexible working thing is about me trying to catch up with a reality that has been imposed upon me. I cannot work full-time any more because I just can't find the energy … the nursery not having a place for my daughter allowed me to say to my husband, 'There's a situation and this is what I am proposing to do about it.'"

"My husband is a feminist so he doesn't think that we should do different things in relation to our work and our kids. And because he wants to work full-time he also wants me to work full-time because that kind of fits his ideological model. I have enormous respect for that, but he works [away from home] three days every week so de facto, when he's away he's out of the picture. So the reality, or practicality of the way we live, doesn't actually make the ideal possible."

"My hope is that [cutting my working days from five to four per week] will give me a sense of entitlement that I've never had, entitlement to not be working. Just a day when I am not working and not feeling guilty about it … that day out will bring us all a little bit of space, a bit of slack in the system."

Like most of the 30 women interviewed for the research that informs this book, Emma is making room for motherhood by going part-time and seeking additional flexibility around when and where she works. Her simple ambition to have both a family life and a career introduces complexity and a level of cognitive, physical and emotional energy that in this moment feels impossible to sustain. Emma's narrative reveals the multiple and intersecting factors that explain the circumstances of her transition from full-time to part-time and flexible work: her relationship with her husband and how they each understand and operationalise their gender roles in the family; a critical event – the breakdown of their childcare arrangements; a gradual slowing of her career progression in a work environment that had speeded-up and become more competitive; being physically and mentally tired having sustained for nearly a decade the lion's share of day-to-day parenting alongside an increasingly intensive full-time workload.

Emma reflects deeply on the significance of her professional and maternal identities to her sense of self and the sense of entitlement she feels to express it through metering the amount time she gives both to her paid work and her family. The sustained experience of work–life conflict has sapped her energy and drive to advance her career. Emma's account encapsulates the modern dilemma for professional women in liberal economies: how to balance breadwinning and caregiving simultaneously as well as advance in their careers?

Women in the middle

This book explores the limits and potential of flexible working arrangements through the lived experience of women in professional and managerial jobs who adjust their employment because of their motherhood. They are part-time, job-sharing, location-flexible, flexi-time working lawyers, doctors, academics, accountants, civil servants, bankers and senior managers in marketing, human resources, communications, research and technology, and they are all mothers of at least one infant or toddler, school-age child or teenager. They are members of a generation of highly educated women starting their careers in the late 1990s and early 2000s who, arguably, are the beneficiaries of family-friendly employment policies and equality rights and protections aimed at them. They are argued to have the potential to achieve economically as much as men and their moves into more flexible ways to work are thought part of a rising trend. Estimates suggest that 63% of the working population in the UK already has some flexibility in either hours, schedule or location of paid work, and 87% of workers want *more* flexibility (Wolf, 2013; Timewise, 2017).

Evidence discussed in this chapter will show that there is a life and career stage when women tend to get stuck or get out of the pipeline to the top jobs in large organisations and it corresponds with motherhood. The women whose experiences inform the research explored in this book are at that stage. They are women in the middle. They are experienced professionals who hold jobs in the middle and upper tiers of organisational hierarchies and they are also mothers and most (not all) are in dual-career couple relationships with men who are the fathers of their children. They are in the middle of organisations and they are also positioned in the middle of a network of social relationships in the family. As Emma eloquently expressed it: the needs, wants and aspirations she has for her career are positioned in relation to those of her partner, to the needs of her children, and to the expectations of her employer, and signal the difficult trade-offs that women make when they become mothers and attempt to craft a life that combines a professional career with family care.

Their planned employment adjustment is not without risk. Persistent inequalities in pay, promotions and prospects over the life course disadvantage women and bite particularly hard on mothers. Approaching 50 years since the introduction of the Equal Pay Act (1970) women remain disadvantaged in the labour market. The gender pay gap currently stands at 18% in the UK and has been largely static for three years, which means that, on average, for every £1 a male worker earns a female worker earns 82 pence. After ten years of motherhood the pay gap widens to 32% and worse in the elite sectors of financial and professional services (Costa Dias et al, 2016). That we know this is a step in the right direction, and the visibility of pay inequalities will increase as new legislation requires large organisations in the UK employing at least 250 people to publish their gender pay gap data for the first time in 2018 and annually after that.

Poor-quality part-time work and the lack of women in the most senior and highly paid roles in large organisations are two key drivers of the gender pay gap (ONS, 2016c). It follows, then, that addressing women's over-representation in poor-quality part-time jobs, and under-representation in the high-paying top jobs should matter to employing organisations minded to close the gap. This study speaks to both these drivers in its close examination of why highly educated and highly skilled professional women choose part-time and flexible working, and how the experience of doing this influences their careers.

Context is everything, and the women whose shared experience of transition into part-time and flexible work informs this study are women living through a shift in cultural context. The second decade of the 21st century is an emergent point for new so-called 'choosing' forms of feminism and conceptualisations of gender progress that emphasise that success in life depends on making the right choices and taking personal responsibility for one's own opportunities and development (Hatton and Trautner, 2015). The cultural image of the professional working mother as Superwoman is receding and Balanced Woman is gaining ground (Rottenberg, 2014). Fulfilment and success in both occupational and domestic domains is presented as something for middle-class women to strive for. This balance quest is perhaps no better epitomised than by the rallying call issued by Facebook's Chief Operating Officer, Sheryl Sandberg (Sandberg, 2013) to professional women to hold on to their ambition and *Lean in* to their careers upon motherhood. The implication being that if women made the right choices and tried harder to balance their lives, they would be happier and workplace inequalities would be a thing of the past. Yet it seems that the decision to combine paid work with childcare remains a dilemma for mothers when few would question fathers' employment because the 'idea that paid work conflicts with men's domestic responsibilities simply never arises' (Durbin and Fleetwood, 2010, p231).

When academic and former US government senior official Anne-Marie Slaughter hit world headlines with her reflective essay 'Why women can't have it all' (Slaughter, 2012), her simple explanation about why many professional women continue to feel divided between career and family touched a nerve. Slaughter's essay exposed what feminist cultural scholar Rottenberg (2013, 2014) describes as a hidden truth: that the field of play for men and women at work is not quite as level as mainstream liberal discourse implies, and the contemporary cultures of business, management and politics remain as gendered as they ever were. It seems that equality of choice and the opportunity to develop organisational careers and be at least a 'good enough' parent (Chodorow, 1978) remains an enduring challenge for working mothers who continue to carry responsibility for the 'hard labour' of family care (Gatrell, 2005). This challenge, and how greater flexibility at work assists its resolution, is at the heart of this study.

Exploring narrative

This chapter begins with elements of Emma's first interview because women's narratives, their stories of their transitions from one work–life configuration to another, form the core of the material explored in this book. Exploring narrative has proved fruitful in the study of motherhood, assisting discoveries of how women's identities form and transform through becoming, adapting and moving through motherhood over the life course, and exploring the sense that women make of their feelings and experiences (Miller, 2005; Thomson et al, 2011). Personal narratives are equally revealing of the social and cultural contexts in which individuals operate, offering a window into the complex dialectics – the interactions and tensions – between the individual and their social environment (Tuider, 2007; Bold, 2012). In using personal narrative as a window into the links and compatibilities between the individual and the social, I place emphasis on its content and interpretation, not its dialogic construction. In other words, I explore what professional women *say* in a series of research interviews about their experiences and attend less to *how they say it*. This story-telling use of narrative is reflected in my treatment of the rich qualitative data generated in a series of narrative interviews with women over one year. Their words and their stories illuminate this text.

In the evolution of qualitative research approaches, narrative and related biographical methods had taken hold by the beginning of the 21st century, inspired to some extent by the tradition of oral history that facilitates people in telling their own stories. The so-called narrative turn in the social sciences also reflects moves to increase the role and power of participants in research (Cresswell, 2013), offering a way of retaining faithfulness to the told stories and placing participants as experts in their own lives (Chamberlayne et al, 2000). The narrative form of research interviewing has proved illuminating in its attention to context and also in its application to research that attempts to access people's inner worlds as well as the explicit contexts in which their decisions and actions are taken (Wengraf, 2001; Bold, 2012; Hollway and Jefferson, 2013). Narrative methods have offered deep insight into a wide range of social issues in the context of people's own accounts of their personal development and histories and are much employed in the study of transitions and processes of becoming, for example Walkerdine et al's (2001) seminal study of the intersections of age, class and gender in *Growing up girl*, and Miller's (2005, 2011) narrative studies of men and women becoming parents.

The research that informs this book draws on over one hundred hours of rich and detailed narrative insight. It illuminates the ways in which professional working motherhood is steeped in and shaped by moral and cultural framing of who mothers and professionals *should* be and what they *should* do, and wider cultural scripts about good and good enough mothering, about professionalism and careers, work–life balance and flexibility.

Looking at individual situations in a common culture permits analysis of the forces and influences that produce women's common and distinctive experiences of professional, flexible, working motherhood. This approach puts the everyday experiences of doing professional work and mothering into focus and locates in a wider system of meaning the things that women do that might be taken for granted as normal. This is important because understanding how what we do every day complies with or resists what is socially expected of us signals both the target and the potential for change and transformation. Philosopher de Certeau (1984) argues that the agentic ways in which we practise, or 'do' everyday life may either reproduce or resist social norms. The social context for the 'doing' in this study is the family and the workplace. These are not understood as static institutions; rather I conceptualise them as sites of social practices where individuals, in their actions and interactions with others, comply or resist conventions, and in so doing may reproduce, sustain and occasionally transform them (Morgan, 2013). This work therefore engages with narrative to explore the transformational potential of flexible working as it is currently understood and practised by women in the context of the family and the workplace. Reay (2005) argues powerfully that the work of social reproduction is located in the interlinking of the domestic sphere with public institutions, and if this is the case then women are on the front line.

Choices within constraints

Debate about the extent to which individuals have agency and choose the life they live, and the extent to which social structures enable or constrain those choices, are central in sociology and fundamental to this analysis. The link between the individual and the social has been articulated in many ways across the disciplines of the social sciences. Theories of structure and agency pivot on the tension and interactive dynamism between voluntarism and determinism in shaping human experience. Structures can include legislative and policy frameworks, workplace processes, and material circumstances such as financial and non-financial resources including education, skills and status; and McRae (2003) argues structures can also be normative, and include the limitations we place upon ourselves and on others to comply with social expectations. Through McRae's lens then, shared ideas in society about gender roles within families, about mothering practices and about 'breadwinning', 'caregiving' and careers become structuring influences on both men's and women's opportunities and choices. For Giddens (1984, 1991), structure and agency are two sides of the same coin, both the mechanism and the outcome of the practices they organise, and structures can be both constraining and enabling. Margaret Archer (1982, 2007) is critical of Giddens' emphasis on agency and the enabling qualities of social structures, arguing that Giddens' structuration thesis fails to account for the conditions under which individuals' choices are *more* enabled or *more* constrained. Archer views social structures, institutions and conventions not as what people produce, but 'what people confront and have to grapple with' (1982, p463) and argues for the *analytic* distinctiveness of agency and structure, rather than what she considers their misleading conflation. Archer's realist account emphasises the interactive dynamism of structures and agency through time as what leads to either reproduction or transformation of social structures, what she terms the morphogenic cycle. The theoretical framing of this study therefore, pivots on that dynamic interaction of agency and structure through time. It explores how women negotiate and construct the maternal and professional lives they seek and, in so doing, comply with, resist or even transform gendered structures and expectations in employment and inside the family.

A simple assumption underpins this study. It is that being able to engage in productive and meaningful work and to be an active participant in family life are desirable outcomes to be achieved in most industrialised societies (Sen, 2000; Bailey and Madden, 2017). The concept of work is central to this analysis of women's lives and labours, and in this is informed by the relational and inclusive framework developed by scholars promoting the 'new sociology of work' (Pettinger et al, 2005), which includes paid market work and unpaid labour in the home in a holistic definition of 'work'. In the tradition of feminist scholarship I extend the definition of work to include both the work of the body in reproduction and infant nursing, and the cognitive and physical activities of mothering and caring as work (Oakley, 1974; Gatrell, 2013; Phipps, 2014). Other forms of work extend my definition still further to include the expanding repertoire of 'emotional work' that mothers do to manage their own and others' feelings in the family and in the workplace (Garey, 1999; Hochschild, 2012), and to the 'identity work' in which mothers engage to make sense of who they are at different points in their lives (Miller, 2005; Bataille, 2014; Hollway, 2015). Conceptualising work in this holistic way permits my analysis of the *effort* involved to achieve it and in so doing addresses what Thomson et al (2011, p175) propose is a missing sense of the 'kinds of emotional, psychic, and creative work involved in being a good enough parent and a worker' in debates about what activities constitute work in contemporary society, and which, Thomson et al (2011) argue, are inadequately served by the concept many might assume highly relevant to this debate, that of work–life balance.

Despite its entry into mainstream discourse there are problems with work–life balance as a concept. Notions of work–life balance promote a false possibility of an objective and equitable division of life and self across what are positioned as two competing and conflicting domains (Smithson and Stokoe, 2005; Gambleset al, 2006). Feminist critique argues that work–life balance is a flawed and simplistic concept that underplays the complexities, constraints and trade-offs that characterise women's lives, and their attempts to reconcile the competing tensions between work and family demands. The conceptualisation that paid work exists in binary opposition to life, rather than being one part of it is, therefore, particularly diminishing of women's worldview. Crompton et al (2007c) suggests the phrase work–family conflict as a more accurate description of women's struggles and reconciliation more meaningfully reflects the compromises involved.

As a work–life reconciliation strategy, the opportunity to reduce paid working hours and adjust working time schedules and locations under a formal or informal flexible working arrangement, is appealing to those for whom it is as an available and affordable option. Indeed 75% of 14,000 working women in the UK aged 28–40 surveyed by Opportunity Now (2014, p26) said they were "grateful" for the opportunity to adjust their employment participation in these ways. Part-time working is the most prevalent form of flexible work arrangement in the UK, undertaken by 26% (8.5 million) of the economically active population (ONS, 2017b). It dominates maternal employment and is clustered at lower occupational levels: less than 10% of the 25% of all working women who have progressed to the level of manager and senior official are formally recorded as working part-time (ONS, 2011). Any gains in work–life reconciliation associated with part-time work are offset by long-term losses in pay, prospects and promotions over the life course that are well evidenced in a substantial body of research (Fagan and Rubery, 1996; O'Reilly and Bothfeld, 2002; Cousins and Tang, 2004; Walters, 2005; Tomlinson, 2006a; Connolly and Gregory, 2008; Gash, 2008; Manning and Petrongolo, 2008; Gangl and Ziefle, 2009; Bianchi and Milkie, 2010; Holt and Lewis, 2011; Lyonette et al, 2011; Bukodi et al, 2012; Dex and Bukodi, 2012; Fagan and Norman, 2012; Janus, 2013; Lanning et al, 2013; Cory and Alakeson, 2014; Harkness, 2016; Rubery et al, 2016).

Theorising why more women than men apparently 'choose' poorly rewarded part-time work over better quality full-time employment led Catherine Hakim (1991, 1998, 2002, 2006) to suggest that doing so reflects women's intrinsic desires (or 'preferences') and natural orientation towards family life. Hakim's preference theory categorises women as either home-oriented, work-oriented or somewhere in between as 'adaptive' identifying insufficiently strongly with one pole or the other. Adaptive women are the largest of her three preference groupings comprising around 60% of working women. Controversial for many reasons that will be discussed further in Chapter 2, Hakim casts the individual as a free and informed, rational economic agent who approaches each employment decision with full information about the potential costs and consequences of their actions. Preference theory has been influential, although widely and robustly criticised for, among other things, gender essentialism and overemphasis on women's freedoms to choose the life they want to live (see Crompton and Harris, 1998; McRrae, 2003; Leahy and Doughney, 2006). This study offers further critique of preference theory and rational choice-based theories of women's employment and labour market outcomes. It finds support for the reformulation of professional women's agency as *choices within constraints*, as proposed by Crompton and her collaborators (Crompton and Harris, 1998; Crompton, 2002; Crompton et al, 2007a; Crompton and Lyonette, 2011b) and Tomlinson (2006b).

This study contributes a sociological analysis to the contemporary situation of motherhood and professional employment. The foundation thinking that informs this work has its origins in feminist theory and sociology, and also draws on concepts and empirical insights from a range of disciplines in its treatment of gender, equality, identity and subjectivity, work, family and careers, including: cultural studies, social psychology, psychosocial studies, social policy, and management studies. The sections that follow draw upon this framework and explore the central themes of this book: modern motherhood, time and work–life balance, maternal employment and careers, and flexible working policy and practice.

Modern motherhood

Although not every woman becomes or wants to become a mother, a cultural assumption that women do shapes the experience of being a woman in society whether they become mothers or remain child free (Phoenix, 1991; Gatrell, 2008). Feminist scholars have long argued that the maternal body and the family remain sites of power and negotiation between women and men (Butler, 1990; Phipps, 2014). Radical feminist scholars of the 1970s and 1980s argued against notions that relations between mother and child are naturally occurring and biologically inevitable, and called for dual parenting to enable boys and girls to associate nurturing as a parental quality from an early age, rather than a specifically feminine role. Second-wave feminists through the 1980s and 1990s further disputed the notion of biologically determined roles by drawing attention to the social construction of gender roles that maintained the subordination of women within heterosexual couples and confined women to the home. Concluding her narrative study of transitions to parenthood, Miller (2005, p56) concluded that in 40 years the dominant ideologies that 'powerfully and pervasively surround and shape motherhood' appear not to have radically changed and ideas that caring is intrinsically female imbue dominant models of motherhood today.

Mothering models, or ideologies, are socially and culturally constructed and what it is to be a good mother relates to what is considered socially appropriate with regard to childrearing and has varied through history. Social psychologists Johnston and Swanson (2007, p 6) explain how mothering ideology 'is based on beliefs and values about mothering that mothers must either embrace or reject, but can seldom ignore'. For women who embark on motherhood today there is a sense that motherhood itself has become professionalised and intensive (Hays, 1996; Thomson et al, 2011; Christopher, 2012), and yet reproductive labour and the effort of good mothering remain largely hidden from conceptions of what constitutes work in contemporary society (Gatrell, 2013; Van Amsterdam, 2015).

Intensive mothering

Research suggests that intensive mothering expectations define the dominant mothering ideology in US and northern European cultures, and are held up as a standard for good mothering. Hays (1996, p21) first identified intensive mothering expectations:

> The model of intensive mothering tells us children are innocent and priceless, that their rearing should be carried out by individual mothers and that it should be centred on children's needs, with methods informed by experts, labor-intensive and costly. This we are told is the best model, largely because it is what children need and deserve.

Intensive mothering ideology was further expanded by Thomson et al's (2011, p277) intergenerational research with mothers in UK as an 'intensification of responsibility' that describes both the commercialisation of motherhood and a new duty to be an informed and professional parent; that is, to respond to the pressure to buy goods and to engage the help of so-called experts ranging from tutors and coaches to writers on childcare, journalists and mothers writing blogs. They also noted 'the inflation of parental expectations and the proliferation of interventions aimed at improving children' (Thomson et al, 2011, p277), and observed this trend as an expression of a desire to help children become more competitive, which itself has become an outlet for competition between women who are more home-centred and those who work longer hours out of the home. The competitive development of children also features in Baraitser's (2008) conceptualisation of motherhood as being played out in public in mothers' desires to mould their child into an individual who stands out from others and is fully prepared for life's competition.

The intensification of motherhood in Europe and North America is in part attributed to economic liberalisation and the rise of neoliberal ideology. This is reflected in a twin shift in national policy to a pro-family focus and an increased emphasis on personal obligation, such that now it seems maternal care is idealised and mothers' economic activity is essential (McRobbie, 2009; Lewis, 2010; Gill and Scharff, 2013). Individualism works in opposition to a pro-family focus in its emphasis on personal responsibility for one's future, self-improvement, and the obligation to emancipate oneself through paid work, and therefore pulls women in two directions. Crittenden (2001, p61) persuasively argues that this paradox of obligation and liberation contributes to an economic devaluation of motherhood and serves to make mothers' unpaid work at home disappear. Women's actions to reconcile their dual responsibilities for mothering and paid work are therefore held in tension by contradictory discourses that simultaneously emphasise maternal care as important *and* oblige women to fulfil their emancipated economic destinies.

It is in this space that a new postfeminist discourse has proliferated. Postfeminism can be understood in many ways, as a theoretical orientation, as a new moment in feminism, or a straightforward backlash that attributes women's continuing struggles to failures of feminism (McRobbie, 2009; Gill and Scharff, 2013). Gill (2007, p147) approaches postfeminism as a discursive formation rather than a theory or movement with a defined aim, describing postfeminism as 'a sensibility' that comprises interrelated themes including 'an emphasis upon self-surveillance, monitoring and self-discipline; a focus on individualism, choice, empowerment ... and a resurgence of ideas about natural sexual difference'. An example of feminism remade in this way is the bestselling self-declared feminist manifesto *Lean in* (Sandberg, 2013), which calls on professional women to work on themselves and build confidence and assertiveness, to plan their lives and relationships such that they can achieve both careers and fulfilling family lives. Achieving such a balance, however, still places a requirement on women and not men to be present in both domestic and professional spheres. Viewed in this light, promoting balance as the aim of professional women's lives becomes a risky business and, as social commentator Traister (2012) argues, represents a potential undoing of feminine gains.

The inherent incompatibility of society's expectations that mothers will work outside the home with intensive mothering expectations that propose mothers provide the best care for children puts women in a difficult ideological and practical position (Adkins, 2002). Psychologists

Johnston and Swanson (2007, p447) describe the 'cognitive acrobatics' that women experience in their constructions of a coherent worker-mother identity and the challenges of doing so in a cultural climate that promotes both a strong worker identity and the intensive mothering ideology. The moral emphasis of intensive mothering as the right way to raise children has proved hard to resist however. Mothers must therefore construct a worker identity that justifies their decisions to work outside the home against this demanding standard of good mothering that insists they should provide an informed, involved and continuous maternal presence.

Time and work–life balance

For mothers the crux of the depiction of employment decisions as a quest for work–life balance is the measurement and management of time, that is the number of hours given to motherhood and to the workplace (Crompton and Lyonette, 2011; Thomson et al, 2011). Time and, more specifically, a lack of time, is a common theme in work–life balance literatures. Time scarcity is often discussed as the cause of work–life tensions and conflicts, which is a position significantly influenced by systems theory and the idea of objective scarcity of temporal resources (Luhmann, 1971).

The meaning and the value of time in contemporary professional and managerial work is an equally important context to consider. Work demands have intensified in globalised economies such that employers now expect adaptability and flexibility in managerial employees to respond to rapidly changing demands (Sennett, 1998; Perrons et al, 2005, Colley et al, 2012). Scholarship on work–life balance that explores the difficulties workers experience reconciling ever increasing work demands with everything else in life has flourished in this environment (Sveningsson and Alvesson, 2003).

The amount of time spent at work in the UK is almost the highest in Europe with 42.7 the average usual working hours for full-time employees (ONS, 2011). The effect of long working hours on subjective well-being remains unclear. Some studies have suggested a positive impact of the number of hours worked on life satisfaction up to a certain point, and others have shown a negative impact of the number of hours worked on happiness and health outcomes (Voydanoff, 2005a, 2005b; van Daalen et al, 2006; Burke and Fiksenbaum, 2008).

The value of time is symbolic and well as material, and is central to professionals' demonstration of commitment and success in their chosen fields. Long hours are a proxy for, and often taken for granted as evidence of, an individual's commitment to their work, to their employer and to their career (Williams et al, 2013). Long hours and continuous availability are characteristics associated with the stereotyped 'ideal worker' (Acker, 1990). This is the idea that the ideal worker is someone full-time, available to work longer than the prescribed hours, and is free from responsibilities for care and household work. Acker (1990), argues that the ideal worker assumptions provide the blueprint for ways of managing people and systems for organising work. Men and women without outside responsibilities are better able to fulfil the ideal worker construct; and those with responsibilities other than to their paid work are vulnerable to exclusion.

How we experience time is highly relevant when considering the context in which professionals and managers are making decisions about work. Technology has developed that changes the way work is organised and performed, simultaneously alleviating and compounding the experience of being squeezed for time. In the context of intensified 24/7 global economies, time becomes non-spatial territory. Work time is no longer zoned in offices and public spaces, and schedules become more open, facilitated by technology that provides anytime, anywhere access. Collapsing the physical boundaries between home and work can cut deeply into human lives and work against efforts to minimise stress and achieve work–life balance (Strazdins et al, 2004, 2011; Colley et al, 2012).

There is a subjective side to work–life balance in that people differ in their perceptions of balance and the same situations can lead to different experiences of work–life balance and perceptions of time scarcity (Schilling, 2015). In other words, even if you and I both work the same number of hours in a week, we might experience those hours very differently and have different ideas about how successful our work–life balance is. In this way, perceptions of time availability and scarcity, and of work–life balance, operate at a much deeper level than a simple book-keeping of hours, connecting to profound concepts of identity, values and to notions of success.

Time equality

The variable ways in which time is used, controlled and understood are fundamental to the nature and understanding of gender inequality in paid and unpaid work. Crompton and Lyonette's (2011) research focuses on the experience of working long hours and the consequent need for negotiating arrangements for care of the family. They argue that female professional and managerial employees experience particularly high levels of work–life conflict because they work long hours and mothers among them are likely to be in partnerships with men who similarly work long hours and yet the women are likely to take the major responsibility for childcare and domestic chores. Women's unpaid responsibilities for the time-consuming practices of caring and domestic work prevent them from behaving like 'ideal workers' and therefore deny them economic rewards. As Bryson (2007) deftly argues, gender inequalities in ways that time is used and valued form part of a vicious circle that leaves many women economically dependent and vulnerable to exploitation.

Feminist scholars and social policy experts have long argued the point that equality and empowerment in the arena of paid work will not offer genuine opportunity and choice to women unless accompanied by shifts in the gendered division of domestic labour (MacDonald et al, 2005; Crompton et al, 2007a; Lewis, 2010; Lyonette and Crompton, 2015). Time use is bound up with gender identity, in that the prevailing sexual divisions of domestic work and the allocation of caring work to women is argued to be a central element of 'doing gender' (West and Zimmerman, 1987, p144). This is the idea that gender is constituted in our everyday interactions and activities and reflects a deeply embedded set of cultural assumptions. In other words, sex is biological and gender is performed. Following this logic women do childcare and laundry and cleaning because doing childcare, laundry and cleaning is what makes women women. These assumptions have important economic consequences for women's participation in paid employment and, following this gender performativity thesis, to undo them means undoing gender (Butler, 2004).

Economistic explanations for gendered divisions of domestic labour emphasise resources and the carrying out of domestic tasks as a function of who has more time available to do them. It also reflects economic power in a relationship, the assumption being that if breadwinners are out breadwinning they will have more power and be able to get the spouse or partner to do more housework (Becker, 1991). Economistic arguments should mean that if women increase their breadwinning, then men will undertake more domestic work. There is some support for this in quantitative analysis that suggests that as women earn more, men do more housework, although not as much as women (Coltrane, 2008; Harkness, 2008). This indicates that a more realistic position is that it is a combination of economistic and gender performance factors that determines prevailing divisions of domestic labour between men and women.

Parents in the UK today spend more than treble the time on childcare in the 2000s than parents in the 1970s. Research by the Centre for Time Use Studies at the University of Oxford shows that the time spent on domestic chores that are in part generated by having children is more than double the time spent on the childcare itself (Sullivan and Gershuny, 2011). Fathers are doing more than they did in previous decades, but mothers are doing the most. British fathers now spend around 36 minutes a day on childcare and up to 100 minutes on housework, DIY and shopping. British mothers spend up to 86 minutes per day on childcare and up to 158 minutes on housework. Simply by multiplying the maximum additional time spent by women on domestic work and care (although it should be noted that not all the women in Sullivan and Gershuny's study are in paid employment), it seems that women undertake an additional 27 days, or almost 4 weeks of 24-hour days, of care and domestic work per year compared to their male partners.

Maternal employment

Historically, women's participation in employment has been distinct from that of men's and with different rewards. Gender progress can legitimately be claimed in employment participation at least, with high and rising rates of maternal employment in the UK: today 73.7% of mothers are in paid work (4.9 million women with dependent children) and 92.4% of fathers. In comparison, 3.7 million mothers were in employment in 1996 which was equivalent to 61.9% (ONS, 2017c). The demographic and social drivers of the dramatic shift in the economic behaviour of women are well documented and explored only briefly here. The contraceptive pill since the mid-1960s and the legalisation of abortion enabled women to gain more control over their fertility, to delay child rearing, and to limit the number of children they had (Barrett, 2004). The expansion of higher education and the broad-based curricula offered by the new universities appealed to women, whose participation increased significantly. By the early 2000s, nearly 6 in 10 higher education entrants were female, 57% in 2015/16 (Universities UK, 2017). The increasing number of skilled and qualified women entering the labour market and going into professional work both influenced and was influenced by delays in starting families. Increased participation in the labour market helped women to accumulate the economic, psychological and social resources to better support becoming a parent (Miller, 2012), and the general trend in the UK today is towards having children later. The average

age for women to have their first child increased from 23.7 in 1971 to 28.1 years in 2012, with over half of all live births in 2016 (54%, 376,000 live births) to mothers aged 30 and over (ONS, 2017a). There are differences in the social circumstances and age at which women become mothers, the average age at first birth is older, typically over 30 among highly educated women compared to women with lower level qualifications (Joshi, 2008). Women becoming mothers today do so having accumulated many years' experience of paid work that they might identify as a career. Careers in the sense of a sequence of employment experiences that offer reward, development and growth are now an established norm for graduate women and career attachment, therefore, is potentially significant with regard to the employment choices women make when they have children.

Leaky pipelines, sticky floors and glass ceilings

From an earnings perspective, by the mid-1990s the traditional one-breadwinner family ceased to be the most common family type in Britain and dual-earner families became the norm (Brannen et al, 1997; Klett-Davies and Skaliotis, 2009). Dependent children today live in families in which at least one parent and more likely both parents are in paid employment. The employment rates for mothers and fathers differ significantly. The employment rate for mothers of a child under 5 years old is 57%, compared to around 90% for fathers. Women with children aged between 3 and 4 have the lowest employment rates (65%), and of these 59% work part-time. As children get older mothers are more likely to be in full-time work (ONS, 2017c).

Despite increasing levels of labour market participation, women are still under-represented in the upper levels of organisational leadership and management: 35% of managers, directors and senior official roles are filled by women (ONS, 2017d), and women hold only 1 in 10 of executive positions in the boardrooms of FTSE 100 listed companies (Vinnicombe et al, 2017). It is noticeable that women disappear from the pipeline to leadership roles in significant numbers around the middle management tiers and they remain longer in grade before getting promoted (McKinsey & Company, 2012; KPMG, 2014). In the financial services sector, for example, almost half of all employees are women but their representation shrinks by more than half at middle management level to 22%, signalling the 'sticky' nature of middle management jobs that fix women's feet firmly to the floor of those roles (McKinsey & Company, 2012).

The effect on gender diversity at managerial levels is often referred to as a 'leaky pipeline' to leadership, after Kanter and Roessner's case study (1999, revised May 2003) and is explained by scholars in a variety of ways, indicative either of features and factors about women themselves or about the environments and cultures in which they work. For example, assumptions that women have intrinsic preferences for 'doing' roles rather than 'leading' roles; women lack ambition to climb the ladder (Sandberg, 2013); lack of role models and the unappealing lifestyles of those in power (Singh et al, 2006; Kelan and Mah, 2014); or indicative of a failure of meritocracy in organisations and institutionally gender-biased promotion processes (Cech and Blair-Loy, 2010).

The greater proportion of women than men who take absence from employment for maternity and parenting is often assumed to contribute to the leaky pipeline. This assumption is challenged by Ely et al (2014), who found women's lower representation in senior management roles could not be explained by the fact that they took more breaks from the workplace than men. Their survey of Harvard MBA graduates found that 28% of Generation X women (born in the 1970s and early 1980s and the birth cohort corresponding to the women in focus in this study), and 44% of baby boomers (born in the 1960s) had taken breaks compared to 2% of men across both generations. When controlling for a range of factors such as age, sector, size of organisation, and factors relating to family status and parenting, including the presence of part-time work in work histories, they could not find a statistical link between these factors and women's lower representation. Insights from psychology point to unconscious, or implicit, gender bias as explanation for why employers judge women's competence and potential in ways that restrict their access to influential networks and positions of power. Psychologists Ridgeway and Correll (2004) argue that mothers in management jobs are vulnerable to normative discrimination arising from implicit assumptions that they will make less valuable contributions in employment than other workers. Normative discrimination is thought to arise because success in the labour market, and particularly in jobs traditionally considered masculine, signals stereotypically masculine qualities such as assertiveness or dominance. These qualities are inconsistent with those that are culturally expected of mothers, such as being warm and nurturing (Blair-Loy and Wharton, 2004). It follows therefore that when a mother violates these norms by showing a high level of professional competence and commitment she will be disliked and viewed negatively. This is consistent with other research on women managers in which women acting 'gender inappropriately by fulfilling a masculine work script' (Kelan, 2010, p182) presents them with more problems in masculine work areas, where they are doubly punished for not being woman enough.

Women's careers

The deeply contextually embedded ways in which women make decisions about what success in personal, family and work domains means to them at different points in time has been emphasised in much research into women's employment transitions (Greenhaus and Powell, 2012; Brimrose et al, 2014). Tomlinson's (2006b) studies of women managers' transitions through part-time work found that mothers make decisions about work and career in relation to the needs of their children and relative to the work and career opportunities of their partners, and not single-mindedly in pursuit of status or self-actualising fulfilment. These aspects of relatedness in women's subjectivities is under-emphasised in traditional age-and-stage theories of career construction that tend to view psychological forces and social expectations at different ages as influencing individuals to address particular accomplishments and issues (see for example, Super, 1981; Levinson, 1986).

The prevalent logic of career-making is linear and cumulative; an uninterrupted and upwards trajectory within the professional sphere (Evetts, 2000). This is arguably particularly diminishing of women's worldview, which may well include a work career that is more typically experienced as an interdependent part of life rather than a separate component of it (Crompton and Harris, 1998; Sullivan and Mainiero, 2007; Durbin and Tomlinson, 2010; Maher, 2013). The emphasis on paid work as central in careers constructs what is perceived as the normal and the desirable way to progress in employment and is problematic for many whose life circumstances do not permit such a neatly linear pattern. Much research shows that women's work career patterns appear more heterogeneous and complex than male patterns, characterised by interruptions and transitions in and out of the labour market, changes of occupation, and moves in and out of full- and part-time work that are tied to caring responsibilities over the life course (Crompton, 2002; Kirchmeyer, 2006; Bukodi et al, 2012). The living of a life is rarely a smooth, staged progression nor is it unproblematic. Many metaphors and symbols have been invoked to communicate the non-linear patterning of women's lives, such as careerscapes (McKie et al, 2013), kaleidoscopes (Mainiero and Sullivan, 2005) and patchwork careers (Halrynjo and Lyng, 2009). Sabelis and Schilling (2013) propose the notion of 'frayed careers' to address the deeply temporal character of careers as part of a life course, as well as to expose the intersections of gender, age and class that produce the interruptions that fray women's career paths. While acknowledging that the term 'frayed' produces negative connotations, Sabelis and Schilling (2013) argue that this is both realistic and that an intentional focus on notions of deficit and disruption renders the linear age-and-stage career logic irrelevant. They call for new whole-life career models that attend to the rhythms of life in theorisations of career, rhythms that require constant adaptation of spatial and temporal arrangements. Maher (2013, p172) argues that far from being a sign of 'fraying careers or fracturing family lives', multiple changes and reformations of family and career can be understood as adaptive and resilient responses to the everyday nature of disruption and the consistency of family change, and not always signalling conflict and breakdown. Similarly, O'Neil and Bilimoria (2005) describe women's career development phases as a sequence of idealism, endurance and reinvention. In both models, temporality is emphasised but a chronology of careers is retained since the model does not appear to allow for how a young woman may seek authenticity or reinvention, and an older woman challenge.

The 'boundaryless' career model offers a description of contemporary careers of both men and women that encompass movement in and out of the labour market, as well as across occupational roles and sectors (Arthur, 1994). The boundaryless career model emphasises agency and choice, and attends little to the conditions under which there may be more or less of these things. At the heart of notions of the boundaryless career is an image of the individual as a self-propelled career-agent, for whom career is not a pathway or an occupational position that an individual temporarily inhabits; rather, it is constituted *within* the individual themselves through their accumulation and expression of multiple skill sets, interests, networks and resources. As Cohen et al (2009) have argued, boundaryless career models cannot be a true celebration of individual freedom and independence to create or find opportunities from the widest possible field because individuals do not have free rein as to how they enact their careers.

Part-time penalties

It remains an issue that women's peak child-bearing years, their twenties to forties, correspond with the period when they are most likely to be developing their organisational careers. Despite a trend towards gender parity in attainment in higher education and in patterns of graduates' early career employment, the transition to part-time working hours upon parenthood remains one that mothers are more likely to make than fathers (Brannen et al, 1997; Sheridan, 2004). The comparatively high proportion of mothers who make the shift and the endurance of a part-time working pattern in their lives beyond the age at which children go to school marks maternal employment in the UK as distinctive compared to other countries with the highest rates of female employment. Just over 50% of mothers with school-age children work fewer than 20 hours a week in the UK compared to an Organisation for Economic Co-operation and Development (OECD) average of 30% (Hegewisch and Gornick, 2011), and less than 20% of British mothers of school-age children work 40 hours or more per week compared to 45% OECD average (Alakeson, 2012).

Having children marks not only a drop in participation in paid employment among mothers compared to fathers, but also the start of a ten-year decline in earnings relative to men and to women without children. This is attributed to women's high rate of part-time employment and the poor quality of the part-time labour market in the UK (Brewer and Paull, 2006; Manning and Petrongolo, 2008; Costa Dias et al, 2016). It is reasonable to assume a greater degree of upward social mobility among women without primary responsibility for children and, in pay terms, this is borne out by evidence that the full-time gender pay gap is almost nil in the under thirties age groups (Costa Dias et al, 2016).

Substantial evidence links the poor-quality part-time labour market in the UK with women's diminished pay, prospects and promotions over the life course (O'Reilly and Bothfeld, 2002; Tomlinson, 2006a; Connolly and Gregory, 2008; Gash, 2008; Manning and Petrongolo, 2008; Holt and Lewis, 2011; Lyonette et al, 2011; Bukodi et al, 2012; Dex and Bukodi, 2012; Fagan and Norman, 2012; Harkness, 2016; Rubery et al, 2016). Part-time working for employees still means long hours, often more than are remunerated (Stone, 2007; Kelliher and Anderson, 2010; Lewis and Humbert, 2010), and for women managers and professionals, a move into part-time work is associated with occupational downgrading and marginalisation in low-status and marginal roles (Gatrell, 2008; Neuberger et al, 2011; Cahusac and Kanji, 2014). Lanning et al (2013) found that women's moves into part-time work after the birth of the first child often entails a change of employer and a move into lower status work below their previous skill level and seniority. This is the part-time hidden 'brain drain' (Equal Opportunities Commission, 2005), which has been described as a waste of education and skills (Connolly and Gregory, 2008) and as contributing to gender inequality (Rubery et al, 2016).

Working in ways that reduce an employee's physical presence in a workplace and limit their availability to respond to employers' demands challenges conventional notions of productivity, giving rise to stigma and negative assumptions about part-time workers' level of work commitment and professionalism (Dick and Hyde, 2006; Evetts, 2011). The overwhelming weight of evidence suggests that going part-time in professional and managerial jobs is a high-risk activity with significant and lasting consequences for careers.

Flexible working policy and practice

In 2000 the term 'work–life balance' was introduced into UK policy under a Labour government and is widely used in academic literature to describe a basket of employment and social policies at the level of the state and the employer that support the combination of paid work with unpaid family care and also voluntary and leisure activities for employees (Lewis, 2010). These policies included childcare provision, early years education, maternity and paternity rights and leave, and framed one part of the policy package in particular: the legislation concerning flexible working patterns that was introduced in 2003 (Lewis and Campbell, 2008). The Right to Request Flexible Working gave parents of children aged under 6 (or of children with disabilities aged under 18) the right to apply to work flexibly and required employers to consider applications seriously. It also increased the generosity and reduced the eligibility conditions for paid maternity leave. Amended in the Work and Families Act (2006), the Right to Request Flexible Working was extended to parents and carers of children under 18 in England, Wales and Scotland. In 2014 the Right to Request Flexible Working was further extended to all employees, irrespective of parental or caring status. Economic benefits of around £450 million in ten years are anticipated to flow from this adjustment as a result of increased productivity, lower labour turnover and reduced absenteeism, as well as improvements to employee health and well-being (Department for Business Innovation and Skills, 2012). The legislative right afforded to employees with at least six months' service is to *request* flexibility, not for employers to grant it. How employers evaluate and prioritise potentially competing demands for flexibility from a more diverse group of employees is an issue raised by those concerned that leaving the decision about the relative merits of flexibility requests for care or for leisure purposes to local managers may risk further making the challenges for working families disappear from the contemporary workplace. Managerial discretion has been shown to be an important enabling and constraining influence on employee access to flexible working policies (Den Dulk et al, 2011). If acknowledgement of family responsibilities is replaced by validation of the rights of all individual employees to competing interests, the vicious cycle of barriers to participating in both paid work and care is likely to be reinforced. This is because placing less pressure on employers to be part of the solution to the challenges of caring pushes responsibility further towards the individual and the family.

On the whole, researchers have found that worker autonomy to manage personal work schedules, or to vary the timing and place of work, generates positive outcomes for individuals, organisations and communities (Strazdins et al, 2004; Brannen, 2005; Voydanoff, 2005c; Shockley and Allen, 2007; Hill et al, 2010, 2013). Aspects of organisational culture, management processes and operating context mediate these effects, for example the constant on-demand requirements made of workers in elite, client-service occupations of finance and law has been shown to all but eliminate the well-being benefits for individuals (Blair-Loy, 2004, 2009). Research has highlighted the tensions and incompatibilities between satisfying employee requirements for work–life balance and organisational goals of resource agility, efficiency and responsiveness. Some forms of flexible work arrangement may suit the employee but are not favoured by the organisation, particularly those that impinge on worker availability to the organisation, its clients or customers. In these circumstances, part-time working and restricted schedules may only be acceptable to the business if they do not impact negatively on the client (Michielsens et al, 2013). This pressure to prioritise the clients' needs contributes to sustaining norms of long working hours and presenteeism, and works against flexible working, and against part-time working in particular. Valuing employee responsiveness over employee rights to private time could account for the reported under-utilisation of flexible working practices at managerial levels, even in the most encouraging of environments (Smith and Gardner, 2007). There is a marked difference in seniority of those who say they would take up flexible working if they had the chance according to the Chartered Institute of Personnel Development's (CIPD's) formerly bi-annual flexible working survey that was last issued in 2012. The majority (60%) of male and female senior managers reported that they would not, compared to over 60% of lower ranking managers who said they would. This finding is consistent with the comparative review of flexible working policies undertaken by the Equality and Human Rights Commission (EHRC) that found much less appetite for flexible working among senior staff, and that senior staff who do request flexibility are more likely to have their request refused (Hegewisch, 2009). It could also be that senior managers do not feel that they need to avail themselves of organisational policy to access flexibility and have sufficient autonomy and discretion to manage their own schedules. The evidence suggests that there is an uncomfortable coexistence of flexible working within workplace cultures that value the ideal worker norms of availability and visibility, and that associate high inputs of working hours with high work commitment among managers. It is in these environments in particular that the continued uptake of flexible working arrangements by women only, serves to reinforce gender inequality rather than transform the situation (Sheridan, 2004; Crompton and Lyonette, 2011b); a situation described succinctly by Phillips (2008, p 7): 'as long as flexible working is offered to women and uptake is strongest among women, it continues to create a female ghetto of flexible workers'.

In her comprehensive analysis of the development of work–life balance policies in the UK in the 1990s and 2000s and their role in enabling gender equality, Jane Lewis (2010) concludes that the access and reconciliation focus of UK employment policy has achieved its aim of increasing the numbers of mothers in labour market. Policy has made it possible to combine work and care in ways that were not available to previous generations, but the implications for gender equality are questionable because there are clear penalties for labour market absences through maternity leaves, breaks and part-time work. Penalties take the form of reduced pay, under-utilisation of skills, promotion opportunities foregone and pensions out of reach. Lewis (2010) concludes, in agreement with other social policy analysts (see Perrons, 2006; Lewis and Humbert, 2010), that on the whole, policy packages in the UK, in common with most European approaches, have been more concerned to permit mothers to shoulder their dual and often conflicting responsibilities for both paid and unpaid work, than to facilitate *real* choices over how to reconcile work and care. The implications for the pursuit of gender equality have not been wholly beneficial.

Introducing women in the middle

Thirty women's experiences as they told them, as they lived them, form the basis of the material explored in this book. It is a study of the lived experience of transitioning into, implementing and sustaining a part-time and flexible working arrangement among professional mothers living and working in the UK in the second decade of the 21st century. Despite their differing stances on the significance of personal preferences, choice and structural constraint in determining women's work–life configurations and outcomes, Crompton and Harris (1998) and Hakim (2000) concur that *most* women who are mothers will seek some sort of combination of work and family. They also suggest that this group will in itself be heterogeneous. It is this majority group, that they describe as **maximisers** and **satisficers** (Crompton and Harris, 1998), or **adaptives** and **drifters** (Hakim, 2000), that this study targeted for participation. Given the acknowledged heterogeneity of this majority group of women, my concern was to design a sample that would be sufficiently homogeneous to allow themes to emerge and, simultaneously, to permit analysis of the distinctiveness of women's circumstances and experiences. Thirty is a large sample for this type of qualitative exploration of individual experience through time and, as such, the sample offers sufficient breadth and depth, richness and resonance of insight to be able to generalise to similar cases and situations.

Transitions are an important site of study in employment and careers research generally, and specifically in the context of motherhood (Evetts, 2000; Tomlinson, 2006b; Gash, 2008; Fenwick, 2013), assisting in discoveries regarding the link between social and personal change and transformation, and regarding personal continuity and discontinuity, and gains and losses through time. Seventy-six individual interviews with 30 professional mothers generated over 100 hours of rich narrative insight into their 'before and after' anticipations and reflections of their experience of adjusting their employment to something flexible. Their adjustment can be described as voluntary in so far as it was initiated by them not their employing institution. My reference to **professional mothers** applies to their occupational classification as either managers or professionals, and not to their approach to their mothering. The descriptors 'professional' and 'managerial' align broadly to Standard Occupational Classification (SOC) 1 and 2 (ONS, 2016b) although the SOC was not used prescriptively. My definition of professional and managerial roles follows that of Evetts (2011, p5) and relates to the 'knowledge based category of service occupation, which usually follows a period of tertiary education and vocational training'.

Given that this study is about mothers it is important to carefully define mothers and mothering. 'Mother' is defined as both social role and identity, in that to be a mother has social, political, cultural and moral meaning, status and relative influence. It is not necessary to have given birth to become a mother or to perform a mothering role, yet it is an identity position socially ascribed only to women's bodies.

'Mothering' is defined for the purposes of this study, after Doucet (2006), as taking responsibility for children at emotional, community and moral levels. For the purposes of this study I define 'professional mother' as a woman with a biological or adoptive relationship to dependent child or children and who is employed in a professional or managerial job in a large organisation and who is usually resident in the UK.

It is mostly women who work part-time and flexibly in professional and managerial jobs; research has demonstrated that the opportunities to do so are limited and overall the population is small and reportedly hard to find (Durbin and Tomlinson, 2010). The dearth of part-time and flexible working opportunities in more senior occupational roles and the political ambition to make more available to facilitate women's labour market mobility and progress underlay my focus on women in roles in the middle of organisational pipelines to leadership (Tomlinson et al, 2009; Durbin and Fleetwood, 2010; Timewise Foundation, 2013). My aim was to focus on highly skilled and professionally experienced women occupying roles under the glass ceilings in large organisations and at the level and life stage when women's representation diminishes across a range of industries. They represent the cohort of women whose potential could be lost if the reported 'pipeline problem' in large organisations is not addressed (Women and Equalities Committee, 2016). As such they are prime targets for the current wave of inclusion interventions aimed at them that include government-sponsored returners' programmes, workplace trials of different types of flexible working (Gascoigne and Young, 2016), unconscious bias awareness training, and women's development, mentoring and coaching programmes. In many cases in this study, women were the first and only employees to work part-time or flexibly at their levels in their organisations. The additional pressures of being a role model are brought to life in their stories.

Much academic and industry research points to the significance of the late twenties, thirties and early forties age groups for women starting families. It is a life transition that women today approach having already accumulated perhaps 10 to 20+ years of professional experience and so it is reasonable to assume that career attachment might feature in their decision making about work. I focus on professional women's transitions because they are heavily invested in education and work experience and therefore professional identity is likely to be an important element of their sense of self. The decisions about work and motherhood they make are likely to impinge at deeper level than a strictly economic one, and to be about core aspects of identity and selfhood. As other studies have observed, professional women are also likely to experience ideological and practical tensions between their responsibilities as mothers and as workers (Blair-Loy and Wharton, 2004; Haynes, 2008; Crompton and Lyonette, 2011a; Bloch and Taylor, 2012). This is not to imply that the identity work, employment experiences and work–life tensions of women employed at other occupational levels are less worthy of scholarly inquiry; it is simply that they are not the focus of the present study.

Given that the transition to part-time working in particular is one that mothers in the UK are more likely to make than fathers, and given the persistence of part-time working patterns in women's careers long after the age at which children begin school, I was interested to be able to compare the experience of women approaching the transition for the first time, from their first period of maternity, with that of women making flexible employment adjustments when children are older. Twelve first-time mothers were recruited to the sample who were approaching the transition to part-time and flexible working for the first time simultaneously with their return-to-work following maternity leave. Eighteen mothers were recruited who approached the transition at a later biographical point: upon the birth of a second or third child, and when children were older. The consequences of these criteria for the sample were that most of the women were aged between 28 and 44 at the time of the first interview and were mothers to either one infant or up to four children under the age of 17 who were usually resident with the mother.

Women lived in different parts of the UK, the majority in England and around one third in the capital city of London. They were employed in the public and private sectors in approximately equal numbers. They worked in large organisations that typically employed over a thousand people, and they worked in a broad range of occupational fields as doctors, lawyers, accountants and finance managers; management consultants; managers in technology, marketing, communications and human resources; academics; public servants in central and local government; and in health, justice and the protective services.

Most women were in couple relationships with men who were the fathers of their children. Plenty of research evidence points to the salience of the gender role strategy within couples in women's decisions about employment and careers, and to their satisfaction with their domestic arrangements (for example, Hochschild, 1989; Ely et al, 2014). Domestic divisions of labour and gender role strategies within couples were heavily present in our discussions of relationships. Twenty-eight women were either cohabiting or married to their male partners. One lone parent participated in the project and one lesbian mother took part who was married to her female partner. One woman became a lone parent in the year that we were talking and another initiated separation; as will be discussed in later chapters, relationship pressures and problems loomed large in women's overall assessments of their experience of a year of working flexibly.

Flexible working can be defined in the broadest sense as affording workers autonomy and control over what, when, where and how their paid work gets done. These affordances are operationalised in individually negotiated flexible working arrangements. In US management studies literature, such arrangements are referred to as idiosyncratic deals or 'i-deals' (Rousseau et al, 2016). I refer to **flexible working arrangements**, a term I use interchangeably with **flexible working patterns** and in abbreviated form as **FWAs**, and which I define after Hill et al (2008) as an individual variation in working time, space, place or job structure that makes it distinct from a full-time (typically between 30 and 48 hours per week), permanent, fixed day-time working arrangement on the employer's premises.

In policy, there is little agreement about which FWAs constitute flexible working. UK labour market statistics distinguish 8 types of flexible working arrangement in addition to part-time working hours and home or tele-working (ONS, 2016): flexible working hours, job-share, term-time working, nine day fortnight, zero-hours contract, annualised hours, four and a half day week, and on call working. Industry surveys offer anything between 8 and 18 specific types of arrangement with variation typically around the inclusion of various forms of contract flexibility such as self-employment, temporary employment or zero-hours contracts as flexible work arrangements. The definition can further include irregular or extended breaks and leaves, such as formal career breaks and unpaid leave. Flexible work arrangements are not mutually exclusive, and survey data indicate that multiple forms of flexible work arrangement are used simultaneously by managers, for example part-time work hours in combination with a flexi-time schedule (CIPD, 2012). By my own calculations, combining the most common temporal, location and structural flexibilities gives rise to 330 possible combinations only one of which represents the default under Hill et al's (2008) definition. If contractual flexibilities, which are not the focus of this study (that is, contingent workforce contracts such as zero-hours, temporary and 'gig' or fixed-term contracts) are included in the calculation, the possible combinations reach 720. The possibility of hundreds of flexible working arrangements in permanent employment signals something of both the opportunity to customise how, when and where we work, and also the dramatic adjustments that organisations structured around the singular default work pattern need to make to integrate and manage such diversity.

This diversity was reflected in the study sample and just nine professional women varied the 'full-time, fixed schedule, employers' premises' default by only the number of weekly hours they work. Part-time working was more typically used in combination with either schedule flexibility, that is, control or specificity about the timing of core hours and days of paid work (in 12 cases), and/or location flexibility, that is, control or specificity over a place of work, in 18 cases; also, in three cases, part-time working was combined with job-sharing, that is splitting or sharing the responsibilities of one job with another person.

The work circumstances of women's transitions were just as diverse as their individual working arrangements. Connolly and Gregory's (2008) longitudinal quantitative analysis of women's moves through part-time and full-time work suggests that there are two tracks at least for part-time workers; part-time work can serve as short-term support to career and as a trap or a dead-end. Fairly consistently in the empirical literature it appears that the most advantageous part-time positions are with same employer; reduce hours but not use of skills; and endure for a relatively short period of time. The definition of 'a short period of time' however, is ambiguous in the literature (Lambert et al, 2012).' Twenty-five women in this study were embarking on what Connolly and Gregory (2008) suggest may prove to be a more advantageous position of remaining with their present employer. Of those 25 women who remained with the same employer for their transition, around half (13 cases) were converting their previous full-time jobs into part-time and flexible jobs, and the other 12 women were simultaneously embarking on a new job and a new flexible working arrangement. Unusually, five women were navigating three new experiences simultaneously: beginning new flexible working arrangements in new jobs with new employers; their working hours, schedule and location flexibilities were negotiated as part of a recruitment process. These are important distinctions, and comparison of the processes and practices women use to implement and 'do' their arrangements, reveals much about the readiness, capabilities and organisational resources women are able to draw upon in each of these scenarios.

Gender equality is the core theme underpinning this work, for which I adopt a definition based on Lewis (2010), that gender equality 'respects agency and seeks to enable real choice', that is, the capacity to make alternative choices about how to care and how to work.

This is not a definition that is restricted to women's work–life choices and career advancement, since I view the opportunities for and the outcomes of gender equality in employment and inside the family as beneficial to all who experience bias or exclusion on the basis of gender stereotyping. The issues in focus are the limits and potential of flexible working in professional and management jobs for gender equality at home and at work.

A number of women involved in this study held prominent positions in their organisations and became more visible by their pioneering of different forms of flexibility in their roles. Great care has been taken to protect the identities of all 30 women who shared their stories and views. Pseudonyms are used and only limited biographical detail and information about their professions is provided (see Appendix 1; pseudonyms in the text are followed by the participant's identification number in square brackets). For the women who met with me two and more often three times over a year in their lives, many spoke of how the opportunity to participate in research of this type and on this theme, had given them welcome pause for reflection in busy lives. Some women had experienced penalties and discrimination in subtle and not so subtle ways. This surprised them because many believed gender discrimination was a thing of the past. These experiences motivated them to share their stories in the hope of making motherhood and work work better.

Structure of this book

This book is concerned with two broad aspects of motherhood and professional work, that can be summarised, colloquially, as the 'choosing' and the 'doing' of part-time and flexible working arrangements. The first part of the book, up to Chapter 4, is concerned with the choosing and the remaining chapters are concerned with the doing. Verbatim quotes and longer extracts from interviews vividly illustrate the analysis.

Chapter 2: Choosing Flexibility dissects the framing structures within which professional mothers are making decisions about work, motherhood and careers. Extracts from Anna's story illustrate the strength and direction of influence on her work–life opportunities and choices of five intersecting factors: money and finance, age and maternal biography, childcare networks, the gender role strategy within couples, and women's status and influence at work. These are discussed in turn. The influences of dominant cultural ideologies of mothering are central to this discussion about *why* women engage in paid work (Hays, 1996; Thomson et al, 2011), as is the relational frame within which women make decisions about *how* they will work relative to the practical and temporal requirements of their children, their childcare providers, and in the context of their partners' employment patterns and careers (Greenhaus and Powell, 2012; Brimrose et al, 2014).

Chapter 3: Seeking Balance explores what the ubiquitous concept of work–life balance means to professional mothers and its elision with part-time and flexible working arrangements. In discussing balance and work choices made in its pursuit, I engage with feminist critique of contemporary discursive formulations of choice and empowerment associated with postfeminism (Gill, 2016; McRobbie, 2009), that urge women to seek fulfilment through balancing professional and family goals (Rottenberg, 2013). A significant and original contribution to this analysis is the formulation of women's motivations into four 'intention narratives' that express what women hope to achieve with their employment adjustments and why it matters. Three of the four are discussed in this chapter, brought to life by Jane, Olivia and Sarah, and Andrea's powerful case illustrations. These are: *resolving work–life conflict, protecting careers* and *expanding careers*. This analysis concludes that transition holds far greater meaning and significance in professional women's lives than an apparently minor fractional adjustment to the contract of employment might suggest. Close examination of how professional mothers explain their motivations for their particular working arrangement reveals the layers of meaning attached to it and the complexity of the practical and ideological settlement it reflects.

Chapter 4: Compromised Choices discusses the fourth intention narrative, which relates to the circumstances of eight professional mothers that afforded them little or no real choice about how to work and how to care for the family. Compromise is a feature of all women's decisions and transitions through part-time and flexible work, however compromise stymies some women's intentions in more marked ways. The twin contexts of the workplace and the family are sharply in focus here, and the strength of influence on professional mothers' opportunities are vivid in Jenny's story of failed negotiation with her new manager over her desired working pattern, and Meera's story of frequent and occasionally furious negotiations with her husband over domestic chores in an effort to release herself from some of the routine and repetitious responsibilities for family life. This discussion extends to examine the circumstances under which women had greater access to flexibility at work and operationalised a more egalitarian model of the couple relationship (Hochschild, 1989; Lyonette and Crompton, 2015). Analysis of these compromised transitions offers important challenges to assumptions that the ways in which professional mothers work reflects their deeply held preferences (such as Hakim, 2000).

Chapter 5: Doing Flexibility benefits from the longitudinal perspective and, drawing on women's narrative accounts between 3 and 12 months after embarking on their flexible arrangement, shifts the focus from intentions to practices. Surprisingly little is known about how flexible working arrangements work in practice, on the ground, in professional and managerial jobs (see one exception, in a limited field: Gascoigne, 2014). This chapter explains how women redesign their jobs, create new workspaces, and manage the temporal and spatial boundaries between their professional work and their family work. It deals with the work-related experiences and outcomes of women's transitions under three scenarios: converting a full-time job into a part-time job, job-sharing and working from home.

Chapter 6: Feeling Flexibility extends the discussion of practices to the physical and emotional labours involved in doing flexibility. In the tradition of feminist scholarship this analysis makes visible the intense and varied kinds of emotional, cognitive, physical and practical work women do every day to implement and sustain the work–life arrangements they have, and the terrific responsibility they feel for doing so. Women's experiences navigating the return-to-work post-maternity transition simultaneously with the first-time flexibility transition reveal the intensely physical and emotionally vulnerable characteristics of a period of profound change. The concept of *quiet responsibility* is introduced to conceptualise the expectations placed upon and assumed by professional mothers for implementing their non-standard arrangements in work contexts not designed to support them.

Chapter 7: Stresses and Success discusses outcomes, in the sense of how experience of transitioning to a part-time and flexible arrangement tallies with expectations. It records the dominant themes that characterise the experience of implementing and sustaining flexible working patterns in professional and managerial work. Why women make further adjustments to their work arrangements or why they quit evidences how the sustained experiences of work intensity associated with working fewer hours in largely unadjusted full-time jobs, and frustration in marginal part-time jobs deemed more suitable to fewer working hours, reveals systemic inattention to how work is organised and performed and how jobs are designed. Job-sharing emerges as flexible job design with potential to support a part-time work pattern in a role that demands continuous availability and responsiveness to its requirements. Women report moments of success when everything seems to work, and frequent periods of stress which make situations feel fragile and any sense of balance fleeting. Discussion in this chapter extends to the stresses and successes in the domestic sphere and the rich seam of data that relates to women's experiences and satisfactions with their couple relationships.

Chapter 8: Making Professional Motherhood, Careers and Flexibility Work considers the implications of the research findings for professional mothers, partners-in-parenting, employers and policy makers in order to challenge gendered norms and responsibilities for earning and caring that frame women's work–life opportunities and choices. I propose that systemic inattention to how we work and what needs to happen to make jobs *genuinely* flexible is damaging women and organisations. I make the case for interventions that may support individual transitions through part-time and flexible working arrangements, alongside more structural interventions at the level of the organisation and national policy that shift the default job design from fixed and full-time to flexible and, in so doing, create the conditions for more equal lives across domestic and professional spheres.

2

Choosing Flexibility

Chapter themes

It is often assumed that professional working mothers are well-resourced women who have made choices. The concept of choice, however, is highly problematic in the context of motherhood and paid work. There are two competing accounts concerning women's disproportionate involvement in part-time work. One account assumes that choosing part-time work is a reflection of women's personal preferences and intrinsic desires (e.g. Hakim, 2002, 2006). Others foreground the social and structural influences on women's preferences and employment choices, and underline the difficulties women with family responsibilities face reconciling paid work and family care (e.g. Ginn et al, 1996; McRae, 2003; Crompton et al, 2007a).

This chapter investigates professional women's choices about how much, where and when they work, and unpicks the complex and intersecting factors found to complicate and constrain their capacity for professional work in the context of their motherhood. The influences of dominant cultural ideologies of mothering are central to this discussion about why women work (Hays, 1996; Thomson et al, 2011) as is the relational frame (Greenhaus and Powell, 2012; Brimrose et al, 2014) within which women make decisions about how much and when they will work relative to the practical and temporal requirements of their children, their childcare providers, and in the context of their partners' work patterns and earning power.

The chapter begins with Anna's story and then moves to discuss five intersecting economic, social, cultural and personal factors that are material to women's working hours and flexibility choices. The strength and direction of influence of: age and biography, money and mortgages, childcare, couple relationships, and women's work status are discussed. Anna's story underscores the complexity and the myriad of influences surrounding the decision to adjust employment in early motherhood.

Anna's choice

Anna and I met towards the end of the full year that she had spent on maternity leave from her senior management job in a large private sector business. Anna is married and owns her home with the help of a mortgage loan, and had enjoyed a 17-year professional career before her longed-for first pregnancy at age 38. She had risen fast through the ranks in a traditionally masculine industry and was one of few women embarking upon her profession in the late 1990s. Anna and her husband have been together over 15 years and for much of that time Anna was the main breadwinner in the couple. As the eldest daughter of a lone parent, she had provided financially for her younger siblings during her twenties. Anna said that she had initially planned to take six months maternity leave from her job but had extended it following health problems caused by her pregnancy. In three weeks Anna is going back to work for the first time since her son was born and simultaneously she will transition into a three-day part-time work arrangement in a new internal role that the company found for her when she asked to reduce her work hours. There are a lot of firsts marking Anna's next few weeks. We met in a coffee shop near where she lived and, with her infant son settled in a highchair, I asked her to tell me her story about how she got to where she is now and about the significance of returning to work and of going part-time for the first time in her work career. Anna said:

> "I've never entertained the idea of going back full-time because we wanted to have [my son] for a long, long time and it's taken a lot of heartache and effort to get to this stage. I didn't really feel I could go back and not enjoy him for at least half the week. So that was the decision for the three days as well. It was massively stressful though working out whether to put him into nursery whether that was the right thing for him, or whether we should go down the childminder route."

Tracing the origins of her decision to return to work part-time to her long, exhausting and medicalised journey to pregnancy, and to the experience of a difficult birth, the opportunity to be with her son is the welcome reward. A recent employment change for Anna's husband has brought him some career success. She says he is enjoying his work and is now earning significantly more than he has ever done before, which means the family can be supported by his income from a full-time job without making major adjustments to their lifestyle and financial commitments. Their roles have changed, as Anna explained:

> "He's the main breadwinner now. He works in banking so there is no flexibility whatsoever, so if we were ever going to have any flexibility it would be on my side [rather] than his and he's always been very supportive of that. I think secretly he'd hoped I wouldn't go back to work at all and I'd just stay at home full-time … I think it's because he's a bit of a traditionalist at heart. I think he likes this idea of having this full-time mum at home to look after Max. I mean all kids are precious to their families, but in particular in our case because we waited so long, I think my husband would rather keep Max's care with me, someone he trusts completely … Yeah, he has slightly traditional values but he's open to kind of being supportive of me wanting to go back and he's definitely a lot more comfortable now I have convinced him of the value of a nursery and Max being with other children as an only child."

Anna was passionate about the job she was doing full-time before she left on maternity leave, "I absolutely loved it!" she said, and having been employed in various roles in the business for over ten years, she had good relationships with her managers and colleagues to return to. Her ambition to continue working was clear. Her professional work was part of who she was and she didn't want to give up. The negotiation of her return to work was justified to her "slightly traditional" husband as presenting social opportunities for their son, which would be good for his social development. Her dilemma was how much work outside the home she should and could do at this point, in the context of her husband's deepening work commitment, their mutual expectations of her maternal role, and doing the right thing for their son.

The balance that Anna seeks to strike, she measures by metering time in a typical working week, and on this she says: "three days at work, four days with the family, that feels like the right balance". Despite having expressed a passion for her job, she said she had privately anticipated that it would be more difficult to do it when she couldn't be available around the clock. She knew that she would need to leave the office at 5 pm to collect her son from nursery because it closes at 6 pm and would then take over his care through to bedtime. She felt her job was unsuitable for part-time working and found this was something that she and her employer agreed on:

"I had sort of thought and didn't really want to face it, but when they [her employer] said it, it did feel like a bit of a rejection. I did feel a bit sad and it had a bit of an end-of-an-era feeling to it. And I did worry that I am never going to get such a great job again, but then you very quickly kind of put it in perspective and you come home and think, 'Well actually I wanted to be in this position to have my son, to be a mum so I had better get on with it.' Maybe you can't have it all sometimes."

There is palpable disappointment in Anna's account of coming to the end of the work life she knew and enjoyed. Anna is embarking on a new and unfamiliar work experience and assuming a new professional identity as a part-time worker, which appears in her eyes to have instantly narrowed her professional opportunities. Her reference to a widely circulated cultural myth of professional women's capacity to 'have it all', meaning to successfully combine motherhood with an interesting and well-rewarded career job, exposes how her own lived reality is less about having it all and more about making hard choices.

The transition to motherhood is a time of significant change in a woman's life. Research that compares women's post-birth experiences with their expectations and ideals for motherhood during pregnancy, consistently shows that becoming a mother can concurrently be described as hugely disorienting, overwhelming, deeply fulfilling and enriching, and a profound shock despite being anticipated (Miller, 2005; Lupton and Schmied, 2013). The transition to motherhood begins long before the event of a birth and continues long after. The social status of mother and the responsibilities of motherhood are conferred upon birth or adoption but becoming a mother is a generative process that demands learning, adaptation, and social and economic resources. *Feeling* like a mother is considered to be a lifelong reflexive project that is often in flux (Miller, 2005), and Anna is at the beginning of that project. Expressing the transition to motherhood in narrative terms, Bailey (1999) describes the sudden transition from woman to mother as 'a narrative pivot in the construction of a reflexive biography' during which women experience a heightened awareness of different aspects of themselves. Identity transformation, Bailey argues, is not inevitable. It is possible for a woman to feel like the same person, but different upon motherhood, and as such to experience a sense of continued self rather than encountering a disjuncture or a splitting of the self as postmodern accounts of identity fragmentation would suggest. This is not to suggest that there are no disruptions. There are tensions between different aspects of women's lives, and between their identities as workers and as mothers. These tensions inhibit women's opportunities to express a globally whole identity as professionals *and* mothers and push them towards one or the other.

Dynamics of choice, preference and agency

It was evidence of downward occupational mobility, lower pay and restricted promotions associated with part-time work that led Hakim (2002, 2006) to theorise about why it was that women appeared, paradoxically, to choose it over better quality full-time jobs. By equating women's working patterns with their preferences, Hakim suggests that in choosing part-time work a woman is demonstrating her intrinsic desire for mothering and domestic life and hence her weaker work and career commitment. One of the many reasons that Hakim's theory is so controversial is its implication that women working part-time are less committed to their paid work and to their professional identities. Hakim grouped what she termed women's 'work–lifestyle preferences' into three ideal types thought to reflect closely held personal values: the home-centred woman represents 20% of women for whom family life and children are the main priorities throughout life; the work-centred woman represents another 20% of women, mostly childless and whose main priority in life is employment or equivalent activities in the public arena. Hakim's majority group are the adaptive women, the 60% of women who seek to combine work and family, because, Hakim offers, they are less committed to their paid work than their full-time counterparts and less committed to work in the family as is evident by their attempts to limit time in both spheres. The many critics of Hakim's preference-driven theory of women's occupational choice and decision making do not deny that women can and do make choices, rather they see those choices as more constrained by practicalities and circumstances, norms and conventions (see McRae, 2003). Failing to sufficiently examine the framing structures and constraints within which choices are made positions the individual as responsible for the outcomes they achieve. In effect women can be blamed for their own exclusion from the workplace by making the 'wrong' choices (Lewis and Simpson, 2017). Robust criticism of Hakim's theory came from feminist sociologists Rosemary Crompton and Clare Lyonette (2007b) who, along with many other scholars (see for example Ginn et al, 1996), critiqued the theory for its inattentiveness to the complex web of competing pulls and constraints that mothers have to face, and to the significant identity work required in reconciling mothering and working. McRae (2003) makes the compelling argument that women may have similar attitudes and orientations but their differential capacities for overcoming constraints lead to different labour market outcomes. Studies that track women's work–life trajectories through time have been helpful in demonstrating that women do not end up doing what they would have chosen, and their work–home arrangement does not necessarily match their orientation towards mothering and working. Houston and Marks (2003) found that some women seemed to have withdrawn from working to *preserve* rather than compromise their professional identities, some remained childless and not necessarily due to a strong career orientation, and some returned to full-time work after one child and reduced to part-time after two.

In response to Hakim's overemphasis on voluntary choice, and her conceptualisation of working pattern as an expression of work or family preference and, by implication, career commitment, Crompton and Harris (1998) developed a six-category typology of personal styles of managing work and family combinations. This is an important distinction, between Hakim's 'types of women' and Crompton and Harris's emphasis on 'styles of managing', the latter locating women's approaches firmly within an external context, compared to Hakim's more intrinsic treatment of working patterns as a reflection of deeply held values. Crompton and Harris, and also later Tomlinson's (2006b) research with women managers, identified a minority of women giving primacy to domestic life and some to their careers. Importantly, they also identified much more nuanced differentiation within the majority group of women whose circumstances, identifications and strategies were directed towards reconciling the two. Tomlinson concluded, in agreement with Crompton and Harris, that most women attempt to 'satisfice' their work and family lives. A satisficing approach involves a conscious and unconscious scaling up and down of goals for family life and professional career such that neither is maximised at the expense of the other. In both studies, women's transitions through part-time work were found typically to be a reaction to changing external circumstances such as divorce and redundancy, or a restricted framework of opportunity compromised them (for example, a lack of affordable childcare). Overall, women's employment transitions were much less likely to be strategic, planned or, as Hakim might argue, a reflection of personal preference. By foregrounding factors in individual life biographies such as divorce, pressure of work and organisational restructuring in the shaping of personal styles of managing home and work, Crompton and Harris (1998) and Tomlinson (2006b) positioned individual choice as socially constructed, and that women's options are gendered, classed and constrained in ways which may not be fully appreciable by the individual at the time.

Research on identity transformation and motherhood in the psychosocial field has been particularly useful in positioning internal understandings of motherhood and mothering within the social context as mutually constitutive, that is, forming and informing one another. Attempting to bring the cultural and economic rationales for maternal employment together to explain worker-mother identity construction, Duncan and Edwards (1999) and Duncan and Irwin (2004) termed the construction of employment and mothering choices 'gendered moral rationalities' (GMRs), referring to the moral guidelines of the appropriate and responsible decision a mother should make in regard to employment, shared parenting and childcare. These 'socially patterned understandings are gendered in that they delegate childcare to mothers, moral in that they recommend cultural values, and rational in that these values are used as the basis for making decisions about how children are raised. In their study of lone mothers' caring and work decisions, Duncan and Edwards (1999) found that GMRs take three forms: primary-mother (physically caring for the child yourself); primary-worker (separating the identities of mother and worker); and mother/worker integral (defining employment and financial support as part of good mothering). They found that rather than the task of care being viewed as simply a constraint on participation in paid work, for mothers it was often a deeply felt moral obligation and commitment. This complicates the notion of choice by introducing an element of agency that simultaneously structures decisions about work and care. Himmelweit and Sigala (2004) similarly found that mothers making the interlinked decisions about childcare and their own working patterns had both internal and external constraints; in other words, individual attitudes (which the authors use analytically as a proxy for identity) – as well as dominant external factors such as finances, childcare and working hours – limited mothers' choices. They observed how mothers' attitudes informed how they construed their decisions so that they did not consider options for childcare or working patterns that did not accord with their identities. For example, in couching views about mothering and working in statements that begin 'I'm not the kind of person/mother who ...' behaves in a certain way (Himmelweit and Saga, 2004, p490), women ruled out possible courses of action such as not working and becoming a stay-at-home mother, and confirmed their position by the process of ruling them out, so would not consider full-time employment or full-time institutional care for their children.

Age and biography

The transition to motherhood is pivotal in a woman's evolving biography and prompts personal evaluation of the meaning and significance of paid work in life at that moment, and which they carry on re-evaluating throughout their careers. The significance of age and biography in shaping women's situations and how they talk about them is important in this discussion. This is understood in terms of embodied age at first and successive pregnancies, and the age-related circumstances of the journey to pregnancy. The trend towards later motherhood in the UK is reflected in the women's stories, a small number of women participating in this research having given birth for the first time in their late thirties and early forties. In medical terms this marks them as 'older mothers' and positions them simultaneously as having accumulated the necessary social and economic capital to support motherhood, and potentially risking their own health and shaming their children by being 'too old' (Thomson et al, 2011).

For some women interviewed in this research the long and difficult path to a successful pregnancy and birth or adoption influenced their preference for working less by going part-time. A significant minority of the women (seven) talked about their experiences of difficulty and delays getting pregnant. The long, physically invasive, emotionally and financially draining medical pathway to pregnancy shaped women's thoughts about the amount of time they felt they could and should put to their paid work, and about who should be trusted with care for their longed-for children.

> "I've been trying for a long time to have children and then seven years later it finally happened. So I'm like what's the point in me having children if I'm not going to be around to bring them up? So mentally I'm going through that dilemma of really working out how many days do I want to work." (Olivia [5])

If we return to Anna [24] for a moment, Anna feels her career, or at least her first career, is behind her, however she remains deeply committed to her professional identity emphatically claiming, "I will never not work." The transition to motherhood, and the series of employment and personal transitions that characterise combining motherhood with career, take place in multiple unfolding biographies: of the individual, the couple and the family. The timing of first birth or adoption of a first child in the context of establishment of women's professional careers is material to their employment decisions in terms of whether they feel they are on the ascent, at a satisfactory point, or have reached an unsatisfactory plateau. Tomlinson (2006b) identified a 'career-behind-me' work–life trajectory among older women working part-time in management roles that she describes as an emergent trajectory with potential to arise in greater numbers because of women starting families later in life. Tomlinson's research showed that some women try to achieve a work–life balance in a biographical sense, by constructing different periods in their life course (career phase, family phase) and in this way rectifying the competing tensions by refracting their goals for work and goals for life in a way they can articulate and make sense of.

Money and mortgages

The relationship between women's part-time and flexible working choices and their financial needs is not straightforward. The economic drivers of professional mothers' employment were significant; their participation was not driven purely by financial necessity, however. It is the amount of paid work in these women's lives that is structured by the family's financial commitments and a perceived need to achieve a desired level of income. Eleanor [13] illustrates this point. She is aware that her lifestyle choices had constrained what she felt was her ideal choice of working arrangement and described a need to earn a minimum amount for the family as determining the amount of work hours in her life:

> "I need to work 80% to earn the minimum we need so that absolutely isn't a choice, but it is my choice to go on holiday, and drive a car, and live here and it's that and how we live that's driving how much we need to earn … we have three children, we have by no means a luxurious lifestyle but we have more than a lot of other people." (Eleanor [13])

For the year ending 5 April 2016 the median gross annual earnings for full-time employees were £28,600 (ONS, 2017e). Individual and household earnings information was not requested of the women taking part, but where offered the range appeared to be great and significantly higher than the national median. One senior manager employed in the public sector volunteered information about her gross annual pro rata salary of £22,000. Another senior manager in the private sector said she earned in excess of £250,000 salary and bonus. Lower and higher earning women alike described an obligation to service the family's ongoing financial commitments, such as mortgage loans and other credit, and to maintain a standard of living. Social psychologists Johnston and Swanson (2007) suggested that financial need is relative and socially constructed. While, in practical terms, women in better-off households are more able to choose not to work, their study of 98 professional women showed that middle-class women may well feel a need to contribute and not to be completely dependent on their partners, or they may describe as a *need* a desired standard of income or one they had been used to before children. Amanda, a senior manager and mother of two children aged 4 and 6, illustrates this point in her reflection of the need she feels to be financially independent and how being at least an equal earner elevates her status in her relationship with her husband:

> "I didn't want to be in a situation where I wasn't earning at least close to the same amount as him because I'd just been so used to it. When I was an equal earner I felt I had more authority in our relationship. I felt very uncomfortable being financially dependent on my husband during maternity leave … I didn't like being answerable to how money was spent and I *really* didn't like having to ask him to put money in the joint account." (Amanda [10])

Juliet [29], a senior manager in the private sector and mother of four children aged between 6 and 17, similarly articulated her motivation to contribute financially to the family: "when I'm contributing financially I feel more part of decisions … it is kind of how I put a value on myself." That women's perceived financial need was relative in the context of their lifestyles and earner status is not to suggest that any pressure women felt to sustain a level of income was not real. Hayley [14] recalled hard financial times for the family, and how the expenses associated with travel to and from her employer's premises and the cost of childcare supressed her free choice of employment:

> "He lost his job when I was on maternity leave so stuff like what I really personally wanted to do with my career got pushed right down, I just needed to get back to work … I remember doing constant calculations about childcare versus commuting versus childcare vouchers versus stopping working. I just needed to know that we had 'x' amount coming in and that we wouldn't starve and then I could sleep at night." (Hayley [14])

Lara [6] applied an accounting logic to calculating the affordability of her working pattern by off-setting costs of childcare against her income.

"By the time you consider tax and the cost of childcare I worked out that the difference between me working five days a week and three days a week was £5000 [per year], it's not a lot really. I mean obviously it is a lot of money to a lot of people but it's not a lot to me if the price is being away from my children the whole week." (Lara [6])

There were no examples of this arithmetical approach being applied to household income, or to father's income, only to the mother's income. This signals that reconciling the costs of care is considered an extension of maternal responsibility. This finding echoes that of Harkness (2008), who found that in heterosexual dual-earner couples the costs of childcare were typically borne by the mother and couples apply a rational, economic evaluation of whether it is worth her while going out to work.

Women who earned less than their partners, not even significantly less, often referred to their secondary earner status in the household. Some referring to their income as providing for the extras that make family life nice and not for the everyday fundamentals, "I am working so we can have better things … I'm giving us lifestyle choices" (Charlotte [26]). Gemma [8], a senior manager in the public sector and mother of two pre-school children, was not content with that situation and the power imbalance that plays out in her relationship:

"Because he earns more than me, actually probably more than I ever could in my job, there is this sense that my income is secondary and it's his earnings that keep the household afloat. It feels like decisions about my work are then also relegated to second place and become all about paying for childcare and holidays." (Gemma [8])

Income inequalities within male and female couples are an effect of the persistence of the gender pay gap and a legacy of lower earnings for women in the UK. The gender pay gap widens among the highly educated, and for men in their thirties their wages continue to grow rapidly while women's wages plateau. Among parents the gender pay gap yawns open at a potentially unrecoverable 33%, which means that, by the time the first child is 12, women's wages are a third below men's (Costa Dias et al, 2016). These gendered wage inequalities intersect with gendered assumptions of care that position women as responsible for children and the domestic sphere and, I would argue, perpetuate inequality inside couple relationships in terms of the division of chores and also the rewards of labours inside and outside the home. In making decisions about working hours, it was common for the women in relationships with higher earning men to privilege the continuity of the highest earner's income trajectory over that of the lower earner because it seems more immediately affordable to reduce women's less well remunerated working hours than men's better paid time.

While these relatively well-resourced women were in principle freer to choose not to, the affordability of work in the context of ongoing financial commitments and lifestyle aspirations remained an important consideration in decisions about how many hours to work outside the home.

Childcare

Childcare is the scaffolding around professional women's lives. Who provides it, where it is provided, the quality of care, how much it costs, how flexible it is, and how children feel about it are questions the answers to which structure women's capacity for paid work and influence the types of workplace flexibility they seek.

> "I couldn't do any of this without the childcare. We have quite a combination to manage over the week. Mondays, they're in all day at nursery 8 'til 6. Tuesday they're in 8 'til 3.30 and Andrew's mum picks them up and has them until one of us gets home. Wednesday they go to nursery in the morning and my husband has them in the afternoon, because he works flexible shifts and can be there most weeks. Thursday they go into nursery half a day and my mum has them in the afternoon. And Friday I'm off work so it's me all day." (Sophie [30])

Sophie was not unusual in combining various forms of childcare within a single day and across a week to increase her capacity for paid work and stretch the length of her working day. Sophie was in an unusual position in another way, because her husband regularly looked after their children for at least half a day during a typical working week. Most women in this study had found solutions to childcare that did not depend on the routine involvement of fathers. The opportunity and the challenge this presents for professional working women in heterosexual couple families is a thread that will be returned to in Chapter 4. The childcare networks in these women's lives involved many actors: partners, nannies, childminders, au-pairs, grandparents and institutions such as nurseries, schools and sports/activity clubs. Tomlinson defined care networks as:

> formal and informal, paid and unpaid, care arrangements, networks and institutions that provide women with the opportunity to work. These resources include care and support by partners, friends and extended family members along with more formal facilities and services such as nurseries, schools and after school clubs. (Tomlinson, 2006b, p370)

Tomlinson views care networks as resources that facilitate women's lives in a similar vein to Bourdieu's notion of social capital (Bourdieu, 1986), whereby effective social networks facilitate mothers in their attempts to reconcile work and family life. When these networks breakdown or are insufficient women face constraints in their attempts to reconcile work and family life. The least flexible and most constraining forms of childcare were provided by institutions at premises outside the home such as nurseries, pre-schools, schools, colleges and childminders providing care in their own homes. Opening and closing times structured the time women had available for work. Commuting distance between home and location of the childcare facility further constrained women's work schedules. Care provided by grandparents now retired from paid work was valued highly by women who were able to benefit from a regular arrangement. Grandparent care was valued for many perceived benefits: for keeping care in the family, for maintaining continuity of care as children grow up, and for the financial benefit of reduced household expenditure on private childcare. Six women received regular childcare support from their own or their partner's parents, or a combination of both:

> "It's a necessity really that our mums have stepped in. It's very difficult to get from and to London from here between 9 and 5 so that's why we asked for their help two afternoons a week, it just means that it's only on one day I need to leave work at 4.30 to pick the children up from nursery." (Sophie [30])

A key finding is that women's decisions about childcare are linked to their decisions about their working hours, schedules and locations, and in this decision tree, the affordability of childcare is a key branch. There were discernible patterns in the types of childcare that women identified as most and least constraining on their hours, schedules and locations of work. The options that offered the women most flexibility were also the most expensive: private live-in or live-out nannies. Nannies or childminders (including live-in au-pairs in this category) were felt to offer the most flexibility, and care provided by institutions such as nurseries, pre-schools and wrap-around school-based care was the most restrictive and least flexible option. An effective childcare arrangement is so highly prized that it becomes a structuring feature of other decisions about the family's future:

> "We actually want to move out of the city but we have a perfect childcare situation here and until the kids are older I'm not going anywhere. Our childminder lives on our street and I drop the kids off at 8 am and she walks my daughter to school, and then takes my son to pre-school. She picks them up and feeds them and then they play at her house with another three kids until one of us can get there about 6.30. The brilliant thing is that there is no extra commute and she can be flexible and has them for extra time here and there." (Olivia [5])

The high cost of childcare for infants and toddlers was mentioned frequently by women interviewed for this study, in terms of its impact on their working hours choices: "it's very expensive and clearly between us we are very high-income earners and at £32,000 a year we still think it's expensive". For some women in managerial roles, the cost of institutional childcare eclipsed her earned income. Avoiding this expense by using grandparents made professional work possible for some women, like Nina [16]:

> "I suppose if we had childcare costs to bear in mind it might have been more of a weigh-up about whether I went back to work at all but because we know that we don't have to pay for that, I mean we might pay our parents something to look after him for food and outings, but it's not the same as paying £50 or £60 a day for a nursery."

Gemma's reflection illustrates the interrelated nature of decisions about childcare and decisions about working patterns:

> "I just decided that if I was going to go into what was a new and challenging job and he was going to continue to be away with work, then we needed childcare that was just a bit more wrapped around and was at home ... it is prohibitively expensive really, I mean it pretty much wipes out my salary but at least it is working well so far." (Gemma [8])

The often commented upon high cost of formal childcare is a reflection of the policy context in the UK at the time these women were making their transitions into part-time and flexible work. The UK is unique among European countries in the way its youngest children are looked after. There is no state provision of childcare for under-2s and high fees for private infant care. The commercial market is now a significant third-party supplier of care and domestic services that are outsourced by the family and it has become fundamental in supporting many dual-earning and working lone-parent families fulfil their 'adult worker' duties (Lewis, 2010). The availability and affordability of quality childcare is a significant enabler and, conversely, its inaccessibility is a significant constraint on maternal participation in paid work, either full-time or at all. The average cost of a nursery place for a child under 2 is now £4.26 per hour across Britain, £5.33 per hour in London and nursery costs for 3- and 4-year-olds in England are only 1.9% cheaper than are costs for children aged 2 and under (Daycare Trust and Family Parenting Institute, 2013). Couples in the UK with both parents working use a median of 19.5 hours of formal childcare for children aged 3 to 4 and 15 hours for children aged up to 2, and most use a pattern of either five days or three days per week (Huskinson et al, 2011). In their analysis of the hours in which children are enrolled in early years childcare in European countries, Plantenga and Remery (2015) identify the UK as an outlier among European countries on two dimensions, first in the low levels of state support for early years childcare (which at the time of writing is 15 hours per week for children aged 3 and 4, extended to children aged 2 on a means-tested basis) and, second, in relatively few weekly hours that the majority of children spend in formal childcare (19.5 hours), when children in other countries experience attendance in formal settings typically for more than 30 hours per week. The costs of childcare are significant in the UK and rising at a rate higher than inflation. The UK has the highest costs of childcare across OECD countries in the West, with the costs of full-time care for one child consuming 25% of the average wage in dual-earner households, while with two children costs rise to 43% (OECD, 2012). This compares to the one-child costs against the average dual-earner wage in Sweden of 5%, and 6% for two children; 20% and 27% in the US; and 15% and 25% in France.

Mothers of infants and pre-schoolers had better access to continuous hours of childcare in a day, and for more weeks of the year than mothers of school-age children. Mothers of school-age children spoke of the changing temporal pattern of institutional care that was triggered by their children's entry to school at age 4 and progression from infant to junior school, typically prompting commensurate change in their own working patterns:

> "When Jack was in Year 2 I switched from four days a week in the office to spreading my four days' work across five. This meant that I could be there for the end of the school day and he didn't need to go to after-school club. This year it's got easier still now he's in Year 4 and walks himself the really short distance to school. I can be in the office by 9.15, which is great." (Cathy [4])

Different types of formal and informal childcare solutions are available as children grow up. Many of the mothers of school-age children found it necessary to patch together a full day of care by combining breakfast clubs and after-school clubs to bookend an 8.30 am to 3.30 pm school day. It was usual to use their own annual leave and an assortment of holiday clubs to cover the 12 weeks of the school holidays per year. Mothers of school-age and older children remarked that not only did formal childcare become harder to access; it also became the subject of negotiation between parent and child. Older children are less biddable than infants and toddlers and express their preferences for the care environments they do and do not wish to attend:

> "The kids go to breakfast club at half past seven, then school and then they're with the childminder until half past six. That's the longest day, that's 11 hours for them in childcare. I've tried different things and we'd settled on after-school club for quite a while as they both liked it but then they started to complain about it and say they didn't want to go. I get that. They're bored, they're tired, they want to be at home or doing other things like swimming but there is no one to take them." (Jane [12])

Noticeably absent from most women's accounts of the structuring influence of childcare on their own patterns of work was a reliance on networks of friends for informal childcare. This is potentially a reflection of these women's class position since it has been shown that informal childcare and local friendship networks feature more prominently in the care networks around working-class women's lives (Walkerdine et al, 2001; Crompton and Lyonette, 2007a). Professional mothers relied upon local friends only in emergencies, but not for regular care. As such, informal care was a weaker influence on the strength and resilience of a woman's care networks than formal childcare, and certainly weaker than partners' working patterns, which are now discussed.

Couple relationships

Often when partners worked long hours or travelled long distances and stayed away from home during the week, women's employment was adjusted to different ways of combining work with childcare. The unreliability of male partners' working patterns is a significant structuring influence on women's capacity for paid work, about which they had a lot to say in our first interviews:

> "He's not here for a couple of days each week and he can't seem to predict when those days are. If he's going to continue to work like that it means that I have got not choice really. I have to count him out of all the logistics and choose childcare that I know I can get to. I mean it is just epically complicated when he is not here to get two children to two different places and then turn up at work on time and ready to go." (Gemma [8])

Women's relationships with their partners-in-parenting, which in almost all cases were the fathers of their children, were heavily present in our discussions of women's decisions to adjust their employment. Gender relations inside the family are a significant theme in this research, and are discussed here in relation to how a couple's ideas about breadwinning and caregiving influence women's opportunities and capacities for employment and careers.

At the beginning of this chapter, Anna [24] talked about how her husband was "open to ... being supportive" of her desire to return to her professional work after the birth of their son and, in common with most male partners of first-time mothers in this study, she reported that he was not making any adjustment to his own working hours, schedule or location to accommodate childcare. How amenable a mother's partner is to adjusting their working pattern and taking on childcare reflects a couple's gender role ideology. Studying dual-career couples in the 1980s led Hochschild (1989) to argue that the gender role strategy between heterosexual couples features prominently in women's decisions about work and family and in their evaluation of satisfaction with their current arrangements. Gender role strategies reflect how couples' gender role *ideologies* are implemented in daily life, and Hochschild proposed they may be egalitarian, traditional or transitional. The egalitarian ideology expects that men and women identify with the same spheres of work, of family, or some combination of the two, and share power within the marriage equally. The traditional ideology expects the male career to take precedence and women are expected to identify with the domestic sphere. In between the egalitarian and traditional ideologies is the transitional ideology, whereby both partners are expected to seek fulfilment from work, although the male partner identifies as the primary breadwinner who supports the female partner's desire to work and she expects and is expected to balance work and family herself.

In generational perspective, Ely et al (2014) noticed a mismatch between the gender role expectations and lived realities among highly qualified women graduates. They found that half the women they described as Generation X (born in the 1970s and early 1980s; the birth cohort that aligns to the birth years of the women in focus in this study) expected egalitarian relationships and a sharing of responsibility for childcare, yet two thirds described a lived reality that was much more traditional. Ely et al (2014) suggest that this dashing of expectations leads to women's lower levels of satisfaction with their careers and is implicated in women's reported lower satisfaction with their couple relationships than male partners.

The mismatch between ideology and reality is perhaps nowhere better expressed than in Emma's [25] description at the beginning of the first chapter in this book: "my husband is a feminist so he doesn't think that we should do different things in relation to our work and our kids" and he was initially unsupportive of her desire to cut her work hours thinking she should continue full-time "because that kind of fits his ideological model". Practically however, her husband worked away from home for three days and two nights, "So the reality, or practicality of the way we live, doesn't actually make the ideal possible".

By contrast, Anna describes, in this chapter, what amounts to a transitional model of one-and-a-half-breadwinners that arises from the from the combination of her husband's traditionalism with her own transitional ideals. Anna and Emma were not alone. The majority of women in this study who expressed egalitarian rather than traditional ideals described a lived experience that was transitional (in 18 of 25 cases), in that women retained responsibility for home and childcare and were supported in various ways by a male partner to take on paid work. Only four of the partnered women in this study described a lived reality that was egalitarian and involved a more equal sharing of power within the partnership as well as the demands and rewards of work and looking after children. These arrangements will be discussed further in Chapter 4.

The persistence of domestic inequalities in the division of household labour and childcare in male and female couple relationships is in focus here, because a family management strategy that relies on the woman's participation in paid work on a part-time basis means that gender inequalities in domestic work allocation are often left unchallenged. The research literature concurs that over many decades little has changed regarding division of labour within the family. Time use studies show that men are doing more domestic tasks than in previous generations (Sullivan and Gershuny, 2011, 2013), however both men and women generally continue to prioritise the male partner's work and place primary responsibility for the home on the female partner when couples become parents. This seems to be the case even when the relationship begins on more egalitarian terms.

The language women in this study used to describe how "fortunate", "blessed" and "lucky" they felt to be able to share domestic chores and childcare tasks with their partners implies that perhaps women did not feel entitled or deserving to do so:

> "I'm very fortunate in that my husband does more of the domestic chores than I do. He can't sit still. We have a clean-up once a week but he does most of the cooking so he's very much busy about the house. I don't have to worry about being the main person who is doing that." (Victoria [21])

Domestic and childcare tasks might be shared between male and female partners, but mothers universally retained overall responsibility for their children and for organising childcare when they did not provide it themselves. Eleanor vividly brings to life what this responsibility means:

> "I guess as a mother you don't have a choice, do you? And a father doesn't either I suppose, but the responsibility for

the children is mine even though I am working almost full-time. He will do things like read them a story every night and if he's back in time we will do baths together, so he's not completely removed, it's not that they don't see him Monday to Friday. But at the heart of it really is that I could never be late for them but he could be." (Eleanor [13])

Eleanor's account illustrates an important theme that sets the scene in which women's working hours and flexibility choices are made. It illustrates the gendered nature of the moral requirements relating to parental care for children and the hold these have over mothers. That childcare was the mother's responsibility was implicit in the majority of women's accounts, explicit in others, of their decision to combine work and care through use of part-time and flexible working patterns.

Women's work status

Accessing flexible working policy and achieving a preferential arrangement remains a privileged position. Rarely did women described the flexible working arrangement that they arrived at as their ideal. Research has shown that high status and senior positions in organisations offer managers greater latitude for adjustment of their working time and timing, and greater ability to negotiate with employers to access preferential working arrangements (Tomlinson, 2006a). Work status can be conferred by grade or rank and also value to the organisation in terms of specialist skills and expertise, and valuable relationships. All the women in this study were in the occupational category of managers and professionals, although by their descriptions of the chains of management above and below them, some women occupied positions much higher up their organisational hierarchies than others. As a consequence, few women in the most senior positions used their organisation's flexible working policy to initiate and enact their request under the Right to Request legislation. Instead they verbally proposed a working pattern to their line manager and later formalised an adjustment to their contractual terms and conditions through relevant approving committees.

In our interviews, many women talked about refused requests and reluctant compromises relating to this transition and previous attempts to access and negotiate flexibility in their work histories. Refusals, which employers are within their legislative right to make for one of seven business reasons (Acas, 2014), plunged women into panic and removed their sense of agency. Gail [20] provides a vivid example:

"I know when they first turned me down going back on three days while I was still on maternity leave, when they said no, I mean, I just, well it was panic really … Not working wasn't an option. Finding another job seemed terrifying at the time, you know, as I don't think there could be one anywhere that I could work part-time and earn a decent wage. It was absolutely horrible." (Gail [20])

Women's access to the flexible working policy was on occasion facilitated by other organisational campaigns and strategies. An example being how some women employed in the public sector and seeking to work from home, benefited from organisational cost-cutting strategies to downsize premises and promote home-working. Other women, like Eryn [3], felt able to benefit from organisational gender retention initiatives aimed at them, "there's a big focus on retaining talented women at the moment and that has helped me I think".

On the whole, the public sector workers were more likely than the women working in the private sector to describe workplace cultures accustomed to and supportive of a greater diversity of working patterns: "There's quite an acceptance generally that most people don't work five days a week" (Victoria [21]). Those employed in private sector organisations and in elite, client-service professions in particular, were more accustomed to operating flexible schedules and working across time zones as a functional requirement of their jobs. How women are incorporated into organisations as professionals, mothers, *and* as part-time and flexible workers is the central theme of this research and will be returned to in Chapter 4.

Conclusions

Decisions about part-time and flexible working are about *how* to work, and are linked to decisions about *how* to provide care for infants, toddlers and teenagers. These decisions are complex and are enacted within a set of circumstances. Five intersecting factors are discussed and how they influence women's preferences, that is, their ideas about how they want to work, and their capacities for employment:

- age as it relates to the timing of maternity in the context of organisational careers and the age-related circumstances of pregnancy and maternity;

- ongoing financial commitments and lifestyle aspirations motivate women's participation in paid work although they are not the sole driver;
- the cost, reliability, location, flexibility and timing of childcare provided by others structure women's availability for paid work;
- couples' gender strategies and, relatedly, men's involvement in childcare, and in providing routine and reliable care in ways that relieve women of their maternal responsibilities, are significant in structuring women's employment and career decisions;
- rarely do women describe the flexible working arrangement they arrive at as their ideal. Women adjust their preferences to what they perceive is tolerable to the organisation and their ability to negotiate access to flexibility is significantly improved by their status within it.

Professional women's choices about how to combine work and childcare are not as open and free as preference-driven, rational choice theories of women's occupational choice and decision making imply. Choice is more complicated than a simple reflection of want. The notion that women's specific adjustments to reduce working hours, control their schedules or alter the responsibilities of their jobs reflects their ideal and signals a 'weaker' work orientation, as Hakim suggests (2002, 2006), is immediately disrupted by the evidence provided in this chapter of ideals (or preferences) adapting to circumstances, and of choices made within constraints.

3

Seeking Balance

Chapter themes

We know that professional women's employment choices are enacted within a framework of opportunities and constraints and impinge at the level of identity as well as practicality. Studies tend to agree that there is a small proportion of women at either end of a spectrum orientating more towards career or towards family, and that these women may experience less of an ideological contradiction when making decisions about jobs and careers (Crompton and Harris, 1998; Hakim, 2000; Johnston and Swanson, 2007), but even so, professional women's choices, and those of the majority, are anything but free. They are constrained instead by economic, structural and cultural factors (Hochschild, 1997; Blair-Loy, 2003; Duncan and Irwin, 2004; Tomlinson, 2006b; Johnston and Swanson, 2007; Gatrell, 2008; Pedulla and Thébaud, 2015), and by their own understandings of the moral, ideological and biographical balance they seek (Himmelweit and Sigala, 2004; Tomlinson, 2006b; Schilling, 2015). Positioning personal 'choice' and understandings of 'balance' as largely socially constructed in this way does not preclude women from having hopes for and attaching purpose to their employment adjustments.

This chapter examines professional women's motivations for part-time and flexible working beyond a ubiquitous balance-seeking goal. Three common motivations form shared **intention narratives** that express what women hope to achieve with their employment adjustment, these are: *resolving work–life conflict, protecting careers* and *expanding careers*. Close examination of how women explain their motivation for their particular working arrangement reveals the layers of meaning attached to it and the complexity of the practical and ideological settlement it reflects. This particular employment transition holds far greater significance in mothers' lives than a simple adjustment to the contract of employment. In this chapter I illustrate how mothers' working hours choices are morally potent, socially informed and internally justified as the right way for them to do things at the time. An important finding discussed in this chapter is the pursuance of part-time and flexible working arrangements with the express intention to *expand* career opportunities. This challenges the conventional idea that in seeking employment flexibility mothers seek to put career advancement on hold. Andrea's 'career reboot' story offers an important insight into the role of workplace flexibility in bringing women back in to organisational careers.

Seeking balance

All the women I interviewed about why they chose the specific flexible working arrangements they did talked about work–life balance in some way. Every one of the 30 women talked about balancing their responsibilities at work and at home, balancing their dual interests and passions for their families and their careers, and they talked about balancing time, that is the number of hours they apportioned to their work and to family. A simple text search of the transcripts from my first interviews with women, when we discussed their intentions and how the employment adjustment they were about to make fitted into their evolving biographies, revealed over one hundred references to balance in 30 individual interviews. Every woman talked about it at least once:

> "it's finding that balancing point that's important for me …"

> "it feels like an ok work–life balance for now …"

> "it just sort of shifts the balance a bit between work and home …"

> "a more predictable balance is what I'm hoping for …"

> "I'm a bit wiser now about the whole work–life balance thing …"

> "we're going for balance across both our careers …"

The pervasive idea that there is a 'right balance' that it is possible to strike between motherhood and professional work introduces a social, moral and competitive dimension to women's employment decisions. It is well established in the literature that women make decisions about combining family care and work within a set of competing discourses of appropriate forms of mothering that form a moral framework of understanding about the right thing to do regarding employment and childcare (Hays, 1996; Duncan and Edwards, 1999; Duncan and Irwin,

2004; Baraitser, 2008; Christopher, 2012). It was very clear that for most of the mothers interviewed for this study, the amount of time they put into paid work was intricately tied in with their moral claims on mothering. It was what they felt was the right thing to do in their circumstances, and especially so among new mothers who are growing into their maternal identities and establishing their mothering practices. Charlotte [26] reflected on her decision to reduce her working hours six years previously, when she became a mother, recalling the social expectation that she felt to go part-time and to spend most of her time caring for her children herself. It's only with hindsight that she can see the social pressure she was under:

> "I *wanted* to go back part-time, three days a week, I really did, I thought that was the 'right thing to do', she says with inverted commas. Ha! People always say you don't have kids for other people to bring them up. I feel like you feel pressurised that if you're going to be a good mum you should be at home more than you should be at work, so four days at home, three days at work. I felt like that was what I was supposed to do." (Charlotte [26])

Charlotte's conceptualisation of being a "good mother" and what "people say" about good mothering accords with one of the central tenets of intensive mothering ideology, defined by Hays (1996) as the idea that the best care for children comes from their mothers. Women less able to put their finger on where their desire to reduce their working hours had come from indicated that the transition to part-time working simply "felt like the right thing to do", which illustrates the inaccessibility of all the influences on individual thinking and judgements.

Discourses that link part-time working with work–life balance appear to have created an unconscious acceptance of the importance of balance to good mothering and of being the best mother you can be:

> "I don't believe in dropping your own life and identity because in some ways my mother did that and I don't feel that's healthy. I think you need to find a balance, you know, I think the mother's happiness contributes to the overall family happiness and that's how I feel. I can't do it all and I will just be the best mother I can be. I can only do my best." (Sophie [30])

In inviting women's stories about what brought them to the point of transition from one work–life configuration to another, Butler's (2004) idea of gender intelligibility is brought to life. In women's stories, it is possible to see how personal biographies synchronise, resonate or depart from discursive formations of what it is to be normal, to be successful, and sensible, and in this case, to be a good mother. Feminist cultural scholar Rottenberg (2013) proposes that women's progress and liberation in the second decade of the 21st century has been re-envisioned as a balancing act. This marks a shift from the 'having it all' standard and rhetoric of the Superwoman model of femininity of the 1970s and 1980s (Conran, 1975). This view represents a critical reading of contemporary motherhood as being loaded with expectation to perform well across both domestic and professional domains, and in effect positions women who seek a combination of motherhood and career as 'a new postfeminist subject' (Lewis and Simpson, 2017). The postfeminist discursive formations that impinge on women's lives reimagines feminine accomplishment as the successful choosing of supportive partners, of rewarding career pathways, and living a well-planned life. This new duty to achieve a felicitous balance across work and family domains draws women towards part-time and flexible working arrangements as a welcome enabler of this balancing act. Policy developments over the last 40 years both reflect and reinforce this, in that the opportunity to adjust working hours did not exist in the same way for previous generations of professional women, such that now part-time working is an option of which both state and society approve. Armstrong's (2017) intergenerational research with Millennial women and their baby-boomer professional mothers emphasises this shift by highlighting the best-of-both worlds appeal that working part-time when children are young holds for a younger generation of professional women *in anticipation* of motherhood. Armstrong's research shows how the metanarrative of balance as something for educated women to strive for impinges early, long before young women embark on motherhood.

In talking about the dilemmas faced making childcare and work decisions, the 30 women on whose lives this study is based were highly aware that their working hours and childcare choices sent a message to the social world about their dedication to their families and to their careers. As such, how a seven-day week splits into so many working days and so many days with the family therefore holds symbolic meaning as well as ideological and practical significance. It also raises the emotional stakes considerably.

There was little consistency across the 30 cases on a magic number of working days as this selection of extracts illustrates:

"It just tilts the balance in the direction of the children doesn't it, three days at work and four days at home?"

"Four days work and three days home is about right I think, I mean three days at work is probably ideal, but I don't know, I think four days is fine, sort of equal, kind of fair ..."

"You've got to have your head in the game haven't you, it really needs to be four days if you want to do a proper job, three days *really is* part-time."

The idea that there was a magic number, a right way to split the week was pervasive among new mothers and mothers of infants in this study. It was clear that most new, as in, first-time mothers felt social pressure not to work full-time five days per week while children were young. Holloway (1998) developed the notion of moral geographies of mothering, which become dominant within localities over time in interaction with the local organisation of childcare provision. These moral geographies consist of institutions and social networks through which notions of good mothering are circulated. Andrea [27], reflected on her own moral geographies in remembering the pressure she felt not to return to work full-time after her first baby:

"I do remember there being a lot of social pressure to work part-time ... I probably wouldn't have wanted to work full-time anyway but I think it would have been socially unacceptable. Nobody I knew went back full-time. We've all just had this thing that we have to go back part-time. It's not quite acceptable to not go back at all but you can't go back full-time either." (Andrea [27])

Andrea's local friendship group of new mothers were influential in her push towards part-time working. They were other mothers and fathers-to-be whom she met through antenatal classes and parenting networks like the National Childbirth Trust (NCT). Within these social networks individual notions of the right way to combine work with mothering are aired, shared, cemented and adjusted. This happens in advance of any formal dialogue with employers about working hours and what a part-time and flexible working arrangement might look like in practice.

The feeling that one *should* work part-time translates into either three or four days at work. If it was mathematically possible for a seven-day week to be divided into an even number of whole days, many women's dilemmas about how much to work outside the home might have been more easily resolved. The point of this discussion about working hours choices in the context of expectations of balance is not to argue there is an optimal number of working or non-working days. It is to illustrate that mothers' working hours choices are morally potent, socially informed and internally justified as their right way to do things. The felt need to be there for children regardless of children's ages and developmental stages was an ever-present theme in women's rationalisations of their working hours and flexibility decisions. Women's ideal ways to combine professional work and motherhood are based in part on notions of good mothering and about what is appropriate care for children at that time (Duncan and Irwin, 2004). The 'at the time' point is important. Scholars have demonstrated that these ideals about motherhood and mothering are actually as fluid and amenable to change as the circumstances within which they are formed (Himmelweit and Sigala, 2004; McDowell et al, 2005). This signals that the meshing of women's professional and maternal lives and selves is dynamic. It is continuously under review as women move through life and react, protect, expand, compromise and make sense of their work–life opportunities and choices.

Narrating intentions

Thirty highly individualised flexible working arrangements, and 30 highly individual motivations for embarking on them coalesce in four shared **intention narratives**. Using a narrative conceptual framework for understanding professional women's flexible work choices is an important and original contribution of this research. It tells us about the outcomes that women hoped they would achieve by going part-time, job-sharing, working from home, or flexing their schedules in a new or existing job. The *resolving work–life conflict* intention narrative describes an employment adjustment that is motivated to relieve or avoid the experience of stress and overspill of one workload into another. The *protecting careers* narrative stories illustrate an intention to defend one's professional identity and safeguard a career from the known penalties associated with sustained part-time work through well-planned, tactical adjustments to working patterns and personal working practices. The *expanding careers* narrative reflects a motivation to expand career opportunities and reclaim a sense of self in the professional sphere previously suppressed by the maternal.

While most women tacitly accept a degree of compromise as an inevitable consequence of combining motherhood and career, for some women, compromise defines their flexible work transition in more marked ways. Employment and domestic circumstances structured their working and their caring patterns in ways that were both obvious to women and that they felt they had little or no choice but to accept. In these highly constrained circumstances, women's intentions are oriented to making the best of difficult situation. This is what I call the *compromised choice* intention narrative, which is discussed in Chapter 4.

My description of what women said about their hopes as intention narratives is deliberate and carefully considered. These are *formative* narratives that are unmediated by the actual outcomes of the transition to a part-time and flexible working pattern. In analysing women's hopes and intentions for their flexible work transitions, I form a dialogue with Crompton and Harris's (1998) often cited typology of professional women's work–lifestyle approaches and Tomlinson's (2006b) reformulation of their important work in her analysis of managerial mothers' employment transitions through part-time work, their work–life strategies and resultant work–life trajectories. Both Crompton and Harris's and Tomlinson's typologies are derived from one-off studies that rely on women's accounts of past employment transitions that are remembered in the present. Studying lived experience through time means grappling with memory and, in the context of a history of women's non-linear career patterns and diminished labour market outcomes arising from sustained underemployment in part-time work, memory has a job to do. Memory protects us from failure and helps maintain a successful life narrative. Memory may smooth or forget the meaning and significance of every employment transition and, through time, intentions and meanings of transition moments in the past may be remembered in ways that perhaps better align to the outcomes achieved. The intention narratives discussed here, by contrast, are formative and anticipatory in character, derived from individual stories told close to the moment and, as such, expand the predominant summative and reflective approach to studying employment transitions.

The event of a transition to a new, flexible, working arrangement typically comes in the context of a wider personal evaluation about the continuing salience of professional identity to one's sense of self and of the economics and practicalities of paid work. Gascoigne's (2014) research on the identity work of male and female managers through transition into flexible work distinguishes between the 'original decision' to work part-time or flexibly and an individual's evaluation of the feasibility of doing so in a particular job. The two processes might not be contemporaneous and, as we have seen, the pull of part-time draws women in in anticipation of motherhood and long before a course of action is worked out. In recognition that there might be two processes of life and of job evaluation going on at once, in our first interviews I invited women to talk about any specific outcomes they hoped to achieve with the particular flexible work arrangement they had negotiated and the meaning and significance it held for them both practically and ideologically in the moment and to their imagined futures.

This chapter is structured around the three most common intention narratives identified and investigated in this research and uses case illustrations of each one. Jane's story of going part-time because work conflicts with family life to an extreme degree is an example of the *resolving* intention narrative (10 cases), which in Jane's case arises out of the experience of work-related stress that exacerbates work–life conflict. Olivia's and Sarah's cases illustrate the *protecting careers* narrative (evident in five cases). Their stories reveal the tactical adjustments women make in an effort to protect their careers and defend their professional identities against harmful social judgements about part-timers' lack of professionalism and mothers' assumed lack of career commitment. Andrea has experienced those judgements and the career penalties that impact women working part-time for extended periods because of their motherhood. Andrea's story of anticipated career renewal with this latest reconfiguration of her employment reveals a professionally expansive intention: a desire to reboot a stalled professional career and reclaim a professional identity for many years marginalised and suppressed by the maternal. This is the *expanding career* narrative and was evident in seven cases.

Resolving work–life conflict

For contemporary professional women, careers and lives appear to be inextricably entwined, work and private life are interconnected, and yet care and career are often in conflict. Consequently, reconfigurations in working patterns are commonly understood as a form of conflict resolution. The pursuit of work–life balance therefore can be understood simultaneously as the avoidance of work–life conflict and a prime driver of women's downward adjustments in working hours, particularly over the transition to new parenthood. Intuitively, we expect that reducing the amount of time given to paid work will release more time for family and therefore will ameliorate or avoid the tensions workers feel due to conflicting demands from work and from family. It seems counter-intuitive to suggest that this type of employment adjustment might actually promote greater conflict, and yet comparative research in Europe finds just that. Workers using certain forms of flexible working (in this case not part-time work but flexi-time, schedule autonomy and teleworking, that is, the ability to choose work location) work *more* hours, experience greater work intensity and worry more about work when they are not at work compared to fixed-schedule workers (Chung and Van der Horst, 2018). Nevertheless, a significant number of professional mothers intend to manage and resolve actual and potential conflict between the competing demands of their professional work and their maternal responsibilities by choosing part-time work and flexible schedules.

Emma's story set the scene in Chapter 1 of this book. She talked about the tensions she experienced between her motherhood and her career that had manifested in taxing and emotional ways and had motivated her to cut her paid working hours. While Emma did not refer to her intention as initiated explicitly to resolve work–life conflict, all the signs of an overloaded life are there in her story: the mentally taxing demands of parenting alone during the week and working full-time, her lack of energy to start new work projects, a feeling of constantly being under time pressure. Her impending transition from full- to part-time work is her strategy to repair and restore herself. Emma is not alone in intending some relief from competing tensions in her work and family life by reducing working hours, adjusting schedules or working from home a bit more. Women's stories illustrate how maternal responsibilities can collide and crash with the professional, and vice versa. Jane's crisis story follows, and illustrates work intrusion into the family and the detrimental effect of work–life conflict on well-being. Both Jane's and Emma's stories are examples of the *resolving work–life conflict* intention narrative.

Jane's crisis

Jane has two children in primary school (aged 9 and 7) and works in a senior management job in the public sector. She has been a lone parent for six years. We met at her home one evening after she had finished work, taken the dogs for a walk, prepared a meal and then put her children to bed. Jane is not new to working flexibly and she describes home and remote working as very much part of the norm where she works. Over the years, Jane has crafted various flexible work arrangements and currently she is full-time and works from home two and occasionally three days every week, which limits her four-hour round trip, commuting to and from her employer's London office. On those long days in the office, her children are looked after by a combination of school breakfast cubs, after-school clubs, and they stay with their father overnight on one set night each week. Jane is about to cut her hours by 20%, or one day a week, and she hopes this will lessen the pressure on one of her commuting days. Her decision follows a period of intense work pressure that she felt spiralled out of control. Cutting her hours is her way of restoring herself and introducing a hard boundary between her paid work and the rest of her life:

> "I think what I actually struggle with is that I'm always doing too many hours and that's what I can't really contain and in the last couple of months that has been really completely out of control ... I had a lot of extra work to do and I was actually working about 55 or 60 hours a week and at that level my life is actually unsustainable because there's nobody else to do any of the other things that need to be done for the kids and the house and I find that incredibly stressful. I really was at a point where I was like I'm just going to have to say I can't, it's actually impossible to do this work or you know, just get signed off sick because I'm really going to lose the plot [laughs]. I can't do that because I need to be a good parent."

Jane is unremarkable for giving more time to her paid work than her contracted hours. The amount of time spent at work in the UK is almost the highest in Europe with 42.7 the average usual working hours for full-time employees (ONS, 2011). Those in professional jobs and, like Jane, at the senior managerial and director levels in organisations, spend more hours at work than other occupational groups when they are not paid for it (ONS, 2011).

At this point in our interview I asked Jane how her experience of work–life conflict showed itself. Her dense, vivid and unedited description of her stress and distress makes plain the crisis she experienced and is an uncomfortable read. Jane agreed in her interview that 'crisis' was an apt description of what she went through; it was an episode. Her aloneness is what is striking in her account, in both the self-management of her paid work and the terrific responsibility she has for her children and their home:

> "I was thinking about work constantly, even during the night. I didn't really feel like I was sleeping I was more

thinking about work half the night. I was incredibly short tempered with the kids and I was really aware I was being like that to the point where I was saying, 'I know that this isn't your fault and I'm sorry that I'm stressed out about work.' I was quite overwhelmed by all the domestic stuff and so things like I went up to my son's bedroom and he had really trashed it looking for something and I just burst into tears which I don't normally do, you know, I don't normally do that kind of thing. The kids were a bit like, what's wrong? I was like, 'I just can't stand the mess.' But what am I *doing* standing sobbing in my son's bedroom about mess? Do you know what I mean? It's just not the end of the world but it felt like it. In the end it came to a head at a team away day at work and I had actually really thought I was completely going to lose control. I felt so much tension and stress rising up in me the night before that I couldn't sleep at all and just kept crying for no reason, and then in the morning I felt terrible and I looked like I'd been up half the night crying. I thought, 'God I can't,' you know, 'What if I lose it on the away day?' But then I thought 'But I've got to go.' So I went and I thought all I've got to do is hold it together today and one of my colleagues was like, 'Are you alright? You don't look your normal chirpy self.' I was like, 'No I'm not, I'm really stressed.' I just couldn't talk about it as I was going to cry and leave again. I had to go to the toilet and then I came out and she'd obviously told my manager and was like, 'Are you alright?' And as soon as I started talking about it I started crying. So anyway it all came out how overloaded I was and my manager kind of said, 'Oh you know you shouldn't be in this state and we need to get more resources to support you' so yeah now after that crisis I'm kind of picking up the pieces. There has probably only been a handful of times that I've been that stressed out about work ever."

Jane constructs herself as ordinarily extremely resilient and together. Her crisis is over but it prompted a re-evaluation and triggered a change in her working arrangement, and an intention to change to her own working practices and manage herself a bit better by saying no to extra projects, working more efficiently and not devoting all those extra unpaid hours to work. She aims to carve out a bit of 'quality time' with her children above what she describes as the minimum.

"It was at that point that I thought living like this is not sustainable for me. Thinking about it, if I work for 60 hours a week the only other things I'm doing are looking after the kids, not in a good way, in a minimalistic way. I'm getting them up and getting them to childcare, it's not quality time. Sleeping and eating, you know, those were the only other things [laughs] that I could do because when you've got kids, and especially when you're on your own and you've got no one else to take up any of the slack, there's no getting round the things that need to be done just as a minimum. I think in some ways I also feel, I mean after that I thought, 'For God's sake why actually are you doing this?' I should just go back to working four days a week, which is 30 hours and manageable if I can keep it to that.'"

Psychologists Johnston and Swanson (2007) found that professional women who work part-time necessarily reframe the omnipresent accessibility demands of the intensive mothering model and reconstruct maternal accessibility in terms of quality time and not quantity of time being what matters most to children. Jane is struggling even to meet the standard of 'quality time' and is aware that doing the minimum for her children is widely perceived as not enough. Laying much of the failure to keep on top of her work at her own door, Jane approaches her transition from full-time to four days each week with cautious optimism that she will be able to make it work. Clearly, she feels it is her responsibility to make it so.

The intersection of working and caring in the lives of couples is highly relevant in this analysis. Jane's relationship circumstances were not typical of the women interviewed for this research in that she was the only lone parent I interviewed. She is not typical in another way: Jane can rely on her former husband's care for their children on a set day and night each week. Very few women in couple relationships with professional men could do that and necessarily excluded their partner's participation from their childcare planning.

All 10 women whose intentions regarding their employment adjustment were directed in these conflict-avoiding/tension-relieving ways spoke in terms of experiencing time pressure, of being depleted by too much work crashing into their family lives, or the demands of their responsibilities for family life zapping their energy and focus on their work. Few articulated a crisis trigger in the way Jane did; more common was an accumulation of pressure over months and in few cases, years, that left women burnt out in terms of their energy and enthusiasm to sustain time-demanding jobs as well as family responsibilities. It is this accumulation and gradual burning out that we hear in Emma's [25] interview extracts with which this book opened.

Protecting careers

There is an enormous amount of advice available to women should they seek it, in the form of self-help books and magazines, blogs and articles about how to combine careers and motherhood. In the self-help genre one of the most vocal and prominent shapers of professional women's attitudes to their careers is professional mother Sheryl Sandberg, Chief Operating Officer of Facebook, whose phenomenally successful self-declared feminist manifesto *Lean in* (Sandberg, 2013) encourages women to hold on to their career ambition when they become mothers. Women are urged by Sandberg not to check out of their careers too soon by choosing less demanding jobs. Planning is key to this strategy; ruthless prioritisation and personal organisation are essential, as is women demanding more of partners-in-parenting to support them in realising their professional ambitions. By implication, any problems women might encounter in achieving these things are put down to women's own limitations. Feminist critique of *Lean in* reads its advocacy of self-improvement and self-determinism as individualistic and unthreatening to capital, effectively excusing patriarchy, capitalism and business for women's diminished position in contemporary culture (Rottenberg, 2013, 2014; Foster, 2016; Lewis and Simpson, 2017). *Lean in* and its genre of self-improving and 'choosing' forms of empowerment has penetrated culture. It was a text referred to as motivating by some of the women interviewed for this study, and was said by some to have prompted a re-evaluation of the importance of professional careers to women's sense of self.

For five women in this study, their career attachment and ability to continue to express their professional identities upon and throughout motherhood was very salient in our discussion about their intentions with regard to their impending flexible work adjustment. All five were 'being strategic' in the sense that they expressed an intended professional outcome from their well-planned job adjustments. Strategy implies control, presumes power and has a definitive goal in mind. Enactment of a strategy requires tactics – intentional manoeuvres designed to achieve a goal. In *The practice of everyday life* (1984) de Certeau thinks about strategy, tactics, power and control in a different way, and characterises tactics as the purview of the non-powerful. He understands tactics not as a subset of strategy but as an adaptation to the environment, which has been created by the strategies of the powerful. Employers are 'the powerful' in that they determine what working time and space options will be available to employees and articulate these in workplace policy, but employees will figure out the lived reality of those options. This is what de Certeau terms the art and craft of bricolage, or 'making do', and thus implies a constant state of reassessment and correction based directly on observations of the actual environment. Through de Certeau's lens, the specific flexible adjustments women make can be considered tactical responses to their workplace environments, informed by their observations of what happens to the careers and the status of men and women who work part-time and flexibly.

The women in focus in this study are all members of the occupational categories of professionals and managers, however they differ significantly in social positioning and economic resources; that is, in the means and the influence to realise the intentions they express. Gaining control over working hours, schedules and locations is the tactical adjustment that is key to implementing a career protective strategy. Some women were in a better position than others to achieve that within their current job because they occupied very senior positions within their organisations and their status afforded them greater control over their own and others' work arrangements. Those who did not have systemic power (Lawrence, 2008) or who occupied job roles that were unpredictable in terms of the level of responsiveness required to clients or customers, made pre-emptive job moves to less intensive roles that they presumed would offer a more predictable workflow. The predictability of workflow and its salience in decisions about and successful transitions into part-time work is underexplored in flexible working literature. It is of particular relevance to workers in managerial and professional jobs (Gascoigne and Kelliher, 2017).

Olivia's and Sarah's stories offer insight into both a tactical adjustment within the same job, and a pre-emptive job move. Women expressing career protective intentions possess insight into the challenging situation for women in the workplace. This is insight that they gained either from personal experience of marginalisation and underemployment through their own previous transitions in and out of part-time work, or by observing what happens to other women. The intent driving these protective moves is to maintain one's professional status and, as such, women proceed with their own transitions with cautious optimism. Their strategy is to insulate themselves from the perceived challenges and failures that befall other women through good planning and thoughtful management of the practicalities of childcare, travel and the design of their jobs. They are *Leaning in* in unique ways that respond to their individual work environments and job demands.

Olivia's tactical adjustment

Olivia is a senior manager in a large private sector firm. She is married with two pre-school-age children aged 2 and 4 and lives in the city. She has worked for the same firm for many years, steadily climbing the ladder, and was recently promoted to senior manager. Every promotion is a step up and this one feels particularly important because she now needs to grow her own business area and lead a large team. She always enjoyed her work and becoming a mother had been expansive for Olivia, finding a new appreciation of how important her work was to her sense of self. Both Olivia and her husband work full-time and she is about to reduce her hours ever so slightly because she wants to find the right balance. She earns substantially more than her husband and her job often requires travel in the UK and overseas. When Olivia and I met she was emphatic about her job and about her family life, and we enter Olivia's narrative when she is describing her plan to combine career and family life using a seemingly small but significant adjustment to 90% of full-time contracted hours and intending to work "four days a week most weeks, and if I have to work Fridays I will do it from home":

> "I knew I always enjoyed my job but the first time, with my son, I didn't know how I would feel about being a working mum when I went back. Second time I had the best time off on maternity leave, a much better time and I enjoyed it so much more … it was so rewarding spending time with both kids, I took longer off … I also realised how much I enjoyed being back at work and there was this sense of almost, the realisation of how much work was important to me … that has only happened post-children, it was unexpected that enjoying my work would define who is me."

Olivia describes an experience of becoming a mother and growing her family as expansive professionally and defining of the self, of "who is me" as she puts it, and this appears essential in orienting her preference towards balance and coherence across both domains and identities that she describes here:

"It's also in my mind-set, the balance between working and family, I mean what's the point in having children if you're not going to be there to bring them up? But I love my job, it's my hobby … it's something that is intrinsic to me and I put my all into my work … that's why I got to four days at work, three days with the family as the right balance … If I needed to I would stop, of course I would. Although I am super career-driven and I enjoy my job, I enjoy getting a pay cheque as I think it gives us options to do nice things as a family, but if I thought at any point it was having a real impact on the family I'd stop tomorrow. I'd give it all up, definitely."

Olivia had been through a promotion process while on maternity leave with her second child. This was a promotion that she felt had been a long time coming. She had first applied and was unsuccessful two years earlier, when she had returned from her first period of maternity leave. Her decision to work Monday to Thursday operationalises the balanced involvement she seeks in both home and professional domains. She acknowledges that she feels confident now that she is in a more senior job, to announce her working pattern and to publicly claim part-time status. At the same time, she offers public reassurance to colleagues and clients that she will always be flexible in the direction of work:

"I think it gets easier as you go up the ladder. I know as I've spoken to a few people, a number of guys who I've talked to and told them I'm part-time and they've sort of rolled their eyes a bit and they're like they've worked with part-time people on projects and it just doesn't work. So I ask why doesn't it work and you get to the root cause of it and it's that the people they've worked with can't be flexible, so they're doing drop-offs and pick-ups every day and having to do 9 to 5 and actually in this industry that's a struggle."

It is that eye rolling of colleagues and managers about part-time and restricted work schedules that contributes to a lived experience of stigma and exclusion for those who break the professional time norms operating in their workplace cultures. This is because time is central to professionals and managers' demonstration of commitment and success in their chosen field and, as such, it has symbolic meaning. Long hours are a proxy for, and often taken for granted as evidence of an individual's commitment to their work, to their employer and to their career (Williams et al, 2013).

Couples' gender strategies are in focus again. Olivia's relationship with her husband she describes as "a team", neither have extended family nearby and so do not and cannot rely on family help with childcare. They share domestic work between them and Olivia organises childcare, which is entirely provided by the market, and she is the "first call" parent in case of emergencies:

> "We try not to prioritise one career over another, we're a team, we're 50:50 on most things ... I'm more career-driven than he is, but he's recently made a move into a career job that he's interested in."

Olivia demonstrates some of the qualities of Blair-Loy's (2003) mavericks, women in elite occupations who orient between two competing devotions, the work-devotion schema and the family-devotion schema. Mavericks are forging careers while being family-centred, flouting the powerful work-devotion schema by reducing their hours and attempting a re-shaping of the rules of engagement with intensive jobs. Olivia's narrative speaks of seniority and influence, as well as self-confidence, financial capacity to go to the market for flexible childcare and an egalitarian partnership. This is most akin to Crompton and Harris's (1998) maximiser and satisficer work–life approaches. The difference between the two being that the maximiser approach speaks of a refusal to compromise in achievement of goals for both work and family. The satisficer approach speaks of compromise in attempting to achieve success in both areas without maximising either.

Where seniority and influence is lacking at work, among middle managers for example, *protective* transition narratives describe orchestrated moves into jobs that women anticipate will be less intensive and more predictable; jobs in which they will not fail to meet the standards of professionalism that they set for themselves and that they are known for within their organisations.

Some women envisioned difficulties resisting dominant cultural time norms and pre-emptively applied for alternative jobs, intending to protect their careers and simultaneously avoid work–life conflict by seeking jobs that are more predictable and therefore assumed to be more manageable. Sarah's story provides an illustration.

Sarah's pre-emptive move

It had taken Sarah a little while to work out what she wanted from her professional work and she'd had a meandering career path to where she is now as an operations manager in a large private sector business. After her degree, she had taken temporary jobs and travelled a bit and then took a postgraduate degree. A few more jobs and projects and she landed where she is now. Sarah enjoys a challenge at work and is ambitious to advance, feeling that she has finally found her niche. Recently married, she lives with her husband and infant son in the country a one-hour commute from her city office. The family moved out of the city during her maternity leave, a move that was prompted by a change in her husband's job that means he now works from home all the time. At around six months into her planned 12 month period of maternity leave Sarah felt she was ready to return to work. This feeling took her by surprise because it contrasted sharply with her joy at being in what she called the "baby bubble" for six months when she hadn't missed work one bit.

> "so I then went through a bit of a rollercoaster, you know, backwards and forwards, feeling oh no I want to stay at home, oh no I want to go back …"

Sarah felt that working four days per week: three in the office and one at home was the right balance for her between time with her son and enough time to do a decent job at work, but this pattern of flexibility, she felt, did not fit with the job she used to do and so she applied for another internal job whilst on maternity leave.

> "I deliberately removed myself from a client-facing role as I didn't want that pressure. I wanted to be able to manage my own time and work from home more and so by not having such a reactive role that was a very conscious decision that I made … I kind of went into it thinking I didn't really have a lot of options and I was quite nervous about it but equally I was still ambitious. That was definitely still there within me as it had been before maternity leave."

No one invites work–life conflict and, if they can see it coming, they use the resources they have to avoid it. Sarah was in this position. Not senior enough in the organisation to have the autonomy to redesign her job to reduce her workload and improve the predictability of her workflow, she made a lateral job move. This is a sideways move into a role in the same internal function and a less reactive job design that she envisaged would offer her greater control over her time. Finding an internal job to apply for during maternity leave wasn't easy. She travelled into the office during her maternity leave and used her established networks in the business to meet people who might be able to help her find a vacancy.

> "There had been loads of changes at work, a new strategy and new people, and because there were so many changes it started to become a little bit intimidating because I just started to think, oh who is going to be there that still knows me? My key sponsor wasn't there and I think I just started to doubt myself. I was really surprised at how that had happened, I hadn't expected it would happen to me but my confidence plummeted … I basically felt like I just want to get back because I'm not really sure of myself … I felt like the longer I was off the worse it was going to get … it was starting to kind of hang over me a little bit and the end of maternity leave was looming quite large and so I decided, I would just bite the bullet and get back a few months early … But secondly, you know, money, so the maternity leave nine-month mark had been hit and so I just thought I'm not getting paid and starting to not enjoy this and I just needed the challenge, I needed something to get my, you know, get my teeth into."

Sarah's visits to the office to keep in touch and research her job options panicked her. The scale of change in her absence made her worry that she might lose her place and people would forget her and her potential. The experience rocked her confidence, which in turn hastened her return. Despite much mention in our interviews of careers and professional status, women like Sarah are not being 'careerist' in the sense of putting professional life *before* domestic life as in the traditional career-woman stereotype. What Sarah intends is to protect her professional self, while simultaneously managing her motherhood. She seeks to keep her career options open by giving herself the best chance to be able to perform a role to the standard of professionalism for which she was known before she became a mother.

Expanding careers

The career penalties that Sarah and Olivia seek to minimise or avoid with their protective adjustments to working time, schedules, location and job roles are the effects that many women in this study had experienced first-hand in their work histories. Sustained periods of underemployment in corporate jobs below their skill level and in marginal roles, or years of reluctant-but-necessary self-employment and 'mum-preneurism' saw women set up businesses that they could fit around the family. Disheartening and poorly rewarded employment experiences were catalysts for some women to make a change and do something that got their organisational careers back on track.

In seven cases, women's intentions with this latest reconfiguration to their working pattern was anchored in a desire to reclaim their careers. This is the *expanding careers* intention narrative, to which biography, that is, previous experience of combining motherhood and careers and of working flexibly, is highly relevant. The expansive intention speaks to a woman's desire to reconnect to her professional identity, to progress a hitherto stalled organisational career and set out on a new professional path. It speaks of an eroded professional identity and represents a desire to elevate social status outside the family, and in some cases inside as well. Juliet [29] who after 12 years of sporadic self-employment that she fitted around her four children's schedules and her husband's full-time work expressed a desire to be valued "for me, for who I am and not entirely for how I feature in someone else's life, otherwise I'm just [his] wife, just somebody's mother". The women expressing their intent with this latest employment adjustment in these professionally expansive terms typically were re-entering the workplace after an extended absence or career break, or following extended time spent underemployed in marginal part-time roles with limited potential for advancement, an experience that Lara [6] reflected on:

> "I spent sort of five years not really caring what job I was doing. But now I've gone back I'm like, 'This is it, I've got to do something I'm happy with now.' I need to start thinking about it again as I'm not intending on having any more children. I need to be a bit more aware of my career and start thinking this is my life now so I need to think about what I want to do with it."

Amanda [10], a former charity CEO quit that job while pregnant with her second child because she had been unable to secure the support from the executive committee for her preference to work part-time. She went on to set up her own internet-based business, and here charts the trajectory to her new career job back in the corporate world:

> "When I look back it does feel like a big cliché, it was totally like something out of *Red Magazine* you know, smart mums making money from home, and there were aspects of it that were lovely. I enjoyed the challenge and doing a business plan and all that kind of thing and I was just totally absorbed in it for a while. After Tom was born, that's when I started to feel like I needed something a bit more engaged with the outside world and I just, it was the money thing as well, not having regular money coming in, and not wanting to have too big a gap in my career, on my CV ... after a while it just got boring, I was really bored and I totally lost my sense of who I was without having a kind of job and a job title so when I spotted the [new job] ad, senior, case work, three days a week from home, well-paid, oh my god, I had to get it!"

The prevalent logic of career-making is linear and cumulative; an uninterrupted and upwards trajectory within the professional sphere (Evetts, 2000). The emphasis on full-time paid work as central in careers constructs what is perceived as the normal or the desirable way to progress, and is problematic for many whose life circumstances do not permit such a neatly linear pattern.

Women articulating expansive intentions with this latest employment adjustment have sought more conducive organisational environments in which they could reinvent and experiment with their professional selves (Ibarra, 1999), in other words they have found new jobs in new places that are supportive of them joining the organisation on a part-time and flexible arrangement from day one. Research shows that this is an unusual position to be in in the UK labour market. Research by Timewise (2017) that indexed job vacancy advertisements in London (offering salaries over £20,000 pa) finds less than 10% of advertisements make any mention of part-time and flexible working options. The restricted, almost invisible jobs market for flexibility in professional and managerial roles is evident in women's accounts of the extended periods of time spent job searching, forcing them to stay longer in jobs they had outgrown or had become unsatisfactory. In some cases, women described how they had been looking for the right job at the right level with the right flexibility for several years.

What is clear in the stories of women reformulating how they combine work and motherhood with professional renewal in mind, is that they have learned from their own previous dissatisfying work experiences about the centrality of professional identity to their sense of self and, in some cases, of the centrality of the organisational career to their social status. Past work experiences were closely connected with their present choices about working hours made for their future selves. This intention did not correlate neatly with ages of children, in that this was not a phase that women only entered when children were of school age and older. For example, Amanda's [10] youngest child was 2 years old when she embarked upon what she called "my way back in to my career". It did seem to correlate with completion of the family, of whatever size, when women signalled they did not expect to have more children. Andrea's story provides an example.

Andrea's career reboot

Andrea is poised to enter a new role in a new sector on a flexible basis and is looking forward to it. Andrea and her husband have three children under 10 and the youngest has just started school. Her husband works full-time locally in the same field as Andrea. They are homeowners with a mortgage and live in the small town near where they grew up and both have family nearby. Andrea's mother retired recently and looks after the children before and after school a few days each week, and a childminder looks after the youngest child occasionally. Andrea worked consistently in her professional field since qualifying 16 years ago. Since her eldest child was born, nine years ago, she has worked part-time in the public sector, most recently in a long-standing job-share partnership. I met Andrea when she had dissolved her job-share and resigned her job and, in a few weeks, was due to start a new job with a new employer on a part-time basis four days a week, with one day working from home. Andrea describes how, after five years in a senior management job-share, she had felt there was nowhere for her career to go: "One of the things that has frustrated me about my current job is that I haven't been able to move up into a more senior role."

She described the transition she was poised to make into a new role in a new sector, with a new form of flexibility as a "moment" of enormous significance in her evolving biography:

> "Many hopes and expectations are resting on this move for me. It's definitely a moment. My husband understands it is

a moment. I haven't really said 'Is it ok if I do this?' I've just said 'I'm doing it'. He's pretty supportive and knows this is the only option unless I stay [in my old job] for the rest of my life and wither and die inside ... I'm also conscious that I've got 30 years before I retire ... my mum and my mother-in-law both retired in their mid-50s and I don't want to do that, it's too young. I think it's been difficult for them to find meaningful things to do. I want to be working and engaged for my whole working life. That might involve moving sideways and doing different types of things and hopefully in my new job that might be possible."

Andrea described the job she was moving into and the addition of a three-hour daily commute into her schedule. She was aware that she had accepted a role that had less management responsibility than her previous role and was in an unfamiliar technical area, but it had been a long time coming.

"It sort of suited me whilst I was having children to stay there but after Isabelle was born I thought, "Ok, finished having children, now my career can start." Then I hadn't realised how difficult it was going to be to find a new job. I just wanted a bigger job with more money, you know, that sort of thing. So initially I was looking for jobs that were significantly better paid than my current job. I applied for about nine jobs in all and I got to the last three for a couple of bigger jobs in [the public sector]. Didn't get them. Middle-aged men got them. And then I applied for this one which is not very much more than my current salary, and got it."

It had taken Andrea over two years to find this job, "Oh God, I mean, the last two years the hours and hours I've spent filling in applications and preparing for interviews." She reflected on the difficulty she had convincing prospective employers of the value of her history of part-time working and of the legitimacy of her five years job-sharing in a senior management role as credible professional experience that positioned her well for a heavyweight role.

"What I think went against me in some of the interviews was being a job-share and having worked part-time. Yeah. The big [public sector] jobs, one of them I was interviewed by a panel of men [on the Board], it was the final interview, and at one point they seemed to be suggesting I might have been lying about doing all these amazing things and it might have been my job-share partner who'd done them. That was difficult and I felt that because I was a job-share I couldn't be seen as the safe option."

For Andrea, these disheartening experiences as an experienced flexible worker have put even greater expectation upon the move she is about to make, although she is sanguine about the new role, viewing it as transitional rather than an end in itself. It offers a way back on to a professional career path and renewal of her professional identity. Andrea's maternal identity is secure in that she expresses confidence in her own style of mothering central to which is "being there", although not at the expense of her sense of self and to which her professional identity is significant:

"Maybe I will feel like I should do more, you know, I know a lot of people worry about seeing their children enough. But you know then I think I've been working part-time for 10 years, they've had a lot of me. I will still be here a lot more than I will not be here. I'm only commuting three days a week. I'm going to have a word with myself if I start getting too sad and guilty about it."

She will retain the organising of domestic life and childcare, and has some well-established domestic systems and processes that support her in that, but the pressure for her children to be there at the right time, for the right event will pass, she thinks, to her husband:

"The burden is definitely going to be shifted to James on the days I will be in [the city] … he's always worked closer to home because of the children and he pretty much takes over the parenting in the evenings, but the pressure isn't on him in the same way … it's really not a massive change for him he just needs to get back half an hour earlier than usual and not travel to [the city] on the same days as me."

Andrea's new start was anticipated with excitement and a small amount of anxiety, but largely with positivity and optimism. It was facilitated by the unusual situation of an employer inviting applications for part-time and flexible working patterns from the point of hire.

Conclusions

A strong moral association of part-time work with good mothering is hard to resist, and the dominant discourses of 'balance' and of 'being there' for children encourage professional women to retain one foot in the family and the other in career and yet offer no blueprint about what balance looks like on a weekly, monthly or annual basis.

Three intention narratives reveal that flexible working offers a lifeline for professional mothers to manage or to avoid the effects of work–life conflict and overspill. Equally it offers a way back in for women seeking to expand their professional opportunities; the extent to which it delivers on this will be examined in Chapter 7. The stakes are high with a move into part-time and flexible work arrangements, and women narrating *protective intentions* are absolutely live to the significant professional risk associated with these moves. They are 'leaning in' and simultaneously attempting to mitigate negative career consequences by using the influence that they have at work to craft a workable arrangement. This is not to suggest that their maternal goals and family responsibilities were not in play, rather the tactical adjustments that women were making to their working arrangements were carefully calculated with professional outcomes in mind.

The fast pace and the dynamism of lived reality calls for equally fluid and dynamic explanations for the moves women make through part-time and flexible work. Situations and circumstances change and it is therefore reasonable to expect that intention narratives will change through time and future employment transitions. The meshing of women's maternal and professional lives and selves is dynamic and continuously under review as women react to, protect, expand, make compromises regarding, and make sense of their work–life opportunities and choices. One person might identify more significantly with one intention narrative or another at different transitional points in life, and from these shifting identifications it becomes possible to discern how individual employment transitions form work–life trajectories over time. A woman seeking part-time working today with a *resolving work–life conflict* intention in mind, when circumstances change and the conflict eases, may well formulate a *career expansive* intention with the next employment adjustment she seeks.

4

Compromised Choices

Chapter themes

Compromise has come to characterise the experience of combining careers and motherhood. Women strike compromises all the time. Between their ideal models of mothering and what is practically possible within their care resources, and between their ideal way of working and what is culturally tolerated and accommodated at work. For eight women in this study, compromise defined this particular part-time and flexible work transition in marked ways and they had a lot to say about it. They are highly aware of the constraints that stymie their personal goals. Jenny recounts her experience of negotiating access to flexibility in her paid work arrangements with a line manager who was unsupportive. Meera explains her success and failures negotiating with her husband to share her domestic workload.

Compromised choice intention narratives reflect working-pattern choices that are structured by external circumstances and are made in situations that are not as open or free as they could be in terms of facilitating women's achievement of their ideal ways to combine work with family life. This is not to suggest that everyone else was more successful at negotiating a preference-driven, ideal arrangement, rather that compromise is a matter of degrees and, for a small but significant proportion of professional women, compromise defined this particular employment adjustment in marked ways. The compromises that these women had made were highly visible to them. They identified more closely with the choice-but-no-choice characteristic of this intention narrative than alternative narratives that foreground intentions to resolve work–life conflict or avoid it, or to protect or expand careers and opportunities.

Workplace negotiations

Access to preferential flexible work arrangements is considerably enhanced by women's work status. Status is one of the important resources women have within their local employment contexts to facilitate access to preferential flexible working patterns. High status conferred either by rank and seniority, specialist skills or valuable relationships is of course not universal, and therefore access to flexibility in managerial and professional roles appears to be a privileged position. This is what Lawrence (2008) refers to as systemic power, the level of bargaining power employees have within their work institution.

Simply having a policy in place at organisational level that supports employee-initiated flexible working has been shown to shape employees' perceptions of likely organisational support for their requests to use it (Macrae, 1989; Dick, 2006). Most women I interviewed felt a strong sense of entitlement to be able to access a flexible working policy when they needed to. They perceived themselves to be the intended and deserving beneficiaries as mothers and primary carers, and as loyal, compliant and previously undemanding workers. This shared understanding is indicative of a widespread interpretation of organisational work–life balance initiatives and flexible working policies that are typically framed in gender-neutral terms as really being family-friendly policies aimed at women (Lewis and Campbell, 2008). Women find, however, that their access to policies is not guaranteed. Access relied on knowledge of the wider system of employee rights and protections and how these apply in local workplace contexts.

Employees' access to adjusted hours, schedules and locations of work is a negotiated process, and it is well documented that positive relationships with line managers are vital in securing access to preferential working patterns. This is largely because trust remains important in securing managers' support for alternative arrangements (Brescoll et al, 2013; Arnaud and Wasieleski, 2014; Daverth et al, 2016). Line managers are the gatekeepers of employees' access to flexible working arrangements (Smithson and Stokoe, 2005; Himmelweit, 2007); they mediate the relationship between the employer and the employee. Den Dulk et al (2012, p 2797) highlight that 'managers' support for work–life policies is crucial for shaping employees capabilities to use them'. The impact of managerial discretion in employee access to idiosyncratic work arrangements has been well researched, and scholars have found that employees whose line managers are supportive of their need to adjust their working pattern to support their responsibilities outside of work tend to express greater job satisfaction, experience less work–life conflict and report lower turnover intentions (Kelly et al, 2011; Masuda et al, 2012; Rousseau et al, 2016).

Some forms of flexibility may suit the employee but are not favoured by the organisation, particularly those that impinge on worker availability to the organisation, its clients or customers. Based on case analysis of four multinational service organisations Michielsens et al

(2013) found that when flexible work patterns impact on worker availability, in the form of part-time work and restricted schedules, they are acceptable to organisations only if they do not impact negatively upon the client, an insight that was also reported by Haynes (2008), studying women's employment transitions in the accountancy profession. This pressure to prioritise the clients' needs contributes to sustaining norms of long working hours and presenteeism, and works against flexible working, and against part-time working in particular. Among the 30 women interviewed for this study it was evident that there were common understandings about certain types of flexible working arrangement. It seems some arrangements and practices are culturally 'ok' in managerial and professional work and others are understood to present more of a problem to employers and hence employers are thought to be unsupportive of them. Working from home on Fridays is ok, for example, while working three days clustered at one end of a week or the other "really is part-time" and not really ok in a responsible job because the gap left is too great; and four days is ok if you are an efficient worker or can make up the time. These understandings and the circumstances under which they come to light will be examined in detail in later chapters. The focus here is on aspects of access and the negotiation of a flexible working arrangement at work because it is this interaction at the level of the line manager that appears crucial in securing women's access to flexibility.

Current patterns of vertical occupational segregation inside large organisations that place more men than women at the more senior levels in organisations mean that the professional and managerial women in this research occupied positions that were line managed by men or committees made up mostly of men. Daverth et al (2016) found that the line managers perceived parents, and specifically women, as the intended targets of work–life balance policies. Although framed as gender neutral and available to employees irrespective of parental status, the 'life' element was constructed by line managers within a heteronormative framework that assumes 'life' means childcare, for which mothers are responsible. This framing both reflects and helps sustain gendered assumptions that underpin organisational cultures. This is not to suggest that motherhood universally enhances access to flexible working policies, and Gatrell et al (2014) found that, despite line managers' associations of maternity with childcare and, rightly or wrongly, with a stronger domestic orientation than work orientation, women still experienced limited support for their need or desire to work flexibly.

Very few of the 30 women in this study had achieved leadership positions that gave them total autonomy and control over their working pattern. Most women did not have advantages such as these, and their access to part-time and flexible working was determined by their line managers' preferences and interpretations of organisational policy. Evidence of localised discretion of this type has been found in many organisational studies and explains why it is that employees can experience implementation of work–life balance and flexible working policies quite differently across different work groups in the same organisation (Dick, 2010).

How well women can match work with childcare seems therefore, to depend on the power of the line manager in mediating their access to flexible working arrangements. Where a line manager relationship is missing or is weak, and women are appealing to someone new and unfamiliar with their circumstances, talent or ambition, women have no option but to negotiate the intricacies of the flexible arrangement they seek with their employer as an institution. This shifts to a much more formal process and an exchange of paperwork and away from dialogue. None of the four women in this position achieved their ideal working pattern under these circumstances.

> "Yes it was my choice [to work part-time] but it's not my choice to work these hours, I had no choice about that, not if I wanted to keep my job." (Gail [20])

Another feature of the *compromised choice* intention narrative that is distinct from the others, is the foregrounding of the family's financial commitments to which women's income contributes significantly. In combination with new and unfamiliar line manager relationships and, as we will hear in Jenny's story, a manager whose preference is for full-time, fixed-schedule working in his teams, there is little potential for exploring women's preferred ways of working and a best fit of work and childcare. There is a strong choice-but-no-choice narrative thread in the accounts of women who emphasise factors outside their control as central to their choice of jobs and the ways that they do them. Jenny's story provides an illustration and emphasises that access to preferred flexible working arrangements is a negotiated process and certainly not straightforward for those who have never done it before.

Jenny's new manager

Jenny's public sector employing organisation has restructured. The restructuring process started before she went on maternity leave and required her to reapply for a senior management post in the new organisation. It was a stressful time, but she was successful and took the job:

> "the level of the job didn't increase so it wasn't a promotion as such, it was almost a demotion really because I got loads more responsibility and loads more areas to manage but without any money ... oh it was an awful time, yeah, new boss, obviously, my first time being pregnant, no idea how that was going to change how I felt about my job or whether I was going to be able to do it. The restructure took ages ... I was about seven months pregnant when I interviewed. I had a fleeting thought of, 'Oh maybe it's just time for me to go and move on', but we'd just bought a house. I had to carry on. I started [the job] about four weeks before I went off [on maternity leave]."

Jenny is married and her husband Jack works full-time in a senior management role in the private sector. They have a daughter now, and when I met Jenny she was gradually returning to work by working first two then three days each week, planning to increase up to four and then five within six months. Moving up to five days and full-time was not her ideal. The couple are in the midst of a home-renovation project. Progress has slowed as their finances dwindled during the three-month unpaid extension she took to her nine months' paid maternity leave. Now the couple are under some financial pressure for her to return to paid work. They plan to keep childcare costs down by using a combination of a local childminder and Jenny's parents to look after their daughter when Jenny is working. Jenny had attempted to negotiate her preferred four-day week work pattern some months previously during maternity leave, when her new manager had got in touch and invited her to meet for an informal lunch:

> "I think I went into the conversation thinking that I would just be able to agree four days because there's another manager in my service who works four days, she's got two children, that's where I was basing my frame of what my flexible working was going to be. So I was then quite

thrown because the first time I met with my boss, he said 'What do you want?' and I said well this is what I'm envisaging is going to happen, he was like 'No, you can't work four days.' It was a flat no ... he said, this is a new role, explained to me that I didn't know the role because I had left after a month after getting it and that, you know, my maternity cover had come in and done an excellent job, he really emphasised that, that really smarted ... he made me, I guess he just realigned my expectations. So, he said the job is very, very busy, the role is very busy, you know, it's grown in a way that he couldn't accept less than full-time hours for the post. He just bombarded me when I first met with him, well that's what it felt like at the time anyway, all these big projects, much bigger team, blah blah blah."

Jenny had one further conversation with her new manager about trialling a four-day arrangement before formally requesting full-time working hours compressed into four days:

"I was really, really torn, and I'll be completely honest with you I was also really confused because I hadn't gone back to the workplace yet, so I didn't know how I was going to feel. We couldn't afford for me to work less than four days and I didn't know how I would cope on five, I mean it was hard enough getting [my daughter] to the childminder and me on the train to come in for one meeting so my formal request in the end was full-time compressed hours over four days ... I suppose with my previous boss I felt it would have been very much more of a conversation, whereas with my new boss it was very much a 'Right, this is your formal request, this is what I legally have to do.' I went in for my next meeting and it wasn't just with my boss, he'd invited HR [Human Resources] as well, and I wasn't told that HR was going to be there so it felt like much more formal. The reason I was asking for compressed hours was because he'd told me he wouldn't accept anything less, and I was thinking that I would be able to work the rest of the hours in evenings and weekends and I was quite clear about that. I'd rather have the day off in the week with [my daughter] and not pay the childminder ... then when I met with him and HR, he just kind of said 'Well to do four days a week, you would have to be in the office for 10 hours a day. How are you going to do that?' In my head I didn't see that I had to be in the office 10 hours a day, I could be in the office for eight or nine hours a day and then I could follow up with maybe an hour or two in the evening or do three or four hours at the weekend, but he was very clear that if I was going to do compressed hours, then that's what compressed hours would mean. It would mean 10 hours in the office because I manage a team and the team are there and it would be difficult to do the job without physically being in the office. I mean the ridiculous thing is that the team are not in the office for 10 hours because the building isn't even open for that long."

The outcome of Jenny's months of negotiation was an agreement to stagger her return to full-time work, working up to a five-day week pattern over six months. Before the end of the period, Jenny was determined to try again to negotiate the four-day week (or 80% of full-time pay) the arrangement that she ideally wanted:

"I'm going to have to sit down and have a conversation with my boss because I don't want to be working five days a week and I don't want to be doing compressed hours on four days a week … he said I had to be physically here in the office every day … it's ludicrous really because [the organisation] is going through this whole transformation process and part of it is getting more people to work anywhere, but this doesn't seem to have reached him.

You know before having a baby I would have just thought, well I'm not very happy with my job, so let's find another one. Whereas now I'm thinking actually I do want another job but I *definitely* want that on reduced hours, how easy is that to find? I'm quite conscious that if I take myself out of the workplace, then getting back up to a position where I'll be in a career that I want will be very, very difficult. I'm stuck really. So a part of me does think, well I'll just get on with it and see it as a short-term thing and then review if or when we have a second child."

Like Jenny, all women who felt compromised by their workplace situations stressed the time-limited nature of this transition, that is, how they hoped – not all were confident enough to expect – that their circumstances would change to something more aligned with their preferences. The future trigger events were speculated to be either securing a new job with a new employer more supportive of women, of care and flexibility, or that they might become pregnant again and, as a result, they would be able to delay finding or negotiating better designed flexibility.

Organisational restructuring during maternity absence impacts women's line manager relationships and, in the examples in this study, the loss of that relationship weakens their negotiating position. Nina's [16] company was bought by a bigger business, and Lara's [6] law firm merged with another and the size of her specialist team reduced. Conversations that they had anticipated would be open and exploratory with line managers about mutually agreeable flexible working options, in those circumstances became process-driven and formal. In most cases the outcomes were that women were expected to work more hours than they would have preferred, or a different schedule. Nina [16] described a request process in her newly structured organisation that to her seemed ill-defined and contradictory. She also felt she lacked guidance regarding the process and did not know how to make a strong supporting case for her application.

> "I sent in a letter to say that I wanted to work three days a week because I was looking after my daughter … I had to put what they called a 'business case' and basically say how me reducing to three days a week was not going to affect my work … actually, it is really difficult to write that letter, to make it sound like working three days isn't going to affect your work, of course it is, I'm not going to be able to do as much in three days as I would in five days. I mean, it's impossible really, it's like I gave them all the reasons to turn it down."

Nina's request was turned down and she accepted a compromise offer to work four days per week, she said, "for the sake of keeping my job". Lara's [6] request for a three-day week on her return from maternity leave with her second child was initially turned down by the new HR function in her newly merged employing organisation. She tried again with a proposal for a split week pattern that meant she would not be out of the office for more than one day and offered to continue to monitor her client work on her non-working days, this arrangement appealed to the business:

"Of course there was always the risk that they would say no again but my team leader had been very open and said to me, 'If we say no will you look for another job?' Well yes, I said, I want to work part-time, what do you think? … I think they had to think 'Do we want her three days a week or don't we want her?', there was no consideration about bringing anyone in to cover my days because the team had been stripped right down after [the merger], or making it so I could finish at five or anything like that. I do three very long days. It's not what I wanted but I've got no choice really if I want to see my kids on two days."

The pivotal role of the line manager in interpreting workplace policy and their discretion in granting access to flexible work arrangements is a theme that will be returned to. For some professional mothers, their compromised choice narrative stemmed not from workplace factors, but from home, from an unsatisfactory distribution of the demands and rewards for family life and work life within a couple. Unequal lives at home are now discussed.

Negotiating at home

Even in seemingly the most egalitarian of couple relationships studies have shown that mothers continue to be positioned as responsible for the emotional and physical well-being of their children and for the regulation of family routines (Hochschild, 1989; Harkness, 2008; Thomson et al, 2011; Alger and Crowley, 2012; Craig and Mullan, 2012; Nilsen et al, 2013), and, it seems, especially so in middle-class heterosexual dual-earner households. In these couple relationships Lyonette and Crompton (2015) identified a phenomenon of 'spoken' egalitarianism, whereby a male partner's intellectual engagement in feminism and his espoused egalitarian values are not matched by his behaviour when it comes to taking a proportional or equal share of routine domestic and childcare duties. In contrast, in working-class households, a 'lived egalitarianism' was evident in that men did domestic chores and childcare, and this behaviour was twinned with more traditional ideas about gender roles. Over time, attitudes caught up with behaviour to a degree, which signals some potential to undo gender traditionalism by men simply doing more domestic and care work (Sullivan and Mainiero, 2007).

Not only are women in Western industrialised economies still mainly responsible for domestic labour, they also perform most of the emotional work in families, for example, listening to and comforting children, giving emotional support to partners and doing things to improve relationships (Strazdins et al, 2004, 2006). These emotional and social activities typically do not feature in definitions of what constitutes work in contemporary society, which serves to make the effort involved invisible. Despite considerable progress in terms of maternal participation in paid employment, gendered allocations of domestic and childcare work have remained stubbornly resistant. Beagan et al (2008) argue that this is because gendered social expectations do not go away, they reinvent themselves in new guises. Studying diverse couples' negotiations of work and family life, Beagan et al found that culturally traditional beliefs about gender roles that they refer to as 'unspoken gender expectations' (2008, p667) appear to be operating just under the surface in many families across many sociocultural groups. These unspoken gender expectations operate under the surface because prevalent egalitarian discourses acknowledge women's economic potential and the inappropriateness of confining women to the home, but not yet the potential of men to 'do' mothering, that is, to take responsibility for children at emotional, community and moral levels (Doucet, 2006). Other studies have demonstrated that male and female partners undertake qualitatively different tasks and practices of day-to-day caring even within egalitarian partnerships that share responsibility for childcare. The conditions of childcare appear to be harder for mothers: 'mothering involves more double activity, more physical labour, a more rigid timetable, and more overall responsibility than fathering' (Craig, 2006, p276). Doucet (2006) argues that even when fathers are the primary caregiver, the dominant paternal practices of care emphasise physical outdoor play, independence and risk-taking. This suggests that mothers typically retain control of social and community activities and emotional well-being.

When I met Meera she was fired up. She had a great job that she was confident doing and she knew her employing organisation valued her. For Meera, the compromises and the troubles she experienced not only reconciling work and family life on a day-to-day basis but advancing her career, were at home. In this extract from our second interview, she explains.

Meera's husband and 'the list'

Meera leads an international division of a large and successful company. Her husband Arun is eight years older than her and works in the same industry in a more senior role and is on the executive committee of his firm. The family employ a live-in nanny who provides childcare for their two children aged 4 and 6 when Meera and her husband are working. Meera has recently moved into a new role on three days per week plus a half day at home. Her work schedule on her three office days is fixed in that she needs to leave by 5.30 pm to return home and take over from their nanny. Her husband's schedule is not governed by that same requirement. Meera feels that in order to perform well in this new role she needs to do a little more team socialising and client networking. These activities typically happen in the evenings and over drinks. At the same time, their eldest child is now at school and has reading to do every day and spellings to learn. Their nanny is not a native English speaker and cannot help with the children's homework. In this interview extract Meera recalls how she has approached negotiating with Arun over their respective domestic duties. She wants more flexibility and more time released from her domestic schedule so that she can do the things she thinks she needs to do to be effective at work and position herself for a promotion:

"We picked Thursday, randomly, once a week when he should come home by 6:30. 'Come home by 6:30', I said, 'so you can put the kids to bed at 7 and I can do whatever in the evening.' So I said, 'If you commit to doing that then I have one evening I know I can actually put something in my diary to meet [my boss], or to meet whichever client.' I mean it hardly worked. It happened so rarely because [sigh and long pause] because there was always something, you know, a meeting with the CEO, or a takeover bid or whatever. And the thing is I get it, I do understand what it's like [pause] I don't think Arun tries enough to make it work, that's, that's still work in progress."

At this point in the interview, I asked how she thought Arun felt about that situation. Meera was succinct:

"I think he, I think, it's a high on intention and a low on execution. I think he's, in his heart he's very supportive of, very supportive of me having a career. He's very proud. He was the proudest person at my graduation. I mean he's very proud of all of that but I don't think, and I don't think it's unique to him, I don't think that leap of 'I have to change what I do in order for her to be able to achieve what she needs to achieve.' I don't think the leap has been made, so

I think he is like, you go off and do it and I will never stop you but I will not enable you by doing things differently. Like the Thursday six-thirties are a good example because I need him to do that. Because the option otherwise is that the kids don't see either parent. Now I could be, I think harsher and just go, well the kids won't see anyone. I haven't made that leap either, I guess. So it's a little bit silly to think I have to step back a little, in order for him to step up. My fear is the kids will fall through the cracks in that time when I've stepped back and he hasn't stepped up."

Meera gave up on the Thursday six-thirties and focused on finding an arrangement between the couple that works. The imbalance in the couple with respect to how much domestic work and childcare she and Arun do is obvious to Meera and she views it as the primary factor compromising her freedoms. Making it more obvious to her husband has become a preoccupation:

"I think it's taken him a long time to even appreciate how much goes on behind the scenes, to run our home. There are things that I have quite bluntly said, need to change but I've been married almost 11 years now, it takes a long time and I'm recognising that. So it's a little bit of nagging and a bit of showing him what needs to happen. Every so often he would complain to me how I was always on my computer in the evenings, and I was like, well yeah, there's all this stuff to do. He kept saying I needed to delegate more, get other people to do that stuff ... so I started a list. It was literally everything from groceries, to [our daughter] has show-and-tell on Thursday. And it's a lot of that stuff. It's a lot of irritatingly small things. That needs to be scheduled, she needs to be dropped off, she needs to be picked up. There's this party and that party, we need to buy cakes for school and send them in, all of that. Every week there are forms from school, consent forms, helping forms, all the time forms. The new clubs list at school has come out, which one is she going to do? Ninety percent of it takes not more than 10 minutes but the list is long. It's a lot of 10 minutes ... So at one point I would send him the list of what happened this week: this is what I've done, this is what you've done, let me know if you've done anything else. And he asked me this once, he was like 'Are you sending this to embarrass me or shame me or irritate me?' So I said, you tell me to outsource more, fine, here's what happened this week. Now you tell me what I can outsource and to who?"

Meera's conclusion was that the list was worth doing, and although few practical adjustments seemed to happen as a result, she felt sure that the constraints on her time and resources had become more visible to her husband.

> "I think it was good to do the list even though it irritated him because it forced him to acknowledge what goes on and stop telling me to outsource. We're not CEOs, so it's not like we have an army of people to help us. We have limited resources. There's nanny, who I think is maxed out, genuinely, she is amazing, she's 54 and she loves our kids. We have to take care of her. She has to have reasonable working hours and we can't drive her to a nervous breakdown because Arun can't figure out the shopping."

When I met Meera, she was embarking on a new flexible working arrangement that she was emphatic was not her ideal, but was pragmatic in the context of her continuing negotiations with her husband to release herself from a small amount of her domestic responsibilities. In her words: "I am doing what I can within the constraints of time and [his] personality." Her free choice of how to work and to combine her career with family life was, she felt, compromised by how she and her husband support each other's careers.

A striking feature of Meera's account is the amount of school- and education-related work. Meera manages the family's relationship with their nanny and with their children's school and nursery. It is clear from her vivid description that the responsibilities, the interactions and the administration associated with managing those relationships adds up to a significant mental load. Reay (2005, p 102) charts the exponential growth of "the educational workload" in families in recent decades, linked to an intensification of the move in educational policy in the UK from parental rights to increased parental responsibilities, such that the assumption that all parents will engage in 'home–school work' with and for their children's benefit has become a normative and common-sense understanding of what being a parent involves. Only those with the time and resources to invest in what were once called extracurricular activities (sports, clubs, tutoring and all round socially improving activities) are able to ensure the future cultural capital and class positioning of their offspring. Those who already have, therefore, are more advantaged than those who have not, thus reproducing and potentially increasing inequalities *between* families on classed lines. Educational success has become linked to the investment of time and resources inside the home in ensuring that success. Mothers are heavily invested in ensuring that success in terms of time and practical, educational and emotional labour to secure their children's ability to exploit the opportunities of public education. Reay (2005) draws on studies of mothers' and fathers' involvement in children's schooling in the UK and finds that children's schooling was seen a primarily the mother's responsibility. Fathers would occasionally help out with homework, and hardly any men got involved with the practical maintenance work that involved mental labour, such as the tasks appearing on Meera's list: form filling, cakes, clubs, snack and uniform preparation. It is Meera, like all the mothers involved in this study, who is on the front line of social reproduction. And middle-class mothers, in turn, are dependent on the paid labour of working-class women to achieve it.

Conclusions

Women's stories about why they are adjusting their employment in flexible ways reveal the strength and direction of influence of multiple factors: of care networks, of workplace policies, practices and attitudes to part-time and flexible working, of complex gendered moral rationalities of care between partners-in-parenting, of identity and sense of self, perceived economic need, biographical life stage and journey to pregnancy, of work stress, past employment experiences and anticipated professional futures. There are issues and factors that women consider meaningful in relation to their decisions about work without defining them. Financial factors, for example, such as obligations to meet mortgage repayments, and to meet lifestyle aspirations, were salient in the majority of women's reflections about their general motivations to engage in paid work on a full- or part-time basis. Money, however, was instrumental in the amount of paid work women did in only a few cases and, as such, economic factors emerged as a less constraining force on *the way* that women work than the scheduling and reliability of childcare, and the attitudes of line managers towards part-time and flexible working.

Compromise is a feature of *all* the 30 women's stories that inform this analysis. What is salient about the level of compromise that characterises the *compromised choice* intention narrative, illustrated by Jenny's story and by Meera's, is women's clear sight of the structuring factors that they see are constraining their choices. It was common for women approaching a compromised transition to part-time and flexible work to express less optimism about the potential benefits of doing so than women seeking resolution of work–life conflict or to protect or expand their careers. Too much compromise and distance between what is preferable and what is possible, it seems, diminishes the confidence and optimism with which women approach the transition at work. They expect it to be difficult and they expect it to be unsustainable. In a workplace context this is important both for gender equality and for organisations managing the cost of employee turnover, because women who approach a flexible work transition from a compromised position anticipate that they will need to quit and exit within a reasonably short time frame. Whether they think the same about their couple relationships will be discussed in the chapters that follow.

In conclusion, the flexible work 'choices' professional mothers make are anything but free. The opportunity to achieve anything near an ideal arrangement depends on women's power and influence both inside the workplace and inside the family. The particular working patterns women arrive at in professional and managerial jobs represent a pragmatic and negotiated settlement of multiple ideological and practical pulls and incentives.

5

Doing Flexibility

Chapter themes

How do you make a big job smaller, or a workload more manageable when you have less time to give to it? Do you integrate or separate professional work from childcare and family work? This chapter and the next shift the focus from the motivations and drivers of part-time and flexible working patterns to how women implement and sustain the flexible working arrangements they negotiate. Surprisingly little is known about how part-time and other forms of flexible working work in practice in professional and managerial jobs. This chapter explains how women redesign their jobs, create new workspaces, and how they manage the temporal and spatial boundaries between their professional work and their family work. It deals with the work-related experiences and outcomes of women's transitions under three scenarios: converting a full-time job into a part-time job, job-sharing and working from home.

Time is the central theme in this discussion. In the context of a sociology of work, a sociology of time extends scholarly discussion of the problems of time in relation to achieving work–life balance to examining how workers experience time in organisational settings and how they accomplish what Flaherty (2003) terms 'time-work', that is, the manipulation of how fast, slow, full and empty time feels. In the professional sphere, time norms determine what work schedules and patterns are culturally appropriate and evidence suggests that these norms override the influence of employment contracts in setting expectations for the number of hours worked and the formulation of a work schedule. Work schedules can be used by employers as a mechanism of control, but they can also be protective and supportive of workers' achievement of protected private time, or what Zerubavel (1989) terms 'niches of inaccessibility'. This idea is helpful to explaining why it was that many women interviewed for this study sought to fix their regular non-work day or days and make their schedules public by declaring in an email footer or out-of-office message, for example, that "My working days are Wednesdays, Thursdays and Fridays" or "My non-working day is Friday." Women embarking upon a part-time work pattern ideally seek private, protected time off work: a niche of inaccessibility. However, very few women in professional and managerial jobs in this study feel it is either realistic or advantageous to their career prospects to be completely inaccessible on non-work days. In this context, a part-time work schedule offers not so much a niche of inaccessibility but rather a buffer, a right to push back against expectations that the woman will be in a work space or doing anything work-related on a certain day or time:

> "What it does is it gives me a buffer. It means I definitely don't have to go into the office on a Friday. They get 120% of me Monday to Thursday and I work some of the weekend to fit in what I need to do, but it means I have most of my Fridays here and I can drop the kids of at school and pick them up and I definitely don't have be in an office. People know that and they don't expect it. That's the buffer." (Olivia [5])

The effectiveness of the buffer, and the achievability of inaccessibility will be discussed further. The analysis in this chapter and those that follow it benefits from a longitudinal perspective and draws on follow-up interviews that were conducted within weeks of women beginning their flexible working arrangements and between 3 and 12 months later.

Converting a full-time job into a part-time job

The experience of going part-time by converting a known full-time job into a part-time job was largely a self-directed activity for the 12 women in this scenario. It was a process that felt to most women approaching it for the first time like trial-and-error, meaning that they would try things without any certainty that their approaches would be effective, and, in some cases, with not a great deal of certainty about what being effective would look or feel like. The intuitive approach of most women towards making their professional workload manageable in less time was to be strategic; to prioritise the task elements of their jobs that were most incentivised and important in terms of alignment to organisational objectives. This meant that some tasks had to go, delegated to someone else or dropped altogether. It was ambiguous to most women whether their employers' agreements to their individual part-time work arrangements extended to granting them authority to reallocate responsibilities and to delegate tasks to other people. This rescoping of a role, potential reallocation of its responsibilities and redistribution of its tasks can be understood as a process of job design. Job design is a key activity of Human Resources Management (HRM), which involves deciding on a job's key duties and responsibilities and formulating these into a job that individuals can do and regard as their own, which is crucial because, 'not only is it the basis of individual satisfaction and achievement at work, [job design] is necessary to get the job done efficiently, economically, reliably and safely' (Torrington et al, 2011, p84).

What women were doing in the early weeks and months of moving into a part-time and flexible arrangement, was on-the-job job design. Importantly, in almost all cases, women approached designing their jobs for flexibility with little or no support or guidance from managers or HRM practitioners, which accounts for the trial-and-error quality of women's transition experiences.

Often women's output targets were pro rata, in line with their proportion of standard weekly working hours, yet with no clear agreement reached about which responsibilities would be reallocated across a work group and to whom tasks would be delegated. Ambiguity, twinned with anxiety about being perceived to be burdening colleagues by delegating work, typically led to women intensifying their work effort in order to compress largely unadjusted full-time workloads into fewer days and restricted schedules:

> "The first month I was attempting to work part-time but was basically working very long days, cramming it all into three. Now I have somebody working with me, however the tasks she's ended up taking are not really the things I needed to lose, so in reality I am still not working part-time. Officially I am, but really I'm not." (Sally [28])

The elements of their jobs thought to matter most to the employing organisations were not always the elements that women found most interesting or satisfying. Extra projects once taken on to expansively craft interesting and stretching roles and build a case for advancement (Wrzesniewski and Dutton, 2001) were now dropped, regretfully in some cases: "it's a shame really as that was one thing that I really enjoyed doing ... I am a bit sad to lose it" (Victoria [21]). Many women reported shedding specific activities, such as personal development, from their work schedules as they felt they could no longer fit them in:

> "I've got to do some sort of training course starting in September so that's kind of one more thing on top of what

I'm doing. They let me postpone it as I was like I don't think I can, I would have had a meltdown if I did that as well." (Sadie [17])

Finding time for personal development and training, attendance at corporate events or conferences, networking and socialising with colleagues was difficult, and this observation echoes the findings of Hoque and Kirkpatrick (2003) and Durbin and Tomlinson (2010) that part-time workers struggle to find time for these activities, and which Gatrell (2005) proposes is potentially detrimental to their future prospects.

Managing other people's professional development and career progression was mentioned specifically as a responsibility that part-time working professionals looked to relinquish or to reduce. Where that responsibility had temporarily passed to someone else during a maternity absence, as in Gail's [20] situation, they were in no rush to take it on again. The additional emotional work involved with managing others' work lives and professional performance can be, it appears, an emotional labour too far in the context of their own retained (and quite often, extended) emotional labours within the family:

> "Oh yes it's a huge relief not to have the people responsibility, much easier just having the projects to worry about and not how everyone else is feeling about their futures. I don't have the energy for it." (Gail [20])

Whether they are flexible workers or not, there is tendency for women to take on (and be asked to take on) more of the 'office housework' than their male colleagues (Kolb and Porter, 2015), which in the 1970s, when the term was invented, involved clearing up after meetings, arranging group social events, remembering birthdays and all the things that make work life pleasant and collegiate. Women who participated in my study observed that the 'people roles' inside their organisations, such as mentoring and managing staff appraisals, tended to fall to women to perform, and the work involved in undertaking these roles was perceived as less valuable than that oriented towards sales or customer service. With less time and emotional energy available, some women were relieved to give them up.

Working more

Overall, women's experiences of converting their full-time jobs into part-time jobs felt more like increased work intensity than a well-managed job redesign process. Work intensity is often associated with poorly designed and managed flexible work arrangements and has performance and well-being implications (see for example Clarke and Holdsworth, 2017). Women routinely worked more hours than their part-time contract. Lack of people to delegate work to was frequently mentioned as the reason they worked the additional hours that many women said they did:

> "I probably do more than my three days ... but it's not like I've got certain roles and bits of it can be taken away and done by somebody else, it's just a matter of resources at the moment and not having anybody below me to delegate to." (Lara [6])

Equally, an unwillingness to delegate for fear of being seen to be shirking their responsibilities was an explanation for the work intensity that featured significantly in women's accounts of their experience. Even when they had control of their workload or led teams of workers, women were caught. They were caught between needing to reduce and control their workload to something commensurate with their available working hours, and a felt need to retain it by way of defence against perceptions of unprofessionalism and the discourses of divided attention and low commitment that circulate around working mothers:

> "I'm in control of my own workload but then it's really hard to just sort of shave off a percentage as I can't give my work to anyone ... and if I do that it doesn't mean I'm doing a good job. I think that's the other thing." (Olivia [5])

Women may be right to assume the ambivalence or animosity of colleagues to their work arrangements. Golden et al (2006) found evidence of co-worker satisfaction being negatively associated with the prevalence of home-workers, and surmised that flexible workers, aware of negative perceptions of co-workers, may feel the need to increase their work effort in an attempt to mitigate such reactions.

In one of the very few studies of transitions to part-time and flexible working arrangements among male and female managers and professionals, Gascoigne (2014) found the conversion of a full-time job into a part-time job the most problematic transition to make. She found that professionals who were supported by their organisations in practical ways to reallocate work at the team or work-group level fared much better in achieving a predictable and uninterrupted pattern of time off compared to professionals relying on their own efficiency and influence to be able to manage and delegate work. The intensity of managing a weekly absence of one or two days while retaining almost full scope and responsibilities was brought into sharp focus by Hayley [14], whose experience draws attention to the additional effort of the part-time and home-working professional to actively manage a routine *absence* from workplace cultures that place value on employee *presence* and visibility as indicators of productivity:

> "Every week, you know, every week I'm packing work into a shorter deadline, I pull it forward because I'm not going be there … every week I have to find free people to farm out my work to, I have to arrange a handover to someone and ask whoever to keep an eye on it, put the out-of-office on … when I was full-time I used to do that the week before I went on holiday and that was bad enough. Now I'm doing it every single week." (Hayley [14])

No women in this study enjoyed complete freedom to adjust their job scope or workload, yet it was clear that some had achieved positions of seniority that afforded them greater latitude for adjustment about the mix between the formal and informal flexibility they could use to meet their own needs. Olivia [5] and Jessica [23] illustrate the affordances of their senior positions within their organisations:

> "We didn't all need to go into the office just for that so I changed the team meeting to a conference call and moved it to Friday … that's my non-working day usually but this is only once a month and it works better like that for everyone I think." (Olivia [5])

> "My team doesn't need to see me — there is a senior manager between them and me who is more hands-on. I am accountable for their work but I don't need to be there every minute of every day and that means that I can control my schedule and where I need to be so much better … my job is not about outputs or process it's about accountability." (Jessica [23])

Calendar-driven deadlines were problematic when women were the named accountable person, for example the signatory to a contract, and completion falls on a non-working day. This accountability was viewed as impossible to be shared or reallocated to another member of the team. This indicates that that the low substitutability of accountable professionals and senior managers is a barrier to a successful conversion of a full-time into a part-time job. No one reported ever missing these deadlines. They made alternative childcare arrangements or adjusted whatever else they were intending to do on those days. In so doing they successfully present a façade of full-time availability and demonstrate their continuing responsiveness to the needs of employing organisation. This compliant and unchallenging approach universally justified as due to 'the nature of the job'.

Far more women in this study occupied management positions that afforded them little latitude for adjustment to their job scope and workload, and many described a typical working week as comprising a rolling 'to-do' list. Women whose work activities contributed to an organisational process upon which other members depended felt particularly vulnerable. Their routine weekly absence due to part-time hours left a resource gap that employing organisations failed to fill. Women who regarded themselves as capable and high-performing found this situation uncomfortable and discordant with their view of themselves as professionals. Charlotte [26] illustrates the felt pressure to perform full-time availability and productivity under a part-time working arrangement. Her account emphasises the emotional management that goes into that performance:

> "It feels like I'm having to cram everything in to a shorter space of time which I am just about managing to do but it feels sometimes like I'm rushing something or I'm not able to keep on top of it … nobody would know because what everybody else sees is that I'm doing everything that I was before. I hide it that I'm feeling more pressured or stressed than I ever have." (Charlotte [26])

Despite the transition from a full-time to a part-time work arrangement being largely welcomed and anticipated by women as enabling of their work–life needs and circumstances, for most women *implementing* their arrangement was a largely self-directed activity that was approached with uncertainty. Considerable ambiguity around how much job redesign flexible working professionals could or should do to adjust their job scope or reallocate its responsibilities, to arrange substitution for key authorities, to delegate tasks and plug resource gaps on an ad hoc or ongoing basis, and anxiety about how their actions will be perceived by managers and colleagues, drives women towards work intensity.

Working from home

Discussed in this section is how women achieved professional work in different places and spaces and how they combined, breached and separated their work and family worlds. A key insight is that strategies for managing time were linked to managing place in professional women's lives. In 18 cases women combined part-time working hours with location flexibility. It was clear that location flexibility facilitated their participation in *more* weekly hours of paid work than they would have committed to without it. Working four days or four-and-a-half days each week is much more manageable if at least one day and ideally two days can be spent working from home. This was described as the ideal arrangement by some: "I think what I'd like to get to is four days Monday to Thursday with the Thursday at home, that would be pretty much ideal" (Sophie [30]).

Most professional and managerial women who had negotiated some location flexibility were thoughtful about their choice of location, selecting locations of work that they felt best suited the task. Individual intellectual tasks such as analysis, reading or report writing were felt best achieved at home or away from busy offices, which reserved group tasks and interaction for collaborative workspaces. Meetings are a hallmark of office culture. Many women in this study described how they had become keenly aware of what they perceived to be time wasting, noticing all the unproductive habits and rituals of organisational life. Amanda [10] described her new perspective on work meetings:

> "I mean it sort of feels like when I'm in the office I'm just in meetings. You know, a typical day I'd have half an hour when I'm not sitting in meetings with people and it feels like it's both utterly exhausting, and really unproductive and it means I'm just not getting round to the things I need to do. So actually, removing myself from the office just is a way of carving out some time to be a bit more productive on the more substantive stuff." (Amanda [10])

'Carving' is an apt metaphor to apply to women's approach to creating time for particular types of work tasks. Southerton (2009) describes how workers create 'hot spots' which condense activities in order to create 'cold spots' which provide time for interaction. There was much evidence of this kind of time-work in women's accounts, that is, conscious and continuous assessing of time, task and place in order to plan for the most efficient and effective outcome. This degree of schedule autonomy that encourages workers to find their own hot and cold spots and make the best use of private and public spaces to accomplish their work is not universal. When this was the case, women made use of culturally compliant practices, such as working from home on a Friday. Taking Friday to work from home or as a non-working day was mentioned frequently and affirms the findings of Gatrell et al (2014) about the symbolic significance of Fridays in British office culture as a slightly more relaxed work day and gateway to the weekend. By choosing Friday as their one day to work at home, women do not disrupt the professional norms of place: "because nobody works in the office on Fridays anyway" (Olivia [5]). Where Friday was designated one of the official non-working days in a part-time fixed-schedule arrangement, this is usually a planned, tactical action to minimise the disruption of their absence to colleagues and clients. In effect it removes non-standard working arrangements from view and, it is often hoped, from harsh judgement.

Minimising commuting time was another important time-maximisation strategy. One woman was permanently home-based, and the 29 others had commuting times of between 30 minutes and five hours on days that they travelled to employers' premises. The longest journey times were to and from London. The longer the commute, the greater appetite there seemed to be to work from home and save that time. In some cases, women actively avoided work projects that required extensive domestic or international travel: "I probably should have gone after that project but I sort of pretended I didn't hear about it because I didn't want to travel" (Jessica [23]). This was especially pertinent to nursing mothers, to women supporting their teenage children through school assessments, and to mothers responsible for dropping-off and collecting their children from school and clubs at fixed times. There were a very small number of exceptions, notably Eryn [3], who eight months into her part-time working arrangement took on an international project that relocated her and her infant daughter four days per week for three months, a situation which, she reflected, was a moment-in-time opportunity only achievable because her child was so young:

"I know that it seems like the craziest thing to do, and I can't imagine being able to do it when she's older or if we have another … it can only really happen because at the moment she is kind of moveable so it's fine." (Eryn [3])

A key finding in this analysis is the interdependency of managing time and managing place of work. Attention now turns to how women work across time and space and manage the boundaries in between.

Managing home–work boundaries

Technology has facilitated a blurring of the spatial boundaries of work, although there is little agreement across empirical studies on the relative benefits or detrimental effects on health, well-being and relationships (Voydanoff, 2005a; Mills and Täht, 2010). For example Carlson et al (2009) found that flexible working may allow job demands to penetrate further into the home domain, particularly through technology that means individuals can work almost anywhere and anytime.

Women in this study achieved being at work without physically being on employers' premises by using the technology that was made available to them. They used video calls and virtual conferencing to collaborate with colleagues in dispersed locations and across time zones. Many women described working fluidly across their domestic and professional worlds; their professional work no longer zoned to take place entirely between rigid working hours. A location-flexible work arrangement was typically combined with part-time working hours and it seemed to mean that when it came to managing workload, boundaries in all senses – cognitive, temporal and spatial – had become more permeable. Jenny [18] contrasted her old fixed and new flexible approaches to her work:

> "One thing that has changed particularly is it is a bit more fluid, the work/home situation. Even on the days I'm not in the office I'll still be answering emails and I'll still check it and if I need to do a bit of stuff over the weekend I will do. Before I would leave work and be like, 'That's it, done now, I don't have to think about that all weekend until I go in.' Whereas now it's very much thinking about both and actually if I need to get something done by Monday and I haven't managed it by the time I leave on Thursday then I will do it over the weekend." (Jenny [18])

Professional mothers value having the schedule autonomy and the technology to facilitate their free movement between work time and personal and family time in a variety of spaces. An important finding is that it was much more common for women to describe this fluidity as essential and enabling, rather than oppressive or intrusive. Sarah [1], for example, described her early morning and late-night work schedule as her preference: "I'm totally flexible about when I work, I actually prefer early mornings in the office and leaving early and then logging back on at night, which is kind of what I do."

Adopting such a fluid approach was very often articulated as a personal choice or a preference, yet it was a choice that women simultaneously signalled that they had no choice but to make. Their *preference* was to feel less stressed and overwhelmed by work and so they *chose* to ameliorate these effects by using their unpaid 'down time' to keep on top of their work, this is an important point very well illustrated by Victoria [21], a doctor in the public health sector:

> "I mean I do actually choose to do emails and things and even things like reports in the evenings and it means I feel I can relax and do it. That was something I worried about, that I'd sort of see it very much as a chore but actually, I choose to do it because it means then my days at work can be sort of less pressured. I could choose not to and then have much busier and more stressful days but I choose to spread it out a bit and it's working out fine." (Victoria [21])

This contradictory choice position seems to draw women further in to privately solving problems that arise from employers' inattention to how professional and managerial jobs are designed (and could be redesigned to support flexibility) and how people could be supported to perform them. A combination of reciprocity and workload justified the additional work in the evenings that Andrea [27], a solicitor in the public sector, routinely did at home:

> "I guess I sort of volley between the two. Like last night I sent two emails that took quite a bit of composing so I worked from about 6 to about half 9 … I feel like because I leave at 5 o'clock I have to make it up a bit at other times and I wouldn't be able to do the work in 9 to 5, there's too much, and quick-turnaround requests come in at all hours." (Andrea [27])

A reciprocity effect on work intensity has been observed in other studies of part-time working. Social exchange theory predicts that employees are grateful to employers for affording them the opportunity to work in a non-standard way, and they demonstrate their gratitude by worker harder or longer (see Kelliher et al, 2013). I would argue that in reality unadjusted workloads and a desire to stay on top of them, in combination with a motivation to avoid stigma and exclusion by burdening colleagues with absences and incomplete outputs, are more likely the drivers of the everyday intensity and anytime working experienced by women in this study. Relatedly, the construction of a part-time and flexible working arrangement in workplace policy and culture as an idiosyncratic adjustment and not a mainstream way of working compounds an understanding that flexible working practices have more to offer the individual than the organisation. It is, therefore, not perceived necessary or beneficial to employing organisations to reorient organisational processes and collective working practices to be supportive of flexibility. These are points that will be discussed further in Chapter 5.

While undertaking professional work in domestic spaces was largely viewed by women as enabling and supportive of accomplishment of their dual roles as professionals and mothers responsible for the domestic sphere, to *not* routinely work from home was viewed by some who had experienced long periods of home-working in their work histories as emancipating. Not physically being at home as much as they were previously freed women from habitually seeing and doing domestic chores, which as Sadie [17] puts it, she does, "just because I am here and it needs doing", and for some women, working more hours outside the home fundamentally altered the bargaining position within the couple, as Victoria [21] explains:

> "It feels a bit more equal now that I am out at work. I feel in a way on a more even keel with my husband and it seems easier to split the domestic chores now than when I was at home a lot more because obviously I was the one who was at home so picked up more ... it has been a bit easier to differentiate and split the things that need doing because we are both not around."

The ability to work at home in the early mornings and in the evenings when children had gone to bed was articulated by most women who worked in this way as an effective way of keeping on top of their workloads. Eleanor's [13] description of her typical Monday working from home provides a relatively extreme illustration of what volleying between domestic and professional work can look like:

"I get up at 5 and work until 7 am when the kids are up, then do breakfast and get them ready. My husband can take them to school and nursery, so I just have the youngest here who usually naps around 9, so that's another hour I can jump on my laptop before I take him to nursery. Then I come back and carry on with work until 3. I might stick some washing on, prep something for a meal later, but that's it really until I get the girls from school. If I have anything left at all I'll log on again after we've put them to bed. Sometimes I just haven't got the energy though." (Eleanor [13])

That women pick up work again in the evenings is significant. It is usually after the time that young children have gone to bed. Occasions when women found themselves simultaneously working and looking after children were problematic and much thought and planning went in avoiding these situations. There were times when it was unavoidable. Claire [2], a solicitor in private practice, recalled a distressing occasion that made her question everything about her professional and maternal life:

"I've ended up having to have telephone conversations with a client to try and keep a deal moving and you know, quite complex things to be talking about, not just, 'Can you send me this? Great, thanks,' in detail conversations and you know, at the same time I've got my daughter at my feet and she's fine for 10 minutes doing whatever she wants to do but then she wants your attention and at one point I remember very clearly, she was not quite 2 then, she started howling because she'd stuck a pencil in her ear. So I let her hurt herself and it could have been really nasty. She could have damaged her ear drum but I was on the telephone trying to have an in-depth conversation about work which wasn't the deal, you know, it wasn't the deal. Actually having *to do* the job on the day you're supposed to be doing another job has been very difficult. Very difficult." (Claire [2])

Crisis situations such as Claire's were pivotal and shone a light on the reciprocity problem: the imbalance in the efforts of the individual to implement and sustain a part-time and flexible working arrangement and those of the organisation to facilitate it. This led Claire to conclude that on the part of her employer, "There is not much buy-in to this three-day week arrangement, not really no, not at all." There were other mini-crises that punctuated women's experiences of combining their paid work with motherhood that placed a strain on them and the family. Examples of missed holidays and shifting work deadlines illustrate these occasional and intense pressures:

> "It was a disaster, they changed the date of the meeting and my husband was away so I had no choice but to get an agency to find an emergency nanny ... it cost £200 for the day to get me to that meeting and the kids were miserable because they didn't know her, yes, that was a low point." (Olivia [5])

Women obliged to monitor their jobs almost constantly by checking emails and answering work calls on their non-working days usually dismissed the possibility of not doing so as unrealistic: "It *would* be great if I could just leave on a Wednesday and not have to be half working when I am off but it is just not possible" (Fiona [9]). The more well-resourced women in this study, in terms of having achieved occupational positions of sufficient status and seniority to afford them greater schedule autonomy, may well have been better placed to manage the practical demands of crises such as these by being able to afford to buy additional flexible childcare for example. However, they were not immune to the cumulative effect of working intensively in largely unadjusted jobs, which caused them to doubt the sustainability of their current arrangement:

> "I feel like my 80% doesn't really equate to every Friday being off however because of various evening things I have to do during the week etc. So I've been back probably about six Fridays, been on holiday for one of them, and on two occasions, well actually on three occasions I've had a client meeting which I couldn't get out of because this person can only have meetings on a Friday at this point in her life and she's a client. Last week we were in the midst of trying to sign a new client so whilst I was completely off I had numerous phone calls. And this week I again have an event on Friday morning so I guess I'm mentioning all that because what I'm doing is I'm testing this at the moment this whole four days part-time thing. It doesn't really feel like it's working." (Jessica [23])

(Job)-sharing the load

A job-share is defined in this study as sharing the tasks and responsibilities of a single full-time role between two people who work part-time. Job-sharing can also be 'teamed' between more than two people, however there were no examples of this model in this study. Job-sharing is most often found in transactional and administrative roles lower down the occupational hierarchy, and is rarely found in management and senior roles. Most often job-sharing is a type of flexible working arrangement performed by two women working collaboratively (Daniels, 2012).

Data discussed here is drawn from the reflections of two women with previous experience of job-sharing in their work histories, and three women whose transitions into job-sharing this research followed for one year. Two of the three women entering job-shares for the first time had found their own partners from within the organisation and then they proposed the model to their employer, and with a particular job in mind. The third case was unusual because the woman had applied as an external candidate to be recruited to join an incumbent job-sharer in a public sector organisation. The two women with job-sharing in their work histories had both worked in the public sector. Their collected reflections on the practicalities of job-sharing in a range of organisational contexts (two private sector, three public sector) and their experiences of the enabling or constraining structures, processes and workplace attitudes provides insight into the lived experiences of this distinctive and collaborative way of working. The potential of job-sharing to emancipate the part-time professional from a challenging five-days-in-three workload is discussed.

The main benefit expressed by job-sharers of working in this way is the achievement of predictable, uninterrupted time off and hence relief from a felt pressure to be always on and available to clients, customers and co-workers on non-working days. Gail [20] provides an example of this benefit in her reflection about how she worked before the job-share:

> "When I was working Tuesday–Friday I would always feel on a Monday that I ought to have a quick look [at my smart phone] at lunchtime if there was something going on. And I'd look again in the evening. So I wasn't really ever switched off from work. It was still there. But now, Wednesday afternoon I do still keep an eye on it to help Sarah take over so if she needs to ask me a question I will

answer it for her. But Thursday and Friday, I don't even turn the thing on." (Gail [20])

The lack of organisational support for job-sharing was evident in the stories told of women finding each other and subsequently proposing their model of collaboration to their managers. Gatrell (2008) similarly found that job-sharing worked well in practice, yet job-sharers had to organise it and establish themselves. Women in the private sector in this study were typically the first and only job-sharers in their work contexts at their levels. Systems and processes did not exist to support two people doing one job. The key challenge for job-sharers operating in elite and competitive workplace contexts is that it is a collaborative model in an environment characterised by individualism. The processes and systems of work organisation, recognition and reward, are aligned to a resourcing model that expects one job to be carried out by one person. Seemingly simple things like getting a joint business card, proved difficult to arrange and necessitated more explanation and more persuasion than a full-time or even a part-time colleague might have been expected to do:

> "It's the things you think are really simple that are actually really time-consuming to sort out, like business cards. There was a policy about one name on one card and that seemed to cause a lot of bother to sort out, and the email account, we wanted one mailbox to share between us ... that still hasn't been set up properly." (Gail [20])

All job-sharers reported a level of introspection about their personal approach to work before they embarked on the job-share and this continued during its early weeks and months. They thought deeply about how they would feel about sharing the limelight with someone else and about how exposing of individual weaknesses such an intimate form of team working could be. Esther [11] captured this when reflecting on why her relationship with her job-share partner worked so well:

> "I think it definitely makes me more effective and accountable in terms of what I actually do at work as I have to 'fess up to times when I have not managed to get something done when I said I would ... yeah, I definitely waste a lot less time ... we've got quite good at making new work habits and breaking old habits that have annoyed

me for years anyway but have never seemed to manage to stop doing ... I think we're both really comfortable with other people knowing a lot about what we're doing, what we're thinking about stuff and how we're performing ... we're both self-assured enough that we're not too worried about what the other person will think about all that and also we've known each other quite a while too, we're similar ability levels and very different but complementary styles. That works really well as well." (Esther [11])

In these women's experiences a blueprint for job-sharing in management and professional jobs did not exist. They needed to work it out for themselves. In this respect job-sharing is little different from any other part-time and flexible arrangement in that, as many studies observe, the heavy lifting is largely undertaken by the employee (see for example Corwin et al, 2001). The practices of job-sharing that job-sharers identified as essential to the effective implementation of their arrangement included: agreeing the time split across the week, for example dividing the week in half with or without an overlapping day. Agreeing privately between the parties an expected life span of the job-share was felt to be important as well. No job-sharers anticipated that their partnership would last forever and all felt that it was better to be up front about a fixed time commitment to working together before reviewing the arrangement. Most settled on a full year or two-year commitment to the relationship.

The design of the job-share needs to be appropriate to the nature of the job. There were a few different models being developed by women in this study. Jobs that manage a business process and require continuity across a week split five work days into two blocks such that a process managed by one partner at the start of the week could be continued seamlessly by the other at the end of the week with a handover in the middle. Job-shares that were designed around project work or case work were more likely to involve a more complete sharing of a portfolio by partners working on different days. It also proved possible to divide projects between the partners according to specialist skill and expertise, thus retaining an element of individuality and avoiding the complete substitutability that characterises a portfolio sharing model.

Job-sharers agreed plans for handover and routinely ran their handover conversations outside of paid working hours. They protected each other's private time on official non-working days by establishing rules about getting in touch on these days. They reported the importance of being united on decisions and of backing each other up. Competition within the job-share partnership, between the partners, was viewed as unhealthy and likely to lead to failure of the arrangement.

Accounts in this study emphasise the positives of job-sharing for the individual, which were felt to be primarily in terms of enabling the individual to be completely absent from work when she is not contracted to be working. It is a flexible working arrangement that, if it works well, offers respite from a felt need for "always being open to the whole organisation all the time" (Gemma [8]), in that a confident and close relationship with a job-share partner appeared to reduce the need to check emails or take calls on non-work days. Many women who were not currently job-sharing spoke in wishful ways about how they imagined this type of arrangement to be the solution to their own in-work challenges. They emphasised the welcome relief from pressure to be continuously available to work across five weekdays, and in some cases saw benefits in job-sharing in more senior roles as an interim step towards full-time employment higher up the ladder when children are older. Juliet [29], for example, was actively seeking a job-share partner although she had had little positive response from prospective employers about the idea:

> "It is clear from the conversations I have been having that asking for part-time fixed hours is pretty toxic … and they don't know how to do job-shares, there's definitely an education process to go through on that … at the moment it's very much a case of you fitting in with us, not us with you." (Juliet [29])

Job-sharing was viewed by many women as a solution to the perceived three-day-week problem, as Sophie [30] concluded, "three days is impossible without a job-share, it just can't be done", again emphasising the idea that jobs are designed as full-time by default.

Little mention of limitations of job-sharing was made by the three women whose transition into job-shares this study analysed. Drawing from women's reflections of their previous experiences of job-sharing offers insight into some of the potential challenges. When one job-share partner quits, only in one public sector organisation did a mechanism exist for recruiting a new partner. Another challenge was negotiating for two within systems that negotiate for one. Ambiguity about pay led to inaction in Andrea's case [27]:

> "My job-share partner and I were thinking why didn't we ask for a pay rise. We'd been on the same salary since 2008

[for 5 years]. I think it was because we had children during that time we felt we couldn't ask for a pay rise and also because we were a job-share I didn't feel I could just ask for a pay rise just for me, I'd need to be asking for her as well but I didn't know if the organisation could give one of us a pay rise without the other, but actually, neither of asked the question so I don't know." (Andrea [27])

Job-sharing facilitates job performance in ways that do not fundamentally challenge the 'nature of the job' or radically challenge the full-time present and responsive professional time norms that dominate the majority of work cultures within which these women are employed. The way that women described implementing their job-shares does not seem to demand too much of their employing organisations. The adjustment required on the part of the organisation is minimal, for example facilitating joint business cards, shared telephone numbers, and colleagues are not tested to remember which days are non-working days because one or other of partners will be there. An effective job-share requires an intense and revealing form of teamwork and trust between the partners, and a consistent message about the model needs to be given to internal and external clients. The women who do it in managerial and professional work regard job-sharing positively. Women spoke of the extra relationship work that comes with being part of a job-share – the effort it takes to manage the relationship within the partnership and between the partners and the organisation. This effort is considerable within organisations that are unfamiliar with, and quite often sceptical about, the expansive impact of two sets of complementary skills and working styles in one professional role. As pioneers and pathfinders in their own organisations innovating with flexible working practices, the job-sharers encountered bias even from seemingly the most supportive of sources, as Esther [11] recalled:

"After a few weeks our boss sat us down and said 'Please stop telling everyone you're a job-share as they'll think you're a bit rubbish', and things like 'I might be a dinosaur but …' We just said, no, and that we were going to carry on telling people that we are a job-share. We are doing this important job with loads of visibility and we're good at it, people need to know that there are two of us and that is why we are so good." (Esther [11])

Job-sharers have a difficult time convincing managers that their collective approach works to the organisation's benefit. An important insight from this analysis is that it is extremely difficult to fit a *collective* job model into progression structures premised on *individual* success and advancement. This contributes to women's own observations that the skills and styles of working that make job-sharing effective were undervalued by employers, and even viewed with suspicion. Andrea [27] provides an example of how she felt that a recruiter's favourable bias towards full-time and continuous employment locked her out of a new opportunity:

> "What I think went against me in some of the interviews was being a job-share ... in the final interview, at one point they seemed to be suggesting I might have been lying about doing all these amazing things and it might have been my job-share partner who'd done them. That was difficult and I felt that because I had been a job-share I couldn't be seen as the safe option ... I was pretty cross, yeah it was pretty hard to take." (Andrea [27])

Job-sharing in managerial and professional work is an opportunity for individuals to better manage time and space and to access more heavyweight roles working three days per week or less than they might have otherwise been able to access with a part-time role. Women spoke enthusiastically about this type of flexible working arrangement while acknowledging the effort that it took, and continues to take, to design and implement their approach. Maintaining a professional and stretching role helped women imagine their future selves in professional positions of at least equal or more responsibility. Their achievement of that vision depends on a more favourable disposition among employers to the benefits of job-sharing for individuals and organisations.

Conclusions

The experience of converting a full-time job into a part-time one or starting a job-share are largely self-directed job-design projects that feel to most women like a trial-and-error process. Uncertainty and ambiguity mark the early weeks and months of the experience. The practical, physical, cognitive and emotional demands of women's labours to do their jobs now extending to working out *how* to do their jobs in less and restricted time and in different places. I will later argue that these responsibilities could and should be shared between employee and employer, and that there is much that employers can do to reduce the ambiguity that marks the experience of implementing different types of part-time and flexible work arrangement in professional and managerial jobs.

There were very few examples of proactive, job-design support offered to individuals. Women worked out for themselves how best to fit in to systems and processes, and align to work cultures that were not designed with flexibility in mind. Inflexibility on the part of the organisation to spend time supporting job design, to backfill routine absences for part-time working, or to facilitate sharing or substitution of accountabilities drew women in to privately solving these problems by working more hours, and working intensively and fluidly across domestic and professional spheres. Job-sharing offers some protection of individuals' private time and creates a highly prized niche of inaccessibility.

6

Feeling Flexibility

Chapter themes

Combining career and family life, and the day-to-day reconciliation of paid employment with childcare places physical, mental and emotional demands on women and are evidenced in a significant body of research (see Gatrell, 2008; Tomlinson et al, 2011; Hollway, 2015). This chapter explores the hitherto underexplored affective dimensions of the lived experience of 'doing' flexible work arrangements for mothers in professional and managerial jobs. The effects on mind, body and spirit are in focus.

For women navigating the transition simultaneously with a return to work following maternity leave, the maternal body was at the centre of the experience. Tiredness was not exclusive to new and nursing mothers, the physical and emotional impacts of working intensively in largely unadjusted jobs or inhospitable workplace contexts are viscerally present in women's accounts. Hochschild's (2012) concept of emotional labour is highly relevant to the professional motherhood project and this analysis shows how the scope and span of women's emotional workload *increases* when they work outside the home.

Attention to the everyday experiences of professional mothers and their actions to implement and sustain their work arrangements in the context of their motherhood raises important questions about the responsibilities of and for workers who are combining care and career. The chapter begins with exploration of that theme and introduces the concept of **quiet responsibility** which characterises women's feelings about and their approaches to their flexible work arrangements.

Quiet responsibility

Women feel terrific responsibility for designing, implementing and sustaining a flexible work arrangement, and they go to considerable lengths to implement a non-standard working pattern in ways that minimise inconvenience to managers and co-workers. Feminist critique of the contemporary phenomena of responsibility and practices of 'responsibilisation' thought endemic within neoliberal ideology illuminates this insight. It assists in interpreting why women experience the pressure that they do to take responsibility and to determine their own successes at work irrespective of their familiarity with the employment circumstances in which they find themselves (Gill and Scharff, 2013; Tronto, 2013; McLeod, 2015; Rubery, 2015).

The everyday language of personal responsibility (Hage and Eckersley, 2012) filled women's accounts of their transition into flexible working arrangements. The personal responsibility women felt for the successful implementation of their arrangements surfaced in talk of "duty", "obligation", "blame", "fault" and "guilt". This point is well illustrated by Sally's [28] concise explanation of the origins of the responsibility she felt:

> "Well because in a way, nobody asked me to and in a way I feel I have a responsibility … I mean I chose to do this, to work part-time, so I feel that it's my responsibility."

The political ideology of neoliberalism frames women's experiences. Individual choice and opportunity is emphasised in a way that simultaneously confers responsibility for the choices made on to the individual making them (Tronto, 2013). When I asked women who was responsible for 'making it work', referring specifically to the implementation of their flexible working pattern at work, universally women answered "I" and "me". Political theorist Joan Tronto (2013) looks at responsibility from the perspective of the care needs of modern societies and argues persuasively that an ethics of care is missing from neoliberal ideology. Tronto sees that overemphasis on self-responsibility in neoliberal times makes the importance of caring for others disappear, and the way modern democratic societies are organised allows some people to effectively pass on being responsible for others, and for the work of care to be differentially distributed along gender, class and ethnic lines. This in turn allows some groups to live in a state of 'privileged irresponsibility' (Tronto, 2013, p52), in which they both depend on and fail or refuse to acknowledge the systems of care and support that make possible their life – domestic labour, cleaning, childcare – while those who do the care work of society are necessarily highly aware of the labour involved in their responsibilities.

Framing responsibilities as 'practices and interactions', Walker (2008, p16) proposes that 'in the ways we assign, accept, or deflect responsibilities, we express our understandings of our own and others' identities, relationships and values'. Practices of responsibility, she proposes, implement commonly shared understandings about 'who gets to do what to whom and who is supposed to do what for whom'. Applying Walker's conceptualisation to this analysis illuminates the collective understandings of women and, by implication, their employers, of part-time and flexible working as a private issue and not a matter of organisational resourcing demanding organisational capability and commitment to provide practical support.

In many cases, women reflected that their organisation's HRM systems and processes were not sophisticated enough to integrate shorter working hours or restricted work schedules, and such limitations were implicated in women's reported experiences of inequitable access to work projects and even to financial reward. Claire [2], a law professional in private practice, reflected on the fuzzy logic that she and her employer had applied to making her annual output target pro rata in terms of her input of weekly working hours. She felt this arrangement had served to disproportionately increase her work effort in order to achieve a lower target that reflected her input of hours and had ultimately disadvantaged her financially:

> "It seems ridiculous now when I look back at this, I mean I accepted a lower sales target because that was roughly in line with my working hours but it takes just the same amount of effort and luck to land a £75k deal as it does a £100k deal. It's harder actually because you need to go looking for lots of smaller clients because you don't get a look in on those big pitch teams because they know you're not there all the time ... and then later they didn't even award me the bonus." (Claire [2])

A few employing organisations were described as having systems and processes that were better able to integrate a greater range of working time patterns, for example Jane felt her achievement of a workload commensurate with her capacity was facilitated by her organisation's new resource management tool:

> "There is a new resource planning spreadsheet that's got all our projects with the number of days needed for each one over the months and then people are assigned to projects on a certain number of days ... it factors in your maximum days a week and the other things you do. So that has all been quite good and does mean that actually I feel more confident in saying I can work four days a week and I

will actually have to have less work than someone who is working five days a week." (Jane [12])

The responsibility women felt for implementing their working arrangement was felt in two directions, for their own benefit, and in many cases symbolically towards the collective category of mothers:

"There are lots of women coming through the ranks; they're looking up and thinking, ok I'm about to get married, I'm thinking about starting a family at some stage ... if she can do it, maybe I can too." (Eryn [3])

Most of these women were breaking new ground in their organisations by originating new ways of working in professional and managerial roles. Being the first and the only people to work part-time, flexibly from home or in a job-share put additional pressure on their performance of both their job and their flexible working arrangement:

"and also I think because my peers, well they're all men, and there are no examples of flexible working at my level ... so in management team meetings I do feel very unconfident, it's hard being the only one ... I don't know, I suppose it's that is part of why it has taken me a long time to get up to speed, longer than I expected." (Jenny [18])

The professional stakes are already high for taking the career risk that is so clearly established in the literature and reducing working hours or increasing absence from the workplace by home-working. The stakes are raised considerably by the added responsibility to role model a successful arrangement and symbolise the possibilities for the working lives and futures of others, as Gemma [8] illustrates:

"I feel that this is a privilege hard-earned ... if our job-share fails because of the way we have managed it, I would feel like I have let the side down a little bit ... you have the responsibility to make it work so that other women get the opportunity to do it." (Gemma [8])

As well as a sense of collective responsibility, there was a relational dimension to the responsibility women felt in the sense that they cared about how their individual working arrangement impacted upon others at work – specifically, on their co-workers and their clients and customers inside and outside the organisation. The solidarity some women clearly felt with their colleagues evoked a sense of responsibility to be working at all times and feelings of guilt when they were not:

> "I do feel that I'm not contributing as much as I used to, I am really conscious of that and sometimes there is a tiny bit of guilt as well because I used to do a lot more ... they definitely get a lot less of me ... it's not just the fact that it's a four days a week and not five, but I'm just focusing on one element of my job whereas I used to do all sorts of extra things." (Sarah [1])

Guilt of this kind was managed by women making themselves available or at least to *appear* available, by responding to emails or phone calls on non-work days, and in effect concealing their absence due to their part-time hours. Professional mothers occupying positions in what many women described as high pressured, always-on work environments, felt the need to present what I term the 'façade of full-time' and minimise disruption to colleagues' usual ways of doing things. This situation has resonances with Blair-Loy's (Blair-Loy and Wharton, 2004; Blair-Loy, 2009) studies of schedule flexibility in the US, which found that the benefits of being able to vary the start and finish times of work were felt least among workers in high-commitment, elite client-service occupations in financial services due to the constant on-demand requirement of workers. Women in this study who operated in contexts such as these often dismissed the pressure they felt to keep things moving during their absence as "just part of the job" (Eryn [3]) or "the nature of the work" (Jessica [23]). This signals a deep understanding of their jobs as fixed and immoveable constructs around which individual working patterns and practices must orient and flex, and not the other way around. The 'ideal worker' norms (Acker, 1990) of constant availability and of responsiveness to the organisation's requirements, and the intensity of contemporary professional and managerial work can be heard in these accounts (Sennett, 1998; Gascoigne et al, 2016). Insights into lived experience discussed here signal that unyielding organisational demands compel women to operate permeable boundaries between work and home, and to develop individual solutions to what are in effect organisational problems.

Extended emotional labour

As well as feeling responsible at work, by their own accounts most women in relationships with men were responsible for organising and managing family life before they changed their work arrangements and continued to do so afterwards. The minority of cases that bucked that trend are discussed in the next chapter.

Women used a variety of tools and techniques to manage their responsibilities and, concurring with Thomson et al (2011), these experienced professionals and managers applied considerable management skill, ingenuity and creativity to methods of organising family life. The language of management permeated women's descriptions of their approaches to their domestic lives: "planning", "task differentiation", "delegation" and "coordination" were words used by women to describe their tactics, indicating a transposition of their professional skills and competencies on to the management and organisation of domestic life:

> "I am still doing the lion's share of organising for sure. I don't do it all but I'm still the planner ... I still want it done properly but I now delegate better. So I'm still doing all the coordinating but it's stressing me out less because I have a bit more time to do it." (Meera [7])

> "I set it all up on Monday ... I write him a list of what meals to give them on what day and like I said to him yesterday, 'You can't deviate from that because things are in the freezer or in the fridge according to what day I've told you you're supposed to eat them.' So yeah I'm still kind of in control but actually I'm quite relaxed about it as I'm not here to worry about it." (Andrea [27])

Successful combining of professional work with the responsibilities of motherhood demanded greater systematisation of household management. Some of our interviews took place in women's homes and they showed me some of their tools and techniques. Esther [11] displayed the whiteboard in her kitchen marked with daily menu plans for her two pre-schoolers that were planned at least a week in advance. Andrea [27] flicked through her lever-arch file that was subdivided with a section for each child and filled with bulging plastic pockets containing timetables for clubs and activities, school information and health and medical details. Amanda [10] pointed to her "control

126

centre", a chalkboard on her kitchen wall marked with days, locations and travel plans for each member of family to ensure that "everyone knows who needs what and when and who is picking and dropping who where."

The effort and time given to emotional work in families has often been overlooked and does not typically feature as a measurable parenting practice in domestic time-use surveys (Erikson, 2011). Women reported retaining responsibility for the social aspects of family life, for managing and sustaining relationships with friends and extended family members. As Sophie recounts "Remembering birthdays, getting gifts, replying to invites, yes that's all me." This tilted emotional load on mothers is evidenced in other studies of family practices (Seery and Crowley, 2000; Gabb and Fink, 2015). Women forged solutions to their capacity problems by engaging the services and support of other women, notably grandmothers providing care for young children and the feminised markets for outsourced family services like domestic cleaning and ironing.

Zelizer (2007, p28) refers to the "purchase of intimacy" to draw attention to the affective dimensions of the economic exchanges of family care. Although framed and regulated as monetary transactions, these exchanges are profoundly social transactions that are given meaning and become part of the web of mutual obligations within the family. In employing the services and support of other women, most professional mothers in this study found that their emotional workload had *increased*. Already largely invisible yet labour intensive, extra emotional work was necessary to sustain new and expanded care relationships and epitomises Hochschild's (2012) definition of emotional labour within families. Jenny [18] talked movingly of how she pre-prepared meals and tried to keep on top of the housework to make things easy and pleasant for her parents when they looked after her child each week. Esther [11] recounted frequent experiences comforting a homesick au-pair, consoling her, helping her with her English language tuition and accompanying her to social events to help her settle and make friends. For many women the additional work to support and sustain these relationships was unanticipated and yet vital if their lives were to function in the way they hoped and planned. Amanda [10], upon starting a new job on four days per week in a new location, recruited an au-pair to live in the family home and perform some of the childcare and domestic duties that she would have otherwise done, such as preparing children's meals, children's laundry and cleaning the house. It was not the solution that she had hoped for, and the effort required of Amanda to direct and coach the au-pair, and make that relationship work, was an unanticipated and substantial drain on her own emotional, mental and physical resources:

> "I think the au-pair plan has not been the solution I'd hoped it would be … just because you have a teenager, even a lovely, willing, enthusiastic teenager, she's still a teenager and needs telling and a lot of management to get her to do the things you want her to do. They're not going to look around and see a table full of crumbs or a wet towel on the floor and think, 'Oh I should sort that' … what I hadn't quite expected was how exhausted I was going to be from commuting and then having to come home every night and sort of do a second management shift with her and how sort of tedious that can get." (Amanda [10])

In all situations where families employed private nannies or au-pairs, or worked with childminders and formal childcare settings, including schools, women reported that they were responsible for managing the relationships and interactions with these institutions and individuals. For mothers of pre-schoolers, the quality of these relationships was felt to be essential both in facilitating their capacities for paid work, and also, importantly, their levels of comfort with the continued execution of their maternal responsibilities to the standard of good mothering that they had set:

> "Let's face it we are bringing my daughter up together, her and me. I need her to be happy and settled or the whole thing doesn't work … she's amazing and I feel utterly dependent … she gets on fine with my husband, but the relationship is definitely stronger between the two of us." (Jessica [23])

That these specific responsibilities, the practices of which were typically established by mothers, were retained by mothers irrespective of their working hours, indicates that the *second shift* (Hochschild, 1989) of domestic labour that working women undertake after and all around their paid work has not been eradicated; its practices have changed but maternal responsibility endures.

Feeling unwelcome at work

For 12 women their transition to a flexible work arrangement was simultaneous with their return to work after an absence for maternity. For eight of these women, these simultaneous transitions back to and into a flexible work arrangement were a novel experience as first-time mothers and first-time flexible workers. It is well established in motherhood literature that women are prone to stress and uncertainty during the return-to-work period, more so than fathers during the same transition (Ladge and Greenberg, 2015). Lack of organisational readiness for their return was a common experience among professional women returning to work in a variety of work contexts, which served to exacerbate their stress during an anxiety prone period. Some return-to-work transitions after maternity leave were more challenging than others, marked by poor-quality dialogue with line managers about return dates and working patterns, and bungled induction processes. Amanda [10] captures the feeling expressed by many women in relation to their first return-to-work experience, "I just felt that it was perfectly clear that no one knew what to do about me." Women returning from a second or third period of maternity leave to the same employer noted that each time their experiences were poor in different ways. They recalled security passes failing to grant access to the office building because they were "no longer on the system" (Meera [7]); not being notified of an office relocation and going to the wrong place on the first day; and not having an allocated desk or chair, or essential IT equipment. In a few cases women arrived without a job to do or a line manager to report to. This was an experience that Anna [24] felt diminished by:

> "I didn't have a very good experience because it appeared they weren't expecting me back when I got there. I didn't have a boss, I didn't have a computer, I didn't have any work for about six weeks … I'm very self-sufficient so I found myself a computer and things to read and catch up. But basically that's all I did for six weeks. It was soul destroying … I wish I had more positive things to say about it but I really don't." (Anna [24])

Anna relied on her own resourcefulness and professionalism to help her manage a difficult transition experience at work, but by describing the experience as "soul destroying" she evidences the undermining of her sense of self. Transition experiences such as these were not uncommon and caused women to speculate that they might not be as welcome back into the workplace as their pre-pregnancy, full-time, 'ideal worker' selves once were.

The few women in this research who were in the situation of starting new roles with new employers on a flexible working arrangement from day one (five cases) experienced similar challenges joining organisations to women rejoining their organisations, indicating that inducting and reintroducing managerial and professional employees is potentially problematic in a range of workplace settings. Andrea [27] for example, an experienced professional and flexible worker who had previous experience of both part-time work and job-sharing, reflected that joining her new organisation felt "a bit daunting, a bit scary ... quite overwhelming for the first few weeks", and she recalled a catalogue of practical frustrations that impeded her ability to implement her agreed flexible working pattern from day one:

> "I didn't have a security pass for the building which didn't make me feel very welcome, I had to be accompanied everywhere, honestly, they've known I was coming for five months why didn't they check I had a security tag? ... Initially I couldn't work from home on Thursdays as I didn't have a laptop for probably six weeks ... that was annoying because it affects more people than just me. My husband couldn't travel for work on a Thursday like we had planned because he instead of me had to pick the kids up." (Andrea [27])

Andrea and four other women had joined new organisations; 13 other women had changed jobs *within* the same organisation and so similarly experienced a hard stop to one role and a period of induction into a new one. The ability to quickly and effectively cross the inclusion boundaries of the new work unit or organisation and transition from outsider to insider status is thought to be important for work performance and worker self-confidence (Ladge and Greenberg, 2015). Working time norms form a significant part of the many inclusion boundaries new joiners need to navigate. Ambiguity about the acceptability of individual working patterns impedes the speed and effectiveness of the transition and, therefore, diminishes workers' performance and self-confidence in the early weeks while they work out what is 'ok'. The information that women would have liked to have had and that in most cases was missing from their induction processes was advice and guidance about working hours and how to integrate a flexible working arrangement into organisational processes. This included information about setting individual objectives, agreeing targets, planning workflow and delegating work. These are the things that women were unsure about and felt that they would have benefited from knowing from their first day, or preferably in advance of their first day. Not everyone felt confident to ask questions directly of senior leaders in their new organisations and work groups about how to manage their personal working arrangements. Those who did ask, however, in most cases received positive and supportive responses from senior managers:

> "I was very anxious at first as I realised I basically needed to leave at 5 o'clock if I was going to see Grace awake and I didn't know if that was ok … it turned out that the head of department works really flexibly and picks her kids up at 3 most days but my immediate manager hadn't communicated that … so after about three weeks I just asked the head of department directly if it was ok, she was fine about it. After that I felt much better." (Andrea [27])

Andrea was reassured by her conversation with the head of her work group about her working pattern only after having endured an uncomfortable three weeks of ambiguity. In Andrea's case, ambiguity arose in the space in between corporate statements of support for flexible working and local line managers' interpretations and communication of the practicalities. It signals a failure of organisations both to cascade communication and to develop capability at the local manager level to manage employee transitions *and* flexible working arrangements.

Tired bodies and charged emotions

The prospect of making room for paid work and adjusting emergent practices of mothering felt overwhelming for many new mothers who were approaching the transition from maternity leave:

> "I remember getting to the nine-month point of my maternity and thinking I'm so focused looking after the baby that I couldn't really envisage how I would fit work into that. It almost seemed like you'd get to the end of the day and if you'd managed to get dressed or out of the house, you know, that was quite an achievement and so the thought of then having to go to work and manage a whole extra

life on top of that seemed just massively overwhelming at points." (Jenny [18])

Evocative and intense, there was physicality in the language women used to describe their experience of the early weeks back at work, which placed the maternal body firmly at the centre of the experience. Hormones "raged", bodies "leaked" and "ached" and energy "lagged" in the fug and fatigue of the first few days and weeks testing new routines and practices of mothering in altered contexts. For mothers of pre-schoolers there was similarly much body talk in our interview encounters about the physical and psychological effects of repeated broken nights. Lack of sleep featured in many women's accounts of their experiences starting and sustaining their new working arrangements while children were young, as these examples illustrate:

"The most difficult thing has been after nine months of being a brilliant sleeper James is being a bit of a nightmare. I'd say five or six times a week I've been having four hours sleep, maybe five hours sleep, and that is hard ... but going to a new place when you don't really know the subject matter, you don't know the clients and you're so dog tired that you can barely even function, that's been quite upsetting." (Olivia [5])

"I've had moments where I feel good and I feel confident ... I've definitely had more moments where I just couldn't handle it and it was all too much. I get tired, I do a lot of work and then I feel like I'm having to work beyond exhaustion. I'm exhausted but I've got to work the next day. My daughter has been teething a lot so there's been a bunch of nights where we've just been up with her and that adds to it you know, and I reach that point where I go I can't handle it, it's too much and I'm overwhelmed." (Sadie [17])

The motifs of hard work and fatigue in body, mind and spirit were ever present. Often women thought they were not functioning at their best and yet felt compelled to perform as if they were. The maternal body was present in new mothers' accounts in specific ways. Some women associated their continued breastfeeding with hormonal disruption and a sense of not quite feeling "back to normal" (Gail [20]). For others, the practical and bodily challenges of sustaining breastfeeding on employers' premises dominated their early weeks, and in some cases, months back at work. How to express and transport breast milk privately, hygienically, and quickly is an intrusive aspect of the maternal experience at work that the male body never needs to navigate. The professional and managerial women in this study had greater autonomy to open their schedules to be able feed or express for the time it takes, but unless mothers had access to personal office space they needed to use the lavatories or leave the premises to find conducive space. The reported lack of facilities and suitable spaces to support continuation of breastfeeding signals employer antipathy towards this aspect of women's daily work experience and has been implicated in early cessation of breastfeeding (Boswell-Penc and Boyer, 2007). Gatrell (2007) argues that the maternal labour of infant feeding is discounted and not articulated as work, obscured within the narrative of good and natural mothering. She argues that pressure to breastfeed as best for children, yet also to conceal feeding from the public gaze renders it hidden labour in the most literal sense, and contributes to women's experiences of their nursing bodies being unwelcome at work. For the women in this study the end of breastfeeding, whether welcomed or reluctantly accepted, appeared to be pivotal in their stories, telling of regained physical autonomy, schedule control, and of a continuity of self:

> "The biggest change that has happened is that I've stopped breastfeeding … before I'd always been the one to put her to bed and feed her in the morning before going to work and then I would dash home to feed her, now I am more free and I don't feel so time-constrained … I'm much more relaxed about my work schedule now." (Jenny [18])

> "With the breastfeeding you don't realise how much it drains you and then you stop feeding and suddenly it's like you have your energy back and then the hormones aren't as bad and you're not as emotionally tired." (Claire [2])

The effects of difficult pregnancies and births, of postnatal mental health issues, infant feeding practices and routines, and broken nights that in most cases, were not routinely shared with partners, had lasting impacts on the female body. Impacts that women continued to manage, privately, well into the first and often the second year of each child's life. For women with two, three or four children of different ages, these effects continue for much longer.

Fatigue was not exclusively the preserve of the mothers of infants; sleep and rest were highly prized and not routinely achieved among women with two, three or more children. The physical demands of mothering intensified for women when children were unwell. Administering medicine, attending hospital appointments and emergency stays in hospital were some of the unpredictable circumstances that pulled mothers' time and energy away from almost everything else. Health emergencies were rare occurrences in women's stories, however stories such as Lara's [6] illustrate the intensity and exhaustion associated with mothering and its reconciliation with professional work during these times:

> "It was my first work project since coming back part-time and then my daughter was sick, and she got sicker and sicker and ended up in hospital. She was in hospital for three nights. I was so worried about having to run out of work like that as soon as she got better I went back into work the next day … I shouldn't have done it. I was completely exhausted because I had spent three nights sleeping on a hard floor in hospital." (Lara [6])

Arlie Hochschild (2012) considers emotions to be the sixth biological sense. Guilt is the emotion often associated with working mothers, which Hochschild defines as an emotional response to mothers feeling that their child or children are enduring a less than perfect experience and seeing their own actions as the cause of this. Feeling guilty was a continuous background 'hum' in women's lives, although few women said they experienced guilt as debilitating. Certain situations brought maternal guilt to the surface more readily than others and the background hum became more prominent and emotionally destabilising. The early weeks and months spent settling children into new childcare settings invoked guilt when women felt their children were distressed by maternal separation. Women whose infants transitioned well to childcare settings were enormously relieved that they did not experience the distress and the guilt they anticipated would arise from that situation.

Feelings of guilt were often suppressed by distraction with work tasks:

> "I feel guilty when I first leave him and when I first get to work … but I think because it's been straight away really, really busy, I think that, in a way, that has helped because I don't have as much time to think about [my son] really as

if I was just sat here with not much to do. I think I'd feel worse and I'd probably miss him more and think about it more if I was in that situation." (Nina [16])

Charlotte [26] related her generalised feelings of guilt to working part-time and not caring for her children full-time herself, which is a central tenet of intensive mothering ideology (Hays, 1996). She carries these feelings, seemingly accepting them as a legitimate consequence of her breach of the social norms of good mothering, although, she adds that she does not feel "bad enough" to change her approach:

> "I still have that constant feeling of guilt about the fact that I'm working all of those hours and I've got my mother-in-law looking after the girls, after-school club, and the little one stays late at nursery ... I have that feeling of guilt, like I'm not really doing what I should be from a parenting perspective ... I think I just have to accept that I'm going to feel like that because there aren't any options for me to do anything different. Well there are. I could change my job. I could say I'm not going to do this any more and I'm going to go back to doing something three days a week and all that, but I don't, and this sounds awful, but I don't feel bad enough that I want to do that." (Charlotte [26])

When I asked women how they managed feelings of guilt, most described being distracted from them; their minds being taken away from worries by daily practicalities, as Nina described above. Sophie [30] defended against guilt by cognitively reframing good mothering in terms of looking after her health and happiness, thus making her a better mother (Johnston and Swanson, 2007):

> "I've always thought that the most important thing in my life is my children. And that's bollocks isn't it? Because the most important thing in your life is you! In everyday life it has to be you, doesn't it? You have to be here to support and do what they need ... if you get to the point where you break you're no good to them." (Sophie [30])

Women were conscious of not passing on their feelings to their children. They avoided expressing their own regret, sadness or anxiety in situations that their children too found distressing. Fixing a smile to soothe an infant's distress was part of the emotional work of working motherhood; mothers managing their own emotions to influence their children's emotions and help them approach the experience of childcare outside the home as normal and fun.

There is a triple load of emotional labour involved in settling an infant in a new care situation simultaneously with women's own resettlement back into the workplace *and* their adaptation to a new, flexible, work arrangement:

> "When I was doing three days a week, always on the Tuesday, which was the first day back in the office, for the first maybe month or so, I'd be coming back home in tears, I'd just be like I can't do it, there's too much to do, I can't do it, it's completely unmanageable … having been back two months now, and although, yes, it is really difficult and not how I had imagined, the thought of it was much worse than the actual reality of it. I thought I would just work the same and make everything else fit around me but actually it doesn't work like that, it is much more the other way round." (Jenny [18])

Undoubtedly difficult, emotional and tiring, the return-to-work transition can be overwhelming to women in this situation, who – regardless – need to carry on.

Conclusions

Women feel terrific responsibility for the success of their work arrangements and for fitting in with workplace cultures and practices quickly and seamlessly. The quiet responsibility that women feel is highly relevant to how they approach incorporating themselves as professionals into the organisation. They apply the tools and techniques of management to organising home and family by systematising household management and delegating domestic and care tasks to the market. Maternal responsibility endures and insights discussed here reveal the scale, scope and span of women's emotional and physical labours in these outsourced and systematised circumstances. Managed simultaneously with the live project of flexible job design (or redesign) and incorporating (or reincorporating) oneself into the workplace, adds up to what one participant referred to as a significant "mental load". Professional mothers feel that the demands of caring are neither welcomed nor understood in many workplaces and most feel obliged to manage quietly and diligently. Given that the flexible work adjustment is being initiated because of their motherhood, and in the context of quality part-time and flexible work in professional roles being hard to find, most women feel a further obligation to fit in and figure it out privately.

7

Stresses and Successes

Chapter themes

This chapter explores the events and the outcomes of a year of combining motherhood and professional work using part-time and flexible work arrangements. None of the 30 women interviewed multiple times for this study were unequivocal about the benefits or otherwise of using flexible work arrangements as a work–life reconciliation strategy. There were stresses and there were successes at home and at work.

A lot happens in a year. By the time of our final interviews most women's lives were different to when we had first met. Seven pregnancies, one adoption in progress, one overseas relocation, one promotion, two house moves, five new jobs with five new employers, one redundancy, two couple separations, one serious illness, and three parental bereavements evidence the constancy of change and the necessity for adaptation in professional women's personal and professional lives. In relation to women's flexible work arrangements, a near universal experience was that the working pattern women had embarked upon when we first met was not the pattern they were working a year later. All but 4 of 30 women had made further adjustments to the time, timing, or location of their paid work, and in five cases had done so in alternative employment. What women identify as the drivers of those further adjustments reveals much about the level of support for flexible work arrangements in important jobs at the pivotal stage in careers when women's progress to the top of large organisations slows down.

Work intensity

Without exception women in this study described working efficiently and, in many cases, intensively when work hours were shorter and schedules more restricted, driven by a felt need to maximise every productive moment of their work time. This is not unusual and in studies of male and female part-time workers, most report a sharper focus and greater task efficiency with less and limited working time

(Gatrell, 2008; Opportunity Now, 2014). Women in this study reported being similarly task-focused, efficient and productive in public workspaces. It was common to cut back on food, rest or social breaks to maximise work time:

> "and I take a maximum half hour lunch break you know, and if I talk to somebody socially for a half hour then I just don't take a lunch break so I can get all of my work done and I don't feel I have skimped on any of the time." (Sadie [17])

> "any spare time, down time, is used up doing all the other things. I don't take anyone for lunch any more, I rarely get to eat myself." (Sarah [1])

> "I just found I'm probably ten times more efficient than I ever was ... my days are pretty organised and I'm normally in for half seven and I leave at half five and those three or four days a week are very busy." (Fiona [9])

Time pressure was felt most acutely when women were compelled to leave communal workspaces at a set time to be somewhere for their children.

> "What I will say is that I've found I use every spare minute of the day much more productively than I used to ... whereas before say, you get to half an hour before you are going to leave work and think, 'Oh well I've only got half an hour left, I can't really do anything so I'll just fiddle about with some emails or whatever', now I think, 'Well I've got half an hour, I can at least write an introduction to a document', or I hammer away at something until literally a minute before I have to leave." (Emma [25])

Women in this study who experienced work overspill into non-work time as intrusion felt that they had failed. They felt they had failed either to keep on top of their workloads or to police the boundaries between their domestic and professional worlds, or both. Blaming oneself for one's own stretched resources, in effect personalises failure. It signals the deep personal responsibility that women feel for the success of their work–life arrangements, of which their flexible working arrangement forms a vital part:

"I am quite upset with myself for not being able to create these boundaries and manage my time better … on my annual review last year it was one of my priorities to become much more structured in the way I manage my time and I'm completely failing on that front … I'm really struggling making this happen basically." (Sally [28])

Sally made a comment later in our interview that revealed how she defended herself against feeling that she had failed with self-talk, she said: "I have to keep telling myself maybe it's not my fault and maybe it just can't work in this way." Sally's self-talk is revealing of the fundamental tension that is at the heart of what so many women feel. The need to prove to the organisation that a personal working arrangement will not disrupt or interfere with the organisation's usual ways of doing things.

Gascoigne's (2014) model of boundary management describes how flexible workers either provide a predictable or adaptable response in two directions, towards work and towards family. Gascoigne (2014) proposes that problems occur when the adaptability is too much in one direction, or there is a mismatch when a consistent response is offered in the direction of work, for example by fixing a work schedule on set days, when a flexible response is required or vice versa.

The women who appeared to be best insulated from excessive work demands were the job-sharers. The three job-sharers were the only group of women who, by the nature of their job designs, were able to provide both a predictable and adaptable response in the direction of work, which as Gascoigne (2014) suggests is beneficial in maintaining a reasonably hard boundary between their work and family time. This was because when one job-sharing partner was not working the other was and fielded organisational demands, and in so doing protected the partner's private time. Despite it being highly unusual in these women's professional contexts for two people to share or split one role, a job-share job design seems to demand very little of the organisation in terms of adjusting its professional time norms and resourcing practices. To fill a weekly absence due to part-time working hours, for example, or to engage in a more comprehensive job-redesign exercise that rescopes the role and reallocates a roles tasks and responsibilities. This observation signals some potential for job-sharing to alleviate the felt pressures of part-time workers in managerial and professional roles to work intensively to maintain responsiveness to the needs and demands of the organisation on designated non-work days. By the same token, enabling a job-share job design does little to disrupt the default job model: that is to offer a continuous, adaptive response to any-time employer demands.

Fine tuning

Jane's [12] aim in adjusting her employment was to reduce the stress and overload in her life. Her reflections about her move to reduce and compress her working hours and increase home-working, from the vantage point of some months on, were largely positive:

> "One of the original drivers was that I felt kind of so overloaded and stressed out that it wasn't just my work–life balance that wasn't working, it was the fact that being overloaded was leading me to being so stressed that when I was with the kids I wasn't really able to be fully present or the sort of parent that I wanted to be. It was almost like they were being doubly short-changed in a way, and that has definitely changed since I've been working compressed hours. I've felt much more like when I'm with the kids I'm focusing on them." (Jane [12])

In the same follow-up interview Jane also said that the part-time working arrangement to which she had transitioned "had not worked at all" and she went on to explain:

> "I think basically what I've achieved by trying to not work on a Friday afternoon is not working at the weekend, which is something, so instead of finishing at lunchtime on Friday I've stopped working at the weekend but I have been working until the end of the day on Friday… so I've reduced my working hours but I haven't managed to ever fit it into four and a half days."

Jane is typical of most women in this study in the equivocal nature of their evaluations of the success of their transitions. At a purely practical level, what women aimed to achieve with a reduction or compression of working hours was predictable periods of time away from professional work. Few women achieved these outcomes to their satisfaction and without further adjustments to their working hours, schedules or locations of work. The most typical subsequent adjustment was to *increase* the amount of weekly paid working hours. Eleanor [13] explains her decision to increase her working hours:

"The whole idea was I'd pick the boys up at lunchtime and have them for the afternoon. I had essentially two and a half hours in the morning when they were at nursery or pre-school where I could do household chores, whatever needs doing that isn't work. So that worked for the first week and then the workload was too much at work so I then started working the mornings and made the decision two weeks ago that I just had to work on a Monday. So I've now gone back to working on a Monday." (Eleanor [13])

The burden of domestic chores twinned with a near-to-full-time professional workload in a part-time contract featured heavily in Eleanor's account and those of many others.

The most problematic conversion scenario was converting the full-time, five-day job women had previously held into a three-day part-time job. Five of the six women attempting this 40% reduction in working hours and without a job-share partnership found personal efficiency could only take them so far and they increased their paid working hours within a few months, including Charlotte [26] who went first to four days and then to five within a year:

"What I've ended up doing is pretty much going back to normal full-time working ... from a working perspective, it's easier as you're around when everybody else is around and things don't get missed." (Charlotte [26])

All the women justified their decision as a need to keep on top of largely unadjusted full-time workloads and a desire to get paid for the extra work they were doing anyway. Only one of the women who had embarked on a three-day week conversion of her previous full-time job continued to work in that way within the 12-month period of study. Having agreed a proportionate reduction in her case load, dropped her interest projects, and identified colleagues she could delegate to and to monitor work in her absence, she found her job was "just about manageable" (Lara [6]) on these terms. More typical however, was Nina's [16] situation:

"It didn't take long to work out that I just could not get through everything I needed to in three days, I didn't have any cover ... going up to four days has made it all a bit more manageable." (Nina [16])

Increasing her paid working days from three to four made Nina's workload manageable and she feels more secure about the sustainability of the arrangement. It does, however, raise an important ethical question about the inequality in pay and reward that arises because the efficient four-day worker is executing their unadjusted full-time responsibilities in less time and for less pay than the fully compensated five-day worker. This and other invisible inequalities that arise from inattention to job design for flexibility are discussed further in Chapter 8.

There were benefits and there were challenges, there were periods of effectiveness and moments of crisis, and in all cases there was a lot of hard work. Emma, whose narrative opened this book, was one of a substantial minority who described her arrangement as "working well" and "really good", and was content that the arrangement had introduced the slack in the system that she felt she needed and had alleviated her work–life conflict:

> "For me the way I try to think about it is in terms of 0.8 of my normal job rather than working four days a week. Generally speaking, I don't work on a Tuesday but sometimes I do and that's fine because very often I have to trim the end of somewhere or go in late or whatever. I don't feel racks of guilt doing that. That is what genuine flexible working is, and that is the key for me, it has been really good, really good." (Emma [25])

It was more typical across the 30 cases to reach a more equivocal evaluation of the experience, as I think it is reasonable to expect given the complexity and the heterogeneity of circumstances, motivations and anticipated outcomes across the sample:

> "It did feel really good to be back in a working environment and to be managing people again, and to have that sense of having a bit of forward momentum, a sense of 'I'm back, I'm in, I'm at a reasonably senior level, I can do this.' That was a big thing and it has been great as a way back in but, on the other hand, the job is not good at all and home, home gets more dysfunctional by the day." (Amanda [10])

> "Mixed, it has been mixed. Overall, it has probably been more good than bad ... I mean going three days has proved that I cannot quit. Quitting would not work for me and

actually I just need one day off to keep on top of things at home … that situation is not going to change and I think I accept that now. I have learned that if I don't hold back a bit on controlling everything at home I just become his glorified home secretary and not the kind of mother I want to be which is actually spending time with my kids not just doing their admin, and having some kind of life for me." (Meera [7])

In general women who had made well-planned and professionally protective adjustments to their ways of working talked of giving the arrangement a full business year before they would feel able to evaluate whether their personal strategies had been effective. Jessica [23] suggested she needed to "get my results to see whether this has really worked", and Olivia [5] said, "I'm just hanging on for my annual appraisal, then I'll know." Lara [6] similarly anticipated more time being necessary to help her work out whether the additional effort she was making by working extra hours in the evenings to stretch her working day and retain her access to "the better quality work", had positioned her well on a career ladder:

"I need to know if I'm going anywhere. I'm giving it maybe a year longer, seeing where I'm going and then considering if it's not something I can go anywhere with, maybe reconsider my career and look at changing it." (Lara [6])

The rewards were not yet clearly outweighing the challenges of working in the way women were. While it seemed that some were awaiting their organisation's judgement of the success of the arrangement, other women had already worked out whether the situation was tolerable and had made firm plans either to stay with their employer and adjust their work arrangement again, or to quit and go somewhere else.

In the 12-month period of study all but 4 of 30 women had made further adjustments to either the time, timing or location of paid work and often made parallel adjustments to childcare arrangements. Twelve women expressed contentment and their intention to stay in their present employment. A remarkable majority of 18 professional women had either already changed jobs or expressed dissatisfactions that they anticipated would lead them to seek new opportunities within months and certainly a year. This is evidence, if it were needed, of the pipeline problem and how professional and managerial women experience it.

Stagnant roles

The three cases of job-sharing had the added benefit of facilitating women's access to professional roles commensurate with their skills and experience, and, in Esther's case, to a more senior position than the one she had previously held:

> "It is great, it is working out *so* well and we've had some really great feedback. People are loving the work we're doing, we're finding it really interesting. We haven't had any blips or things like that." (Esther [11])

Much empirical work has drawn attention to women's underemployment in less skilled and marginal roles, their exclusion from vital work networks, and limited access to progression opportunities as outcomes of the transition from full-time to part-time work, which is thought to contribute materially to the gender pay gap (Costa Dias et al, 2016). This study provides further evidence of the marginalisation that occurs when professional women are moved or move themselves into jobs deemed as more suited to part-time working. The characteristics of these more suitable jobs generally took women away from frontline and customer- or client-responsive roles, reduced their team management or budget responsibilities, and occupied them in back office roles or internal corporate projects. A more predictable work flow and fewer short and no-notice requests are job design characteristics that are attractive to professionals with other pressures on their time, at least initially.

In the main, women who had experienced these types of job moves recalled being bored and under-utilised and felt their skills and experience were undervalued:

> "When I was working three days a week in the job they found me I was completely miserable. My job was absolutely rubbish and I felt like I literally in the space of three months I'd gone back about six years ... I was doing the kind of work that I had done six years ago when I qualified and was like, 'Oh my God, how did this happen?'" (Esther [11])

> "The work thing has been so frustratingly boring. It's just so dull. You feel your brain cells rotting away, it's just one of those like 'Really, really? Is this what you need me to do?' I'm starting to feel frustrated that I'm not progressing

and also frustrated that home life seems to be compromised because I'm in this stagnant role. I'm losing out on the time with my daughter – she probably hasn't noticed that much – but it's having an impact on me. I think well where's my stretch, what's my next step in all of this?" (Sarah [1])

Boredom and frustration were typical expressions of the workplace marginalisation women experienced:

"I had not quite appreciated how much I needed to be mentally stimulated outside of the house. I kept telling myself all I needed was a job, that's fine but I still need the job to hit a threshold of challenging and this is not hitting that. I just think the number of days of the week you work, or can work, is linked to the types of jobs that they will give you, and they gave me a bad one." (Meera [7])

"It is frustrating as I'm probably in a job which is for someone with 10 years' less experience than me and could be done by someone with 10 years' less experience than me ... in a year's time, you know, I want something to change." (Andrea [27])

In her analysis of identity transformation upon motherhood and the renegotiation of professional accounting work, Haynes (2008) found that when women experienced moves into marginal roles, there was a strong sense of retrogression in their oral histories that reflected their feelings of despair. This resonant insight chimes with Anna's account of her simultaneous part-time and return-to-work transition following maternity leave:

"I wish I had more positive things to say about it really but it has been really disappointing ... I am capable of a lot more. I am doing the kind of work I did years ago. I promised myself not to make any knee-jerk decisions about leaving so I am making myself stay for six months and see if it gets better." (Anna [24])

Cahusac and Kanji's (2014) research with London-based professional mothers who worked part-time showed that, over a relatively short period of time, women worked out whether their work situations were tolerable and sustainable and made moves to exit. The inference from their findings in the context of my own is that workplace exit is more likely in circumstances where women, because of their need for temporal, schedule or location flexibility, find themselves in stagnant roles. The serious consequences of these experiences for individuals and for employing organisations will be discussed in Chapter 8.

Opting out

A significant body of research highlights the structural constraints acting upon women's participation and advancement in employment. These constraints include the material realities that determine how women work and the labour market position they achieve, such as the availability, cost and quality of childcare (Nowak et al, 2013); the presence of family and social support networks (Ben–Galim and Thompson, 2013); organisational policies and management approval of flexible working arrangements (Dick, 2010; Fagan and Walthery, 2011); and the gendered moral understandings about what is the right thing women should do that guide mothers' decisions about their labour market participation (Duncan and Edwards, 1999; Duncan and Irwin, 2004). Despite considerable evidence of external constraints operating up and down the occupational hierarchy, there remains a residual belief that the disappearance of women from the upper and middle tiers of organisations reflect women's free choice to opt out and head home. An observation from the field of development economics counters this assumption by highlighting the phenomenon of adaptive preferences. Development economist Amartya Sen (2000) argues that individuals' preferences are adaptive, in that people adjust their desires in accordance with the way of life they know. With reference to women in employment, if the prevailing circumstances of what is known to professional mothers embodies a history of discrimination and disadvantage that is evident in few promotions to senior positions and enduring pay inequalities, then based on that history women might well consider organisational careers out of reach and adjust their desires to take part. This sort of adaptive decision making about careers could be considered giving up on a once-had desire or, as Leahy and Doughney (2006) argue, could simply be making the best of a bad lot.

When I first met Olivia [5] she was emphatic about her career and about how wonderfully accommodating her employer had been about her request to cut her paid hours by 10% and work from home on Fridays. Olivia's story illustrates the *protecting career* intention narrative discussed in Chapter 3. In our interview at around six months into her work arrangement, she was feeling tired and disillusioned:

"As we speak I'm probably feeling a bit under pressure at the moment, yes, I am really struggling to work out how I actually, how can anyone really be part-time … to be honest I am feeling a bit 'we'll see' about staying here." (Olivia [5])

Olivia was not the only one who had come to realise that they lacked organisational support to make their flexible work arrangements work in practice. Hayley felt that she would need to adopt a full-time working pattern if she was to transform her career opportunities:

"I'm thinking about leaving actually … my dilemma is should I stay in this slightly flexible but not very well-paid job with a few issues, or do I go? If I go I'll probably need to go full-time for a bit before I can get any flexibility. It's really tough." (Hayley [14])

There appears to be a normative understanding that flexibility and part-time working in particular, costs careers and is certainly incompatible with advancing in an organisational career:

"If I thought I could be [a director] here next year, barring the money and the prestige, I'm still not sure if I would jump at the opportunity 100% because I look at our directors and they work insane hours and they need to, I mean I get that. So the way I view it now is that I just have a job, I don't have a career. I have to figure out now what my career is going to be." (Meera [7])

It is important to note that it was not any woman's stated intention to exit paid work altogether. The process of professional women leaving their organisational careers is termed 'opting-out' (Stone, 2007) or 'off-ramping' (Hewlett, 2007) and describes the apparently voluntary decisions of successful professional women to leave corporate employment and retreat to the domestic sphere. Stone's work contributes much to debunking the myth of the pull of home by presenting empirical evidence that most women who opted out of an organisation in fact remain in employment when followed up 12 months after their exit. In a 2014 survey of 25,000 Harvard Business School (HBS) graduates, Stone and Hernandez (2013b) found only 11% were out of the workforce completely to care for children full-time, and their stories indicated they were 'mommy tracked' on return from maternity leave, that is given roles marginal to the business or of lower status. In a later study Stone with Ely et al (2014) contrasted the workplace experiences of high-achieving MBA graduate baby boomers (aged 49–67 in 2014), Generation X (aged 32–48), and Millennials (aged 26–31). They found that male and female graduates alike aimed for fulfilling professional and personal lives yet their ability to realise them played out very differently according to gender. Among graduates working full-time, men were significantly more satisfied than women with their experience of meaningful work, of opportunities for growth, and with the compatibility of work and personal life. Women's stymied goals and lesser satisfaction is masked by a competing discourse that emphasises women's willingness to 'opt out', 'ratchet back', 'scale down' and forgo opportunities. The premise that women value career less than men do, and that mothers do not want high-profile or challenging work, does not reflect reality for the women in this study, or indeed the substantial majority of 14,000 working women aged 28–40 in the UK who participated in a survey in which three-quarters expressed intentions to lead and signalled ambition to progress to senior management and the top jobs (Opportunity Now, 2014). The challenge is how to get there while working part-time and flexibly.

Domestic discontent

A rich seam of insight about women's relationships with husbands and partners revealed their satisfaction (or otherwise) with the continuities and discontinuities in divisions of domestic labour and childcare through time. The relatedness of women's lives and the intricate web of relationships that are spun around them are made plain in their accounts. Many women spoke of simmering tensions and predictable flash points in their relationships.

One participant memorably re-told a long-running argument that she had with her husband: "… and I said, you do know, I didn't go to Harvard to do your laundry?" This was one of many conflict stories told by women that related to laundry. Wives laundering husbands' work wear was an issue between couples, holding symbolic significance, epitomising wifework (Maushart, 2002) and exposing the power relationship within couples. In couple interviews Gatrell (2005) found similar frustrations in relation to ironing men's shirts, which was a form of wifework too far for many women she interviewed, who took a stand against it, leaving their husbands feeling a little hard done by.

In early motherhood women often report feeling that it is only fair that they take on the bulk of childcare and domestic work because they are the ones with more time available at home (Lupton and Schmied, 2002; Miller, 2012). The time-availability rationale ceases to be meaningful when women return to work and increase the amount of paid work they do in a day, but the continued unequal division of domestic labour may still be rationalised as fair. Rationalising a fair distribution of earning and housework does not mean that women are content with it. Much research has shown that uneven distribution of housework is a source of conflict and tension within relationships (Alger and Crowley, 2012; Chambers, 2012; Lyonette and Crompton, 2015). Emma [25] described a recurring row with her husband about his apparent inability to execute his set of allocated childcare tasks without her background organisation:

> "I just flew off the handle. I cannot understand why he cannot hold that information in his mind. They have been at school for three years and he still can't remember they finish at 3.15 not 3.30. I genuinely think he doesn't see it, doesn't see the correlation between the two things, my relatively lack-lustre career at the moment, the sense that I can't get any new projects under way because I just don't have the head space and that I am constantly thinking about lunchboxes and who is picking up who and the fact that he is always forgetting where he is supposed to be. His career is on a roll and he doesn't see his impact on mine."
> (Emma [25])

In the heat of the moment, during a busy morning preparing all five family members for their school and work days, Emma held her husband responsible for the daily pressure she was under. The responsibility she had for remembering everything for everyone, she felt, had facilitated his career at the expense of her own. Emma felt diminished professionally by her enduring domestic and childcare responsibilities. Emma was not the only one. Gail [20] exemplified the feelings expressed by many of the new mothers in this study, and with some surprise, that their individual wants and needs had receded in importance in the family. This was fertile territory for conflict:

> "I really resent that everything I ever wanted to do went right to the bottom of the list ... I kept saying to him and it's still something I say to him now is that time to myself does not mean the two hours when [our daughter] has a nap. That's not 'me time'. I'm still responsible for her in

that time. It's not free time. Even though I can sit down and watch something on telly, what I need is to hand over responsibility ... I've had to completely reinvent everything that I do and he hasn't changed his life hardly at all." (Gail [20])

Most women in this study lived transitional relationships when their espoused relationship ideology was egalitarian. Amanda [10] described her mounting dissatisfaction with living with contradiction between her relationship ideals and reality, the inequalities in which she found physically and emotionally debilitating:

"It's quite a miserable existence doing four hours commuting a day for a job that I'm not finding particularly interesting or fulfilling then come the weekend having to pick up all of the lapsed housework and just really not having the energy to manage that ... I've just found myself not having patience at home as I'm feeling really squeezed and really exhausted ... I snap at the children and my husband and quite honestly I just don't want to be around them sometimes." (Amanda [10])

For two women in this research, simmering tensions had become more sustained and serious in the 12 months since our first interview encounters and they were in the process of negotiating formal separations from their husbands. In our final interview their concerns about their relationship eclipsed their concerns for the effectiveness or otherwise of their flexible working arrangement, although, as Hayley explains, her relationship problems were not completely unrelated to her frustrated professional ambition:

"It sometimes feels like we're running a business, a project, you know? I'd rather have a problem like he doesn't do enough housework to be honest. I think that's at least something you can work with. You can accept it or you can change it. But I think ours is an issue you can't just agree to change ... it relates to what I want to get out of my job and career, that stimulation that has been missing for years. I want to get more out of my life and I don't think that we do that for each other. To be honest that is the major drain, strain, whatever you want to call it that has been overwhelming my head these last months." (Hayley [14])

Relationships were under pressure in ways not only related to the inequalities in domestic labour. Their relationship was often relegated below the other time-absorbing priorities of professional work and childcare. Sadie [17] expressed sadness and surprise at the pressure she felt her relationship was under:

> "I didn't expect the main impact to be on my relationship ... the thing that's the hardest to deal with is not prioritising our relationship as you think you can push that aside and it'll be fine, that's probably been the hardest thing and the most surprising as I thought it would just be stress associated with work or something like that that affected me." (Sadie [17])

As a work–life reconciliation strategy, working flexibly can have a positive influence on both work and personal domains, but for some people it can relate to higher degrees of conflict between work and family life as the boundaries can become blurred. Gatrell et al (2014) analysed the relationship between work engagement and personal relationship quality using employee survey data and found that flexible working was predictive of higher work engagement but also of slightly lower relationship quality. This means that the adoption of flexible working practices helps employees achieve a positive work-related state of fulfilment, absorption and satisfaction, yet is simultaneously associated with lower satisfaction with couple relationships, particularly among women.

Despite much mention of the apparent disconnect between women's egalitarian ideals and life as they were living it, there was little evidence of intended radicalisation of the couple relationship and a shake-up of roles and responsibilities. The tensions that women reported in their relationships resonate with Beagan et al's (2008) conclusion that traditional gender roles reinvent themselves in new guises. It is no longer acceptable to view cooking or cleaning as inherently women's work, yet the same gender expectations persist in more complex forms couched in terms of individual choices, standards and preferences. Most women in this study recognised that a solution to the problem of *unlived* egalitarianism could be found in the synchronised actions of their male partners to take more responsibility for childcare and their own actions to step back. This option was often discounted, couched in terms of his perceived preference: "he doesn't want to do it" (Meera [7]); ability: "it's just not his skill set, I'm better at it" (Emma [25]); affordability: "he earns more than me ... it's more affordable for me to be here" (Cathy [4]); timing in careers: "he's on promotion track, he needs to focus" (Eryn [3]); and her personal standards: "I worry things will fall through the net, it's easier if I do it" (Amanda [10]).

Practices of resistance

There were some exceptions that departed from the traditional and transitional couple relationship and practised more egalitarian models of sharing and exchanging responsibilities for care and domestic tasks. In two cases, heterosexual, dual-earning couples had consciously redrawn or reversed the traditional breadwinning-caregiving model. Esther's husband took just over one year out of employment to look after the couple's toddler twins full-time; Sarah's husband regularly worked from home and took responsibility for care of their infant daughter for three days every week. In both cases the practical arrangements were felt to have worked out well and helped the women to sustain their professional jobs and stay on a career track. Esther, her husband having since returned to full-time work and she to a job-share, spoke of how their egalitarian approach to shared parenting and dual careers involved turn-taking, and his turn was next:

> "He took last year to be at home with the kids ... this year we have cordoned off time for him to go through the promotion round that he's reasonably well-placed for, so I definitely think it's his turn next ... I will wait and apply for promotion later in the year." (Esther [11])

Sarah describes what their care-share arrangement looks like in practice. Her husband's working time and location flexibility facilitates her own.

> "It just made everything a bit easier because he was there to take up the slack. He does all the drop-offs and pick-ups for nursery so normally I don't work on a Monday and I am with the baby then, then it's three days in a row coming up to [the city] and she goes to nursery on Tuesday and Wednesday, Thursday she's with her dad and then Friday she's with her dad as well but I'm there and can help with lunch and you know breakfast and all that sort of stuff. I flex as well, so last week I changed my days off because there was an important meeting on a Monday, so I had Friday off instead." (Sarah [1])

The notion that there is someone to "take up the slack" of childcare and domestic work when she is not available reveals that, despite egalitarian practices, the responsibility for mothering, Sarah feels, continues to rest with her. Both women recalled moments of doubt about their arrangements. Esther [11] found it distressing that her children preferred their father to read bedtime stories to them and similarly, in Sarah's case, it was her daughter's preference for comfort from her father that triggered her own deep reflection:

> "I've had some difficulties recently as my daughter has started to talk and she just wants daddy all the time and that's been something that's been really difficult for me to deal with. I know they all go through stages and it will pass, but a few weeks ago it was becoming really hard for me and I was really questioning if I'd made the right decision you know, two voices in my head one side of me still this ambitious person that's worked really hard for a long time and wants to progress, and then there's the other side of me that's a mum saying 'Why are you letting this happen, it's you she's supposed to want?' I've had that real battle going on." (Sarah [1])

Moments of doubt were indeed moments; episodes that women worked hard to minimise. In these moments, they looked to their professional lives to convince them beyond doubt that they had made the right choices about work. If their professional lives were not rewarding, materially or otherwise, and a positive vision of their professional futures was hard to see, then the emotional effort required to defend the self against moments of doubt became much greater. In these moments women needed to mount a robust psychic defence against the idea of the natural, omnipresent mother as providing the best care for children.

Women are combining breadwinning with caregiving in different family forms that are increasingly prevalent and becoming more visible: as lesbian parents. Maya [22] described how she and her wife were aiming for "full flexibility for both of us", such that both of them could work part-time and share the care of their children. Both wives anticipated that self-employment would afford them greater freedoms in this respect than permanent employment. When it came to the domestic division of labour, Maya spoke at length about how the lack of what she called a "gender default" meant that every aspect of living together and raising their family had to be negotiated between them. At times this had caused conflict that she felt was "coming from a different place" to the tensions played out in public that she had observed in the heterosexual couple relationships among her friends:

> "Because we're two women I find that the sort of designated roles are not as clear-cut. I don't mean to sound stereotypical but I've seen other friends and even family members have a little fight in public where they'll go, 'Who is going to change his or her nappy, you're the mum you change the nappy,' and there's some tension. Whereas we've had to work out our own rules because of the non-gender issues … Usually, I've seen in other relationships the man will do the handy stuff and take the garbage out. If I'm free and she's at work I'll obviously deal with it. So what I'm saying I think is that we can't draw on the gender stereotypes to say you do it, I'll do it; we just take care of it … what it does mean I guess is that we have to negotiate every single thing between us, I mean, like we both don't want to do the lightbulbs." (Maya [22])

Giddens (1992, p 135) called people in same-sex relationships "prime everyday experimenters", because visible and out same-sex partners making families are at the forefront of changes to the notion of the conventional family. However, it does not automatically follow that same-sex couples will adopt egalitarian models of the family in practice. Hopkins et al (2013) argue that same-sex couples making families are as likely to embrace a heteronormative framework as they are to challenge it.

Conclusions

The level and frequency of further adjustments to working hours, schedules and locations indicate that the complex settlement of competing ideological and practical pulls that women make is only fleeting. Combining work and care is a dynamic process requiring nimble and frequent adjustments to working practices and to family practices. Yet flexible working policy at the national level permits employees to make only one flexible working request in a 12-month period. Chapter 8 draws conclusions from this analysis and discusses the risks and impacts for individuals, families and organisations from persistence of the themes that dominate this book: of quiet responsibility, of failures of egalitarianism, flexibility fatigue and stalled modernisation of working practices. The final chapter concludes with discussion about the transformational opportunities for workplace and family policies and practices for the future.

8

Making Motherhood, Careers and Flexibility Work

Motherhood, careers and balance

Professional women who are mothers do not see themselves in terms of 'or' but in terms of 'also'; few would describe themselves as career-oriented *or* family-oriented and yet persistent binaries dominate academic and public debate about professional women's employment. Work–life orientation models that position all women along a spectrum with family and career at opposite ends of the axis limit women's potential to be anything other than either/or because occupying the middle ground becomes defined by being or desiring neither one nor the other. The work–life binary also elevates the importance of paid work in individual lives by positioning it in opposition to everything else, and so the best outcome we can hope to achieve is balance of two separate poles rather than integration and expression of a globally unified whole. In a move away from the dominant orientation and type models of professional motherhood, Bataille (2014) reconceptualised professional mothers' orientations to work and family as distinct identities that may be labelled 'professional identity' and 'mother identity' and, importantly, are not always in conflict. This is not to suggest there are not tensions, rather Bataille's emphasis is on change and adaptation and the proposition that the two identities are continuously being worked on as women move towards a better understanding of who they are, who they were and who they want to be through significant junctures in their lives. While this study does not exclusively examine identity and its conflicts and coherence in an evolving life narrative, matters of identity and selfhood, or subjectivity, are important in advancing a more holistic appreciation of women's lived experiences of combining careers and motherhood.

In focus in this study are professional women's experiences through one in the series of continuous transitions that Bataille proposes characterise combining motherhood with a career. It is perfectly possible for women to desire success in both family and professional domains. What this study observes is that most professional women expect it to be difficult to achieve, they anticipate compromise and they personalise failure. Twin goals for professional life and family life are articulated as a desire for balance, and balance is operationalised in women's daily lives by metering and managing time – that is, dividing a finite number of hours between paid work and family work, and crafting how they load each hour. Work–life balance, therefore, is an old concept that seems to have found new meaning in the lives of women who are combining careers and motherhood in contemporary times. Dominant cultural and organisational discourse links part-time and flexible working with achievement of work–life balance and appears to have produced an unconscious acceptance of the importance of balance to good mothering. Every woman interviewed for this study talked about their balance-seeking goals. The effect is to draw women into pursuing a new postfeminist standard of femininity that expects them to keep a foot in both family and professional domains upon and throughout motherhood, and personalises the responsibility for resolving any tensions between the two. In other words, mothers feel it is their responsibility to manage careers and family life. The balance narrative also serves another purpose, it offers women a story that anchors their own entry and passage through working motherhood. If balance becomes the goal, then compromise inevitably becomes part of the means of achieving it. It is the work that this narrative does that is important for equality. It simultaneously lowers women's expectations about what is possible and constrains their sense of entitlement to place demands upon other individuals and institutions to facilitate success without compromise. In essence, it holds women back.

Choosing part-time and flexible work

The complex relationship between policies, normative and gendered social expectations, and individual intentions and practices is revealed in the fine-grained detail of professional mothers' lives as they tell them. Women continue to be positioned as responsible for the emotional and physical well-being of their children and for the domestic sphere. The 30 women whose narratives illuminate this analysis share certain domestic and childcare tasks with partners-in-parenting, and simultaneously they acknowledge that their maternal and domestic responsibilities endure irrespective of their working hours, schedule or the intensity of their jobs. This was unexpected to many women, who found their egalitarian ideals faced with more traditional realities when couples became parents and continued to craft lives that combine two careers and family life. Only four women in this study describe their partners (three men and one woman) making parallel adjustments to their working lives and employment arrangements in ways that might constitute genuinely *lived* egalitarianism, in the sense that the egalitarian ideas couples espoused about sharing power in the relationship regarding both the demands and rewards of work and of care, are matched with egalitarian family practices like childcare swaps or exchanges of responsibilities on a daily, weekly or long-term basis. Little, it seems, has changed in couples' family practices after many years of gender progress in employment.

Women can and do exercise agency and make choices about their paid work. Their agency however, is *boundaried*. It is neither as open nor as unfettered as rational economic and preference-driven explanations for women's employment participation and outcomes suggest (see for example Hakim, 2000). I use the word 'boundaried' deliberately, to relate to the concept of the boundaryless career (Arthur and Rousseau, 1996), which, when viewed in the light of this analysis, offers limited potential for women as an actionable alternative to the upwardly linear traditional model of the organisational career. This is because even these presumed well-resourced women's choices about employment are constrained by the gendered relationships to childcare within couples, by household financial commitments and lifestyle aspirations, by women's work status and the strength of line manager relationships, by the availability of childcare that is flexible and affordable, and by women's own moral understandings about the 'right' thing to do for their children and for their own careers.

Narrating choice

These structuring influences and their relative grip on women's opportunities are reflected in how women narrate their intentions for their moves into part-time and flexible work. Some women are caught in a time bind and seek to avoid work–life conflict and stress by metering the amount they give their professional work (the *resolving work–life conflict* intention narrative). Others make calculated adjustments with protecting professional identities or expanding career opportunities in mind (the *protecting careers* and *expanding careers* intention narratives) and approach their transition with caution and with optimism respectively. All are shades and variations of the overarching balance-seeking goal that dominates professional women's narratives, defines their goals and how they evaluate their experiences. For a small but significant number of this cohort of 30 women, compromise defined their employment adjustment in marked ways. Factors external to the self in the workplace and inside the couple relationship overpowered identity claims and working-pattern preferences. Although likely to be articulated as choices, *compromised choice* intention narratives typically revealed very little choice in how women combine care and career on a daily basis.

The formulation of women's motivations and drivers in these four intention narratives offers a fluid conceptual framework for understanding women's work–life choices. It extends the scholarship of Crompton and Harris (1998), Crompton and Lyonette (2011), and Tomlinson (2006b) by illuminating mothers' negotiations of moralities and identities at specific biographical moments, in specific relationships and employment circumstances. Jane's story provides an example of the fluidity and applicability of this framework.

In our first interview Jane [12] described her voluntary move to cut her hours and work from home just a little more as way of managing the intensity of her job and its excessive workload that had spilled over into her home life and was affecting her health. When Jane and I met again some months later and reflected on our first interview, Jane agreed that her intention at that time characterised the *resolving work–life conflict* narrative. In that second encounter Jane went on to explain how she was feeling much less stressed and overloaded. Overall, she was working fewer hours in a week although rarely had she managed to contain her workload within her contracted hours and schedule. Nevertheless, she felt the arrangement had benefited her by giving her enough space to recover, to breathe, and to think about how to best sustain her restored sense of balance *and* keep moving forward professionally. Jane described a new plan to further reduce her working hours so that she could start a graduate training course. Had Jane and I met for the first time at that point, I am sure we would have agreed that her motivation aligned to the *expanding careers* intention narrative. Jane's mobile narrative illustrates just how much change women can experience in a relatively short time, and the different meanings and significance of part-time and flexible employment transitions at different biographical points and in different life circumstances.

Women's narratives reveal that transitions into part-time and flexible work arrangements are tactical responses to the social context in which women are crafting their lives. They are moves made with intention to restore or at least seek a sense of work–life balance, to protect careers or to expand professional opportunities. In all cases, employment transitions in the context of motherhood are morally potent, socially informed and very often a compromise. The meshing of women's professional and maternal lives and selves is dynamic, it is continuously under review as women react to, protect, expand, make compromises over, and make sense of their work–life opportunities and choices in context and through time.

Doing part-time and flexible work

The transformational promise of flexible working arrangements to facilitate work–life balance appeals to women who see themselves as professionals *and* mothers and not one or the other. Does experience match expectation? Survey data indicate that an overwhelming majority of professional women with children (93%) agree that "it is hard to combine caring and a successful career" and most feel that much of the effort to do so is largely unrecognised and certainly not valued by employers and society (Opportunity Now, 2014). For complex reasons, the cognitive, physical and emotional effort involved in reconciling paid work with unpaid care and other parts of life is considered private and is therefore rendered invisible in the public sphere. This work is essential, however, if women are to cross the inclusion boundaries of masculinised work cultures and perform well in both domestic and occupational domains as contemporary, postfeminist conceptualisations of femininity demand (Gill and Scharff, 2013; Rottenberg, 2013). Making visible the hidden work behind a flexible working arrangement is a key contribution of this study. Much of the heavy lifting involved in establishing, implementing and sustaining a part-time and flexible working arrangement most definitely falls to the individual employee. The nature of the work involved in making a flexible working arrangement work in practice extends beyond just doing the job to active management of the way the job is done within limited hours, restricted schedules and in out-of-office locations. Key findings about professional women's transition experiences and flexible working practices are summarised in these concluding themes that illuminate what we learn from women's approaches, successes and failures to implement and sustain flexible working arrangements in professional and managerial jobs.

Quiet responsibility

Women embarking on a flexible working arrangement take personal responsibility for fitting in to established organisational structures, systems, processes and attitudes. The experience of implementing a flexible working arrangement is a self-directed one, the practical, cognitive, and emotional demands of which are largely invisible to others at work. This is what makes the responsibility a quiet one.

Professional mothers assume it is their responsibility to make their arrangements work in practice and, by their own accounts, they are largely unsupported by their employing organisations to achieve effective and sustainable job designs for flexibility. Women are highly aware of the labours of their responsibility, yet few had assumed that the responsibility should or could be shared with employing organisations. The social construction and apparent mutual interpretation between employee and employer of flexible working policy as an employee benefit and not an organisational capability, locates that responsibility with the individual not the organisation. This is both a reflection of policy and, in broader terms, is entirely consistent with what Gill (2016) describes as the 'personalisation of responsibility' that is endemic in the neoliberal framework around individual lives. The personalisation of responsibility appears to extend to the personalisation of failure as well because it was common for women to blame themselves for failing to make a big job smaller or more manageable by simply working faster and harder. It was equally common for women to dismiss the problems they experienced in achieving uninterrupted and predictable time away from paid work on their designated non-working days as due to 'the nature of the job', implying that their jobs were and always will be designed in a certain way.

The idea that the managerial or professional job is an immoveable construct that offers limited potential for redesign so that it can be performed in different amounts of time, on different schedules and in different places limits ambition for modernisation of working practices and for gender equality. Women's quiet, diligent endeavours to implement their arrangements with minimal inconvenience to others at work makes their considerable effort disappear. This further preserves the fixed and unaccommodating 'nature of the job' rather than transforming it and the ways it is possible to perform it. This is not to hold these professional women responsible for a universally stalled transformation of working practices, rather it is to point out the limited reach and perverse impacts of *individual* solutions to working time and flexibility issues, when *collective* solutions may yield greater beneficial impact in terms of both organisational resourcing and individual working lives.

Efficiency versus intensity

Work status, job insight and considerable management skill are the resources that women need to make the necessary job-design adjustments and convert a full-time job into a part-time job, or to restructure job responsibilities to be shared with a job-share partner, or to regularly work from home *and* keep professional careers on track. These resources are not universal. In this way, accessing a flexible working arrangement and the supports to sustain it continues to be a privilege. Women starting new jobs lack the job insight required to be able to design a great deal of flexibility to their roles from day one. Women in the middle of organisational hierarchies lack status and authority to rescope their jobs and to reallocate responsibilities. In the absence of what management scholars call a 'job redesign response' to flexible working requests by employers (Perlow et al, 2014), by necessity women are compelled to work out on-the-job, by trial and error, how to manage their workflow, workload and work relationships, and perform effectively in their adjusted temporal and spatial boundaries.

Constant active management of time, space and boundaries characterised women's day-to-day experience of working flexibly in professional and managerial jobs. Individuals' strategies for managing time are linked to managing place and, given the authority to do so, women eliminated unnecessary travel from their schedules, minimised home-to-work commuting and chose the best location for the task. Far less time can be found for personal development, training, social activities, networking, food and rest breaks. Working intensively and stripping out the developmental, social and expansive aspects of their professional work over time drained jobs of their meaning, and the women of their energy and enthusiasm for their jobs. Five women had changed their employment because of these difficulties, and almost half, 13 women, were contemplating exiting their organisations at the final interview stage of this research.

A buffering effect

Professional mothers making just a fractional adjustment in work hours of perhaps half a day or even a full day each week, value the buffering function afforded by their part-time status. In the context of high-intensity workplaces and work cultures that value professional norms of constant availability and responsiveness, even the smallest downward adjustment in working hours empowers women to say no to work and (they hope) to not feel guilty about it:

> "What it does is it gives me a buffer … I definitely don't have be in an office. People know that and they don't expect it. That's the buffer." (Olivia [5])

"a sense of entitlement that I've never had, entitlement to
not be working. Just a day when I am not working and not
feeling guilty about it." (Emma [25])

What women appear to be buying by accepting a pay cut commensurate
with their variation to the standard full-time contract of hours, is the
right to protect their private time and to hold work back to some small
degree. Conceptualising a part-time and flexible work arrangement as
a buffer may protect women from feeling guilty about not working in
the manner of the 'ideal worker' (Acker, 1990), but evidence suggests it
does little to enhance and advance careers. This is because the job and
its workload does not get redesigned with small adjustments to time,
and women simply work intensively to deliver their responsibilities
faster. In stripping out the developmental and expansive aspects of
their jobs, and finding little or no time for networking, building and
sharing knowledge, nurturing new work relationships and generally
"doing more" as Emma [25] put it, such arrangements then offer a
weaker case for promotion when compared to the normative standard
by which they will be judged.

The buffering effect of a part-time and flexible work arrangement
relates to how women manage the boundaries between their maternal
and professional lives and selves. Boundaries between work and home
become more permeable for professionals and managers working
flexibly. Women report a new fluidity in the way they integrate
and volley between domestic and work tasks each day, facilitated by
technology that enables anytime anywhere working. An interesting
finding is how *few* women narrate this fluidity as intrusion and a
manifestation of work–life conflict, despite concluding that they
have little choice but to operate this way. It seems the nature of the
professional and managerial job is collectively understood to be bigger
than any amount of time anyone could have to give to it.

Flexibility fatigue

It is hard to be different and to work differently in an environment
that assumes everyone is the same and works in the same way. I define
'flexibility fatigue' as the debilitating impact of an individual's sustained
effort to fit their flexible model of work into inflexible organisational
structures, processes and cultures. Sources of flexibility fatigue range
from the intense experience of compressing an unadjusted full-
time workload into fewer days; to managing feelings of guilt about
declining to attend team meetings routinely scheduled on home or

non-working days; to the pressure of having to figure out (on behalf of the organisation, which does not know) how to measure and reward the collective achievements of a job-share partnership within appraisal systems designed to reward individual performance.

Women described periods of physical, mental and emotional fatigue that they associated with their efforts to fit in, to do their jobs and to protect themselves from exclusion. The fatiguing effect of managing routine work absences due to part-time and home-working is amplified for mothers simultaneously going through significant personal change, such as adapting to or ceasing breastfeeding, or coping with personal or family illness. It is perhaps little wonder that career advancement feels like a less pressing activity for many women in this context.

Few women were unequivocal about the outcomes of their transition to a flexible working arrangement. There were periods when it worked and periods when it was a struggle. Few women achieved the work–life balance that they had sought without further adjustments to their working hours, schedules or locations, and parallel adjustments to the time, timing and location of childcare. Even then, things changed again. Change was a constant and women were certain that their employment arrangements would need to change, again and again, through time.

Rumbling discontent

Our later research interviews, around the end of a year of working flexibly, were characterised by a rumbling discontent both with domestic relationships and with employment relationships. Through time and with frequent experience of formulating and reformulating their approaches to work–life balance, women's awareness increased of the gendered workplace attitudes and structures that produced their lives and experiences, and of the cultural pressures and expectations placed upon them as mothers and professionals.

It was too soon to say whether women felt their careers had been negatively impacted by their working arrangements in the ways in which the considerable body of research discussed in Chapter 1 suggests. There was some evidence already of professional mothers being marginalised in lower status jobs. Some women's pre-emptive and protective moves into less intensive jobs were regretted later when they found themselves underemployed and with limited opportunities to move up or out and retain their status as flexible workers.

Relationships were under pressure and some women's discontent was aimed squarely towards the ambivalence of their male partners with regard to the weight of women's life loads. Domestic disagreements about who does how much of what in relation to home and family life were common, although, the majority of women were entrenched in their gendered ways of doing things and found it difficult to envision how things might be different.

The transformational potential of flexible working

We know that more and more people are working flexibly in the UK, and in these fast-paced, technologically enabled, times it is axiomatic to suggest that the future of work could be anything other than flexible. Flexibility has a dark side however. The rise of the gig economy raises important questions about the ethics and responsibilities of employers towards flexible workers whom they engage to deliver services but who may or may not have the status and protections of employees. Central to this debate is the degree of choice that people have in determining the way they work and the degree of compromise that is involved in securing it. The opportunity for employees to adjust their hours, schedules and locations of paid work as and when life demands it *without* compromising their work status, reward or future prospects seems an eminently sensible, and a beneficially inclusive aspiration.

Women continue to experience significant challenges in accessing, implementing, sustaining and adjusting their ways of working to facilitate their lives and futures as professionals and mothers. Paradoxically, reducing and compressing working hours seems to create *more* work for the individual to redesign their job on-the-job and to actively manage their absences that are left unfilled by the organisation. Flexible working arrangements made these women's professional lives possible in the context of their enduring maternal responsibilities, although not always in ways they felt were sustainable or that they wanted to live. The key risks and impacts arising for individuals and their families, employing organisations, policy and society from persistence of the themes discussed in this study are summarised in the next five points.

Risk of burnout

Reducing working hours without redesigning jobs compels women to work intensively and to privilege organisational priorities over their own satisfactions, career and personal development. Few women succeeded in converting full-time to *sustainable* part-time jobs and many were fatigued by a felt pressure to present the façade of full-time availability to clients and colleagues. Finding themselves managing full-time or near-to-full-time workloads in part-time hours and restricted schedules left those who also carry the domestic, emotional and caring load at home feeling that they are 'leaning-in' (Sandberg, 2013) so far that they are falling over.

Obscured inequalities

The felt pressure to make a reduced hours schedule appear seamless obscures the clear view of the extra effort that women put to managing their part-time absence from work. Some women's acceptance of a less than full-time salary for retained full-time responsibilities and outputs was not an issue that they raised with employers. Instead of being viewed as discriminatory, it was justified by women as a small price to pay for greater personal control over their work time, timing and location.

Weakened ties to the organisation

For every woman in this study work is part of who they are and few want to give it up. Women are particularly vulnerable to the structural signals of employers during the early weeks and months of joining new organisations and rejoining old ones following periods of absence for maternity. Bungled induction processes, lack of equipment, lack of facilities for nursing mothers, and ambiguity about how flexible working works in practice communicates that mothers and flexible workers are unwelcome. When women felt they were going it alone and were unsupported in *practical* ways by their employer to manage the transition and to implement their working patterns successfully, within a year they questioned whether this was the place for them. Conversely, ties to the organisation appear strengthened when support is offered and is practical.

Failure of egalitarianism

Couple relationships will continue to be under pressure and relegated below other time-absorbing priorities of professional work and childcare without intended radicalisation of the couple relationship and disruption of traditional gendered relationships to childcare. Women speculate that their level of satisfaction with their careers and everyday lives is lower than that of their male partners. This study did not set out to test that. The point is that women are not living the egalitarian ideals that they hold, and were encouraged to hold, as they progressed through higher education and into the workplace. Living with contradiction exerts an emotional cost and puts pressure on relationships.

Stalled modernisation of working practices

A vision of flexible working for all feels remote if the hard work involved in making it work in practice is loaded upon the individual and not led, or at least shared, by the employer. A collective understanding among women that appears to be shared by employers is of part-time and flexible working practices as a private issue and not a matter of organisational resourcing that requires a strengthening of organisational capability in flexible job design, as well as structural and cultural change. Making women's experiences visible through this analysis is therefore an important step in a process of transforming and modernising working practices in large organisations. Men need also to consider working flexibly and how flexible working is managed in their work teams, otherwise flexible working practices and the people who use them are inevitably marginalised.

Implications for policy and practice

This study offers insight about how well flexible working policy works in practice for professional women at the critical point in careers when women get stuck or get out of the pipeline to the top jobs. Current claims about flexible working tend to emphasise its transformative potential and the positive nature of flexible working for both employer and employee (see for example *Good work: The Taylor Review of modern working practices* (Taylor, 2017) and the Women's Business Council, (2012)). This enthusiastic approach gives an impression of compatibility between the time, schedule and location requirements of both parties which the evidence presented in this study suggests are in reality potentially at odds.

There is a policy implementation gap that cuts deeply into human lives because employees continue to do the heavy lifting that makes flexible working work within inflexible structures and systems of designing jobs and organising work. Most of these employees are women and are doing that heavy lifting in the context of their maternal responsibilities, which many professional women find *increase* when they take on paid work and have to manage multiple relationships with childcare providers and educators in their expanded care networks.

In economies and cultures that promote freedom of choice for individuals it is important not to be blind to the forces shaping those choices. In being respectful of women's preferences and desires for involvement and success in either or both professional and domestic domains, employers and policy makers should not be blind to the forces shaping those preferences or to the institutional change required if women's choices are to be more open in the future.

By giving scholarly focus to the kinds of employment relations within which responsibilities for implementing flexible working are assigned, it is possible to illuminate the kinds of interactions that create gendered norms and confirm conventional attitudes to productivity and professionalism. It follows then that illuminating these interactions and how employees experience them highlights the kinds of strategies that unpick them. The ideas that follow have unpicking in mind and promote genuine choice for women, and of course also for men, in the flexible work–life strategies they adopt and the occupational positions they achieve.

Rethinking work and redesigning jobs

"we need to demand more from our employers I think. It is not enough for them just to say yes or no to flexibility, managing how it is done is just as important." (Olivia [5])

Olivia eloquently and succinctly describes the missing element to making flexible working work in practice. Professional women figure out for themselves how to customise their jobs and manage colleagues' expectations about their availability and capacity for work. Reducing workload to something commensurate with their reduced input of hours proved the most challenging adjustment to make, particularly for the majority of women in this study who worked in demanding professional environments where unpredictability is part of the culture and employee responsiveness is a core requirement.

Women craft and they carve. They *craft* their jobs, that is, they actively manage the task and relational boundaries of their work (Wrzesniewski and Dutton, 2001), to be able to *carve* out time for family life. Some had greater bargaining power than others and were able to draw on organisational resources to substitute 'cover' for example, or to delegate tasks to colleagues, due to their seniority and status within the organisation. In all cases, however, it was the individual and not the organisation who was responsible for finding a way to make it work. These findings indicate a significant burden on professional and managerial employees seeking and sustaining flexibility, not only to renegotiate the contractual terms of their employment but also the way the job is designed (Gascoigne and Kelliher, 2017). What Gascoigne and Kelliher (2017, p120) describe as a "remarkable" lack of organisational involvement in re-examining workloads as part of a negotiation of a part-time work arrangement risks undermining well-intentioned initiatives to use flexibility to support women's retention and advancement in the workplace.

Flexible working policies at the level of the state and the organisation are "brought to life" by employees in interaction with their line managers (Cooper and Baird, 2015, p580). Training and coaching support for line managers and HR practitioners will build organisational capability in job design and management of flexible working. This will beneficially shift organisations away from what Perlow et al (2014) describe as an 'accommodation model' of flexible working, where the onus is on the employee to prove their arrangement will not negatively affect their role, and then to successfully fit the demands of work into their lives. The alternative is a 'work redesign' model that implements a coordinated and collective re-think about how work is done and how work is valued. Perlow et al (2014) propose that a work-redesign model will have more success opening up higher level jobs to part-time and flexible working than moves to simply assist employees to accommodate the demands of work in their lives. Work–life scholars Bailyn (2011), Correll et al (2014) and Moen et al (2016) agree and similarly promote work and job-redesign frameworks to support gender equality, health and well-being. Rather than placing the onus on the employee to suggest a pattern of work and the organisation to accept or reject it, taking a collaborative work-redesign approach requires a different interaction between institution and individual. It involves line managers working with individuals to collectively rethink the task, workload, time, schedule and location components of a job with the aim of finding a 'best fit' for the individual, the local work group and the organisation.

Women's accounts of their experiences over a year of sustaining a flexible working arrangement signal the fluidity of their lives, made up as they are of many moving parts. Balance as a sustained state of equilibrium across professional and personal domains is rarely achieved. Genuine flexibility in the working arrangements that individuals negotiate should not simply mean replacing one rigid work pattern with another. It should also mean the ability to change work time and timing when life demands it and not only once a year when the policy permits it.

My own simple multiplication of the hours, schedule and location adjustments that constitute flexible working arrangements in official statistics and organisational policies finds over 300 possible job designs, which offers a startling contrast to the one single job design that is considered the default or standard: full-time, 9–5, at employers' premises. Business models, and the people systems and processes that support them in large organisations were typically designed – and continue to operate – with the default job design at the core. Genuinely rethinking work and rethinking the design of jobs for flexibility actually means fundamentally rethinking how the organisation creates value, and how it measures and rewards how people produce it. This is the leap into a flexible future of work that large organisations need to take.

The problems women experienced adjusting workloads, crafting their jobs and carving time were just one of the many challenges for women being incorporated into organisations and being valued for being there. Addressing these cultural barriers requires organisations to be much more proactive about examining and challenging the biased and limiting attitudes of managers and of many workers about part-time and flexible working, about maternal employment and, fundamentally, about the value and entitlement of women to organisational careers.

Job-sharing

Job-sharing, the arrangement between two complementarily skilled professionals to share the responsibilities of one role, has significant potential to alleviate the felt pressures of the individual working part-time in a largely unadjusted full-time job. Job-sharers' reflections about the positive outcomes from their experience identify some benefits, notably accessing 'career jobs' *and* achieving uninterrupted time away from work on non-working days, and relief from the pressure to be always on and available to clients and co-workers all the time.

Well-designed job-shares can support individuals to achieve a 2.5- or 3-day working week in a professional job. There are few practical resources available to employers and individuals about designing job-shares and implementing the arrangement effectively (see for example Cunningham and Murray, 2005). This book expands those resources by setting out the key design features of job-shares in professional and managerial occupations, and the experiences of women implementing this collective approach to how one job is done.

Without doubt, job-sharing demands open-mindedness among employers and a willingness to make practical adjustments so that two people can successfully perform one role or share a client portfolio, share a deal or transaction, or co-lead a team. What it does not necessarily require is an institutional rethink about the fitness and continuing relevance of an organisation's full-time standard model of work and the systems, processes, attitudes and behaviours that support it. Assuming that a job-share is designed so that when one partner is working the other is not, there will not be any routine absences that require colleagues and managers to step in or that compel teams to rethink their routines and schedules. Making job-sharing more widespread in managerial and professional roles could, therefore, be an interim strategy for organisations seeking to take a step towards a more fundamental rethink about what work is valued and what matters about how and when people do it.

Flexibility from day one

Job-sharing arrangements in professional and managerial jobs offer some work–life balance benefits for individuals. There are some difficulties, however, in that women with job-shares in their work histories reflected that promotion was rarely offered to the partnership, and they felt that in order to move up they should to return to full-time work. It seems that it is possible to work part-time in a job-share *within* a job, but it remains much more difficult to move *between* jobs because promotion ladders tend to lead to full-time jobs. This means that women for whom flexibility has become a necessity and new norm are locked out of opportunities to advance their careers.

Moving up might not be top priority for everyone but moving on to new environments and new challenges often is. Moving into a new professional job on a part-time and flexible arrangement is certainly more difficult that it could be. The dearth of part-time and flexible working opportunities at middle and senior managerial occupational levels in the UK was one reason for my focus on women approaching these roles or in them. More flexible working opportunities at the more senior levels in organisations and public life, and more men and women doing them is promoted heavily by policy makers and activists campaigning for gender equality in employment (see Women and Equalities Committee, 2016; Fawcett Society, 2017; Opportunity Now, 2014). Industry surveys indicate that most large employers offer some form of flexible working arrangement (CIPD, 2012; Institute of Leadership and Management, 2013), however these are rarely available to employees from day one in a job and legislation does not oblige employers to extend the Right to Request to new joiners. Less than 10% of quality job vacancies (defined as earning over £20,000 per year) are advertised as suitable for part-time or flexible working according to research by flexible work campaigners the Timewise Foundation

(2017). Forward-thinking employers are joining campaigns and making public commitments to making it simpler to negotiate flexibility during a hiring process, for example the Hire Me My Way campaign supported by 30 large UK employers. Women's employment opportunities and choices would be greatly enhanced by opening up professional and managerial jobs to flexibility *from day one* not only after six months in a job as current national policy permits. Being able to take one's flexible status into a new job on promotion or from outside as a new joiner was an idea welcomed enthusiastically by women in this study.

A culture of flexibility

The women participating in this study were often the first and only individuals working in the way they were at their level in their organisation. This signals something of the distance to be travelled if jobs at all occupational levels and in all sectors are to become genuinely flexible. Some work environments were more hospitable places to professional women working flexibly than others and, perhaps surprisingly, these did not divide neatly into private sector or public sector employers. The distinction between more and less supportive employment contexts seemed to relate to the professional time norms that operate and the degree of substitutability attached to women's roles, in other words how 'normal' it is to swap people, share work and protect private time. Although not well represented in the stories of women in this study, some supportive workplace characteristics were discernible in their accounts. These included: high-trust work environments where professionals and managers benefit from total or partial schedule control; results-based work environments where productivity is determined by the number of outputs produced and not the units of time used to produce them; and workplaces that dispense with the full-time work week for all and describe a four-day week, or home-working, or no fixed schedule at all, as standard or normal practice.

Game-changing ideas that normalise flexibility in professional and managerial work involve changing the defaults. Organisations in the US and in the UK are innovating by trialling flexible working practices in specific roles, and monitoring the impact on productivity, and, in a rounded way, also on collegiate behaviour and employee health and satisfaction (Kelly et al, 2011; Gascoigne and Young, 2016). Similarly, the All Roles Flex campaign that has been taken up by large commercial and public sector employers in Australia changes the default job design from full-time to flexible (Carter, 2016). Every job at every level is considered suitable for flexible working and employers respond to a flexibility request that can come from any employee, for any reason, at any point. Cooper (2017) argues that employers are not adopting this policy out of "the goodness of their hearts"; they anticipate that productivity benefits will flow. Insight from my research signals that in certain contexts, however, productivity benefits for the organisation are gained at the expense of individual satisfaction and accomplishments because women reducing their hours and working flexibly as a result of their motherhood intensify their work effort and move or are moved into marginal roles. Employing organisations need an easy way to understand their capacity for different types of flexibility in different types of roles, and a way of measuring and tracking the impact of better managed working time and schedule and location flexibility on productivity *and* on individual experience and outcomes.

Implications for gender equality

Who does what at home matters to equality and, as feminist scholars have long argued, cannot reasonably be separated from discussions about gender progress in employment. There needs to be a parallel shift in the domestic division of labour if women in heterosexual dual-earner couples are to achieve genuine choice in the work they do, how they do it, and the successes they achieve. This is difficult terrain for couples to traverse because it connects with deeply held values, morals and ideas about gender, femininity and masculinity. The experiences of women told from their point of view signal that genuinely lived gender egalitarianism, that is a sharing of responsibility for earning and caring, requires synchronised action by men to step up as well as women to share what they have learned and step back.

Living gender egalitarianism seems less about who does the cooking and the laundry, although women in this study had a lot to say about how these particular tasks divided, it is about how *responsibilities* within the family can be genuinely shared. Same-sex couples developing loving families without heteronormative gender scripts are writing their own. One lesbian mother in this study described how she and her wife both worked part-time and shared childcare between them. One heterosexual couple in this study *exchanged* responsibility for childcare when their children were infants and into the pre-school years: she took a year then he took a year away from work to provide day-to-day care. Another couple swapped childcare responsibilities on a weekly basis.

The future of work for mothers could look quite different if fathers were proactively encouraged to exchange or share responsibility for children and their care and were supported by state policies and workplace practices to do it.

Closing remarks

In concluding this study, I return to the theme with which I opened: balance, and what I think it means to professional mothers who are using flexible working arrangements to achieve it. Balance is the seductive and coercive mantra of modern motherhood that draws professional women towards flexible working practices. It is seductive because work forms part of a women's sense of self and few want to give up. It is coercive because mothers feel obliged to comply and make balance the quest of their lives. For many professional women who become mothers, achieving balance has become a career aim in itself. What this study has learned is that balance across work and family life cannot be achieved arithmetically by dividing time evenly across two domains because balance is subjective and cannot be measured in working hours. Almost as soon as equilibrium is sensed things change again, and in that way balance is also a dynamic construct; what it means tomorrow will be different from today. Finally, balance is social. It is collective. It means balancing the demands and rewards of work and childcare between partners-in-parenting and balancing the responsibilities for crafting flexible jobs that fit into real lives between employer and employee.

This study has attended to the difficulties and the challenges of combining professional work with family life but these women's lives were not dark, bleak or desperate. It was clearly the case that mothers who participated in this study loved and enjoyed their children. A deeply felt moral obligation to take responsibility for their care was twinned with a pleasure and satisfaction in doing so. Women might have expressed regret for what some considered their own poor choices of working pattern, profession, employer or even their partner, and yet no woman in this study regretted her children. As one woman said, "my kids are the upside in all of this".

The lived experience of highly educated, professionally experienced women who are mothers and work flexibly is not assumed to reflect that of all women or of all mothers; it is relevant to them, however. It is relevant to all women because culturally shared notions of femininity that assume fulfilment through heterosexual partnership, through mothering and a domestic life that feminist scholars and cultural commentators have critiqued for decades, continue to exert a shaping influence on the aspirations of and opportunities for all women. Its influence is present in gendered pay inequalities and patterns of vertical and horizontal segregation in workplaces, and in the political and market economies that reward care work in and outside the home with low or no pay. Its influence is there in the judgemental tone and content of media discourses about working mothers attempting to 'have it all' as at best juggling and struggling, and at worst, greedy and irresponsible. It is present in the reflections of personal sacrifice and accounts of everyday sexism of women who are crafting careers in inhospitable contexts. It is present in the proliferation of advice aimed at women about what good mothering looks like and that very little is said about what is good enough mothering or even fathering. It is imprinted on organisational structures and processes built in a bygone industrial era around the lives and linearly upward career trajectories of the unencumbered male worker. The situation is changing, yes, but the transformation has stalled. The insights and ideas contained in this study will, I hope, advance not only knowledge and understanding, but also commitment to action in pursuit of better work for better lives.

Appendices

Appendix 1: Women's characteristics and circumstances

	Participant job role	Transition scenario	Flexible work arrangement	Decision context	Domestic context	Transition narrative
1	Sarah Operations manager	New job	4 days per week, 1 day from home	First maternity leave	Egalitarian 1 infant	Protecting career
2	Claire Law professional	Conversion	3 days per week	First maternity leave	Transitional 1 infant	Compromised choice
3	Eryn Senior manager	Conversion	4 days per week, schedule and location flexibility	First maternity leave	Transitional 1 infant	Protecting career
4	Cathy Senior project manager	Conversion	80% of full-time, 5 days per week, shorter days	Other part-time/ flexible arrangement	Transitional 2 teenage children	Resolving work–life conflict
5	Olivia Senior manager	Conversion	90% of full-time, schedule and location flexibility	Second maternity leave	Transitional 2 pre-school children	Protecting career
6	Lara Law professional	Conversion	3 days per week	Second maternity leave	Transitional 2 pre-school children	Compromised choice
7	Meera Senior manager	New job	3 days per week, schedule flexibility	Other part-time/ flexible arrangement	Transitional 2 children, primary school	Compromised choice
8	Gemma Strategy manager	New employer	3 days per week, job-share	Second maternity leave	Transitional 2 pre-school children	Expanding career
9	Fiona Human resources manager	New job	4 days per week, schedule flexibility	Career break	Transitional 1 pre-school child	Resolving work–life conflict
10	Amanda Communications manager	New job	4.5 days per week, half day from home	Other part-time/ flexible arrangement	Transitional 2 children, primary school	Expanding career

	Participant job role	Transition scenario	Flexible work arrangement	Decision context	Domestic context	Transition narrative
11	Esther Senior manager	New job	3 days per week, job-share	Other part-time/flexible arrangement	Egalitarian 2 pre-school children	Expanding career
12	Jane Project manager	Conversion	4.5 days per week, 2 from home	Full-time work	Lone parent 2 primary school children	Resolving work–life conflict
13	Eleanor Senior manager	New employer	4 days per week, schedule flexibility	Other part-time/flexible arrangement	Transitional 3 children, 2 primary school, 1 pre-school	Compromised choice
14	Hayley Research manager	Conversion	4 days per week, 2 days from home	Other part-time/flexible arrangement	Transitional 2 primary school children	Compromised choice
15	Joanne Human resources manager	New job	4 days per week	First maternity leave	Transitional 1 infant	Compromised choice
16	Nina Research manager	Conversion	3 days per week	First maternity leave	Transitional 1 infant	Compromised choice
17	Sadie Education professional	New job	Compressed, schedule flexibility	First maternity leave	Transitional 1 infant	Resolving work–life conflict
18	Jenny Programme manager	New job	3 days per week	First maternity leave	Transitional 1 infant	Compromised choice
19	Frances Medical professional	Conversion	2 days per week	First maternity leave	Transitional 1 infant	Resolving work–life conflict

	Participant job role	Transition scenario	Flexible work arrangement	Decision context	Domestic context	Transition narrative
20	Gail Finance manager	New job	2.5 days per week, job-share	First maternity leave	Transitional 1 infant	Resolving work–life conflict
21	Victoria Medical professional	Conversion	4 days per week	Second maternity leave	Egalitarian 1 infant, 1 pre-schooler	Protecting career
22	Maya Project manager	New job	4 days per week, 1 day from home	First maternity leave	Egalitarian 1 infant	Resolving work–life conflict
23	Jessica Senior manager	Conversion	4 days per week, location and schedule flexibility	First maternity leave	Transitional 1 infant	Protecting career
24	Anna Project manager	New job	3 days per week	First maternity leave	Transitional 1 infant	Resolving work–life conflict
25	Emma Education professional	Conversion	80% of full-time, schedule and location flexibility	Full-time work	Transitional 1 pre-school child, 2 primary school children	Resolving work–life conflict
26	Charlotte Sales manager	New job	80% of full-time, home-based, schedule flexibility	Other part-time/ flexible arrangement	Transitional 2 pre-school children	Resolving work–life conflict
27	Andrea Legal professional	New employer	4 days per week, 1 from home	Other part-time/ flexible arrangement	Transitional 3 primary school children	Expanding career
28	Sally Education professional	Conversion	3 days per week, location flexibility	Full-time work	Transitional	Expanding career
29	Juliet Finance manager	New employer	3 days per week, home-based	Other part-time/ flexible arrangement	Transitional 4 children at school	Expanding career
30	Sophie Communications manager	New employer	4 days per week	Career break	Transitional	Expanding career

Intention narrative	Count
Resolving work–life conflict *Resolving or avoiding work–life conflict and stress*	10
Protecting career *Tactical adjustments to protect careers and defend professional identity*	5
Expanding career *Optimistic moves towards new professional futures*	7
Compromised choice *Circumstances overpowering ideals*	8

Appendix 2: Note on methodology

The research questions for the study upon which this book is based were:

- Who and what are the influences on the opportunities and choices professional mothers have to combine paid work with family care using part-time and flexible working arrangements? How do the influences interact?
- How do professional mothers experience the transition to flexible working patterns? What resources do they draw on? How do they implement and sustain the working arrangements they negotiate, and what is the nature of the work involved in doing so? What are the gains and losses through time?
- What can be concluded about the transformational potential of part-time and flexible working arrangements for professional women who are mothers?

Recruitment questionnaire

A pre-selection questionnaire was developed, piloted, refined and distributed through social media (via a dedicated Facebook page, and Twitter), and into workplaces across the UK with the cooperation of five large employers in the finance and professional services sectors (Santander, Linklaters, KPMG, Lloyds Banking Group, Bond Dickinson), and via employee networks in several police forces, local government authorities, the civil service and the National Health Service (NHS). It was promoted widely through the newsletters and social media announcements by flexible working campaigners Timewise, the Prince's Trust's Business in the Community workplace equality campaign Opportunity Now, LGBT equality campaigners and consultants Out Leadership, and the City Mothers network (now City Parents).

The aim of the recruitment questionnaire was to identify a diverse interview sample of women at different stages in their maternal biographies and employed in a range of professional and managerial jobs and industry contexts. The challenge of recruiting for this study was timing. Its aim – to follow women's transitions into flexible working arrangements as they implemented them – meant it was important to find women who would be making changes to their employment arrangement during the period in which I could run a programme of repeat interviews. In addition to demographic data, the questionnaire collected information about the specific type of flexible working arrangements and the timing of the transition. In total, around 400 women completed the questionnaire and volunteered to take part in the study, of whom around 250 met the sampling criteria. Applying the timing criteria substantially reduced the sample population to around 50 potential participants. Volunteers were followed up, fulfilling the requirements of a quota sample constructed in relation to maternal biography (first-time mothers of infants, mothers of more and older children), and industry of employment (private and public sector), and providing diversity in terms of work status, ethnicity, and couple relationship. The first 30 volunteers I contacted to take part in a preliminary discussion agreed to take part in the repeat interview programme that ran between May 2014 and September 2015. Nobody dropped out and in total 76 interviews were completed. Fourteen women were interviewed twice in a 12-month period, and 16 were interviewed three times.

Interviews

In order to gather women's accounts of their experiences a research design was required that made women's voices distinct and discernible, and that captured the sense of change and continuity that moving into a flexible working arrangement had brought. Repeat narrative interviews provided that openness and temporality.

My ideal repeat interview schedule involved three interview encounters. The first interview invited telling of uninterrupted life stories during the first hour and then moved to facilitate discussion of the influences on individuals' real and perceived opportunities and choices to work flexibly, the specifics of their planned arrangements and the resources women drew upon to inform, prepare and accomplish them. First interviews were planned for around 120 minutes and occasionally extended slightly over that time. The second and third interviews adopted a similarly open style, inviting women to narrate their experiences then probing the circumstances, continuities and discontinuities, and their feelings. Direct questions were asked about women's present circumstances and how these related to their expectations and how women explained any differences.

Using lifelines

Lifelines are graphs where important factual events and phases in a participant's life are portrayed chronologically in relation to age and historical time. In some studies lifelines are created with the interviewees after the interview, in other instances the information is derived from the interview and graphs are drawn by the researcher at a later point (Nilsen, 1994). In this study, lifeline charts were used in the first interviews to capture the biographical facts and sequencing of women's life histories, to identify triggers and turning points, and to open up discussion about the present in the context of the past. In this particular inspiration was drawn from Nilsen et al's (2013) use of lifelines in their cross-national study of transitions to parenthood to facilitate comparison of lives across time and place, and to highlight unique and common experiences across multiple cases.

In this study, lifelines were used analytically to compare the life patterning and the contextual influences that were made visible on the charts across multiple cases. I experimented with introducing the lifeline in the interview in a number of ways. I asked women to prepare it in advance because I thought that this might enable more time to be given to their narration of it in the interview, however, as an interview pre-task it was rarely accomplished because this group of women is characteristically time-poor and rarely had enough time to devote to the exercise.

I then took to completing the lifeline chart together with the participant and experimented with its completion. Sometimes I held the pen and completed it while a participant talked, and sometimes participants drew and wrote on the template themselves. It was most effective as a tool to begin a conversation about the past, from which we then moved to the present and on to imagined futures. The lifeline served as an icebreaker in interviews – a gentle way of gathering factual information regarding life events which I then probed for what they meant to participants.

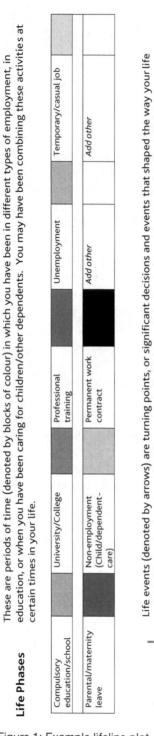

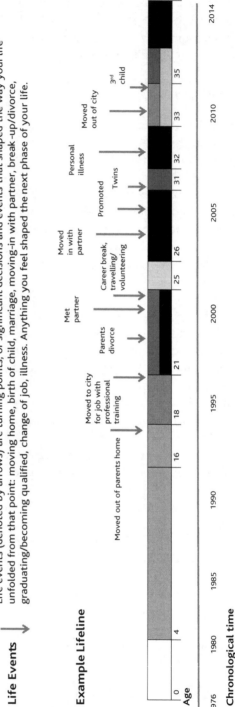

Figure 1: Example lifeline plot

Second and third interviews

Second and third interviews were shorter than the first, around 60 minutes, and were conducted in person except when travel and scheduling made in-person meetings difficult. Skype video calls were used as a second preference, and occasionally telephone when we could not access the Skype video call facility. I structured a topic guide for each interview around core themes yet left it open as to when and how those themes would be introduced and returned to as the interviews progressed. The topic guide featured question prompts that invited women to recall specific situations and occasions when they felt supported and unsupported at home and at work, comfortable and uncomfortable, content and fulfilled, and unhappy and under pressure. The thinking behind these prompts was to apply something of the critical incident interview technique (Butterfield et al, 2005) to help bring to the surface meanings, beliefs and feelings about combining professional work with motherhood that are hard to articulate, and to which individuals may not have conscious access. Demographic data such as age, relationship status and ages of children were gathered at the end of the first interview.

Scholarship about motherhood and combining mothering with working has established that decision making operates at the level of identity as well as practicality and women's lives, as they are lived, involve compromise and complex trade-offs. Life might not unfold in expected ways and to narrate thoughts and feelings about this is likely to be an emotional experience. Hochschild's (1979, 2012) ideas about the emotion work and psychic costs of living with contradiction between lives lived and selves imagined drew me to open-ended styles of questioning and use of probing to ask about feelings as well as practical experience. I sought explanations for feelings; for example in second and third interviews I asked participants to recall when they felt really happy, to visualise the scene and to explain why that was.

In the tradition of ethnographic note-taking (Atkinson, 1990), after each interview I wrote a reflective memo, the content of which was informed by the approach to recording self-reflective field notes adopted by Thomson and collaborators (2011) and which captured observations about access, interview setting, appearances, emotional dynamics and emergent themes. This approach recognises the co-creative medium of the interview situation and allows the subjective feelings of the researcher to become part of that as a way to enhance interpretive meaning (Oakley, 1981; Lucey et al, 2003). Over one hundred hours of rich and fascinating narrative interview data was generated by this qualitative longitudinal study.

Bibliography

Acas (2014) *The right to request flexible working: An Acas guide.* London: Acas.

Acker, J. (1990) Hierarchies, jobs, bodies: a theory of gendered organizations. *Gender & Society*, 4(2): 139–158.

Ackerley, B. and True, J. (2010) *Doing feminist research in political and social science.* Basingstoke: Palgrave Macmillan.

Adkins, L. (2002) *Revisions: Gender and sexuality in late modernity.* Milton Keynes: Open University Press.

Alakeson, V. (2012) *The price of motherhood: Women and part-time work.* London: Resolution Foundation.

Alger, V.M. and Crowley, J.E. (2012) Aspects of workplace flexibility and mothers' satisfaction with their husbands' contributions to household labor. *Sociological Inquiry*, 82(1): 78–99.

Archer, M. (1982) Morphogenesis versus structuration: on combining structure and action. *British Journal of Sociology*, 33(4): 455–83

Archer, M. (2007) *Making our way through the world: Human reflexivity and social mobility.* Cambridge: Cambridge University Press.

Armstrong, J. (2006) Beyond 'juggling' and 'flexibility': classed and gendered experiences of combining employment and motherhood. *Sociological Research Online*, 11(2). Available at: http://www.socresonline.org.uk/11/2/armstrong.html

Armstrong, J. (2017) *Like mother, like daughter. How career women influence their daughters' ambition.* Bristol: Policy Press.

Arnaud, S. and Wasieleski, D.M. (2014) Corporate humanistic responsibility: social performance through managerial discretion of the HRM. *Journal of Business Ethics*, 120(3): 313–34.

Arthur, M.B. (1994) The boundaryless career: a new perspective for organizational inquiry. *Journal of Organizational Behavior*, 15(4): 295–306.

Arthur, M.B. and Rousseau, D.M. (1996) *The boundaryless career: A new employment principle for a new organizational era.* New York: Oxford University Press

Atkinson, P. (1990) *The ethnographic imagination: Textual constructions of reality.* London: Routledge.

Bailey, K. and Madden, A. (2017) Why meaningful work matters. *Industrial Management*, 58(3): 10–13.

Bailey, L. (1999) Refracted selves: a study of changes in self-identity in the transition to motherhood. *Sociology*, 33(2): 335–352.

Bailyn, L. (2011) Redesigning work for gender equity and work–personal life integration. *Community, Work & Family*, 14(1): 97–112.

Baraitser, L. (2008) *Maternal encounters: The ethics of interruption.* London: Routledge.

Barrett, H. (2004) *UK family trends 1994–2004.* London: National Family and Parenting Institute.

Bataille, C.D. (2014) Identity in transition: Women's narrative identity work on the path to professional and mother. Dissertation, Quebec, Canada: McGill University.

Beagan, B., Chapman, G.E., D'Sylva, A. and Bassett, B.R. (2008) 'It's just easier for me to do it': rationalizing the family division of foodwork. *Sociology*, 42(4): 653–671.

Becker, G. (1991) *A treatise on the family.* Harvard: Harvard University Press.

Ben-Galim, D. and Thompson, S. (2013) *Who's breadwinning? Working mothers and the new face of family support.* London: IPPR.

Bianchi, S.M. and Milkie, M.A. (2010) Work and family research in the first decade of the 21st century. *Journal of Marriage and Family*, 72(3): 705–25.

Blair-Loy, M. (2003) *Competing devotions: Career and family among women executives.* Cambridge, MA: Harvard University Press.

Blair-Loy, M. (2004) Mothers in finance: surviving and thriving. *Annals of the American Academy of Political and Social Science*, 596(1): 151–71.

Blair-Loy, M. (2009) Work without end? Scheduling flexibility and work-to-family conflict among stockbrokers. *Work and Occupations*, 36(4): 279–317.

Blair-Loy, M. and Wharton, A.S. (2004) Mothers in finance: surviving and thriving. *Annals of the American Academy of Political and Social Science*, 596: 151–71.

Bloch, K. and Taylor, T. (2012) Overworked or underworked? Examining hour mismatches for women and men in the United States. *Sociological Spectrum*, 32(1): 37–60.

Boejie, H. (2010) *Analysis in qualitative research.* London: Sage.

Bold, C. (2012) *Using narrative in research.* London: Sage.

Bourdieu, P. (1986) The forms of capital. In S. Baron, J. Field and T. Schuller (eds) *Social capital: Critical perspectives.* Oxford: Oxford University Press.

Boswell-Penc, M. and Boyer, K. (2007) Expressing anxiety? Breast pump usage in American wage workplaces. *Gender, Place & Culture*, 14(5): 151–167.

Brannen, J. (2005) Time and the negotiation of work–family boundaries: autonomy or illusion? *Time & Society*, 14(1): 113–31.

Brannen, J. and Nilsen, A. (2011) Comparative biographies in case-based cross-national research: methodological considerations. *Sociology*, 45(4): 603–18.

Brannen, J., Moss, P., Owen, C. and Wale, C. (1997) *Mothers, fathers and employment: Parents and the labour market in Britain 1984–1994.* London: Department for Education and Employment.

Brescoll, V.L., Glass, J. and Sedlovskaya, A. (2013) Ask and ye shall receive? The dynamics of employer-provided flexible work options and the need for public policy. *Journal of Social Issues*, 69(2): 367–88.

Brewer, M. and Paull, G. (2006) *Newborns and new schools: Critical times in women's employment.* London: Department for Work and Pensions.

Brimrose, J., Watson, M., McMahon, M., Haasler, S., Tomassini, M. and Suzanne, P.A. (2014) The problem with women? Challenges posed by gender for career guidance practice. *International Journal for Vocational and Career Guidance*, 14(1): 77–88.

Brown, A.D. (2014) Identities and identity work in organizations. *International Journal of Management Reviews*, 17(1): 20–40.

Brown, A.D. and Coupland, C. (2015) Identity threats, identity work and elite professionals. *Organization Studies*, 36(10): 871–895.

Bryman, A. (2012) *Social research methods.* 4th edn. Oxford: Oxford University Press.

Bryson, V. (2007) *Gender and the politics of time.* Bristol: Policy Press.

Bukodi, E., Dex, S. and Joshi, H. (2012) Changing career trajectories of women and men across time. In J. Scott, S. Dex and A.C. Plagnol (eds) *Gendered lives: Gender inequalities in production and reproduction.* Cheltenham: Edward Elgar, pp 48–73.

Burke, R. and Fiksenbaum, L. (2008) Work hours, work intensity, and work addiction: costs and benefits. In R. Burke and C. Cooper (eds) *The long work hours culture: Causes, consequences and choices.* Bingley: Emerald Group Publishing.

Burnett, S., Coleman, L., Houlston, C. and Reynolds, J. (2012) *Happy homes and productive workplaces: Report of research findings.* London: Working Families. Available at: http://knowledgebank.oneplusone. org.uk/wp-content/uploads/2012/03/Happy-homes-productive-workplaces.pdf

Butler, J. (1990) *Gender trouble.* Oxford: Routledge.

Butler, J. (2004) *Undoing gender.* Oxford: Routledge.

Butterfield, L.D., Borgen, W.A., Amundson, N.E. and Maglio, A.-S.T. (2005) Fifty years of the critical incident technique: 1954–2004 and beyond. *Qualitative Research*, 5(4): 475–497.

Cahusac, E. and Kanji, S. (2014) Giving up: how gendered organizational cultures push mothers out. *Gender, Work & Organization*, 21(1): 57–70.

Carlson, D.S., Grzywacz, J.G.. and Kacmar, K.M. (2009) The relationship of schedule flexibility and outcomes via the work-family interface. *Journal of Managerial Psychology*, 25 (4): 330-355.

Carter, L. (2016) NSW public service promises flexible work hours by 2019. ABC News. Available at: http://www.abc.net.au/news/2016-03-08/nsw-public-service-promises-flexible-work-hours-by-2019/7229238.

CBI (2013) CBI responds to parental leave and flexible working reforms. Available at: http://www.cbi.org.uk/media-centre/press-releases/2013/02/cbi-responds-to-parental-leave-and-flexible-working-reforms/.

Cech, E.A. and Blair-Loy, M. (2010) Perceiving glass ceilings? Meritocratic versus structural explanations of gender inequality among women in science and technology. *Social Problems*, 57(3): 371–97.

Certeau, M. de (1984) *The practice of everyday life*, trans. S.F. Rendell. Berkeley: University of California Press

Chamberlayne, P., Bornat, J. and Wengraf, T. (eds.) (2000) *The turn to biographical methods in social science*. London: Routledge.

Chambers, D. (2012) *A sociology of family life: Change and diversity in intimate relations*. Cambridge: Polity Press.

Charmaz, K. (2006) *Constructing grounded theory: A practical guide through qualitative analysis*. London: Sage.

Chodorow, N.J. (1978) *The reproduction of mothering: Psychoanalysis and the sociology of gender*. Berkeley, CA: University of California Press.

Christopher, K. (2012) Extensive mothering: employed mothers' constructions of the good mother. *Gender & Society*, 26(1): 73–96.

Chung, H. and Van der Host, M. (2018) Women's employment patterns after childbirth and the perceived access to and use of flexitime and teleworking. *Human Relations*, 71: 47-72.

CIPD (Chartered Institute of Personnel Development) (2012) *Flexible working provision and uptake: Survey report 2012*. London: CIPD.

Clarke, L. and Holdsworth, L. (2017) Flexibility in the workplace: Implications of flexible work arrangements for individuals, teams and organisations. Acas Research Paper 03/17. London: Acas.

Coffey, A. and Atkinson, P. (1996) *Making sense of qualitative data: Complementary research strategies*. London: Sage.

Cohen, L., Duberley, J. and Musson, G. (2009) Work–life balance? An autoethnographic exploration of everyday home-work dynamics. *Journal of Management Inquiry*, 18: 229–241.

Colley, H., Henriksson, L., Niemeyer, B. and Seddon, T. (2012) Competing time orders in human service work: towards a politics of time. *Time & Society*, 21(3): 371–94.

Coltrane, S. (2008) Fatherhood, gender and work–family policies. In J.C. Gornick, M. Meyers and E. Olin Wright (eds) *Earning and caring: Creating conditions for gender egalitarian families*. New York: Verso.

Connolly, S. and Gregory, M. (2008) Moving down: women's part-time work and occupational change in Britain 1991–2001. *Economic Journal*, 118(526): F52–F76.

Conran, S. (1975) *Superwoman: Every woman's book of household management*. Harmondsworth: Penguin.

Cooper, R. (2017) Why employers embrace the all roles flex policy. *HRD Australia Magazine*. Available at: https://www.hcamag. com/hr-news/why-employers-should-embrace-the-all-roles-flex-policy-233904.aspx.

Cooper, R. and Baird, M. (2015) Bringing the 'right to request' flexible working arrangements to life: from policies to practices. *Employee Relations*, 37(5): 568–81.

Correll, S.J., Benard, S. and Paik, I. (2007) Getting a job: is there a motherhood penalty? *American Journal of Sociology*, 112(5): 1297–338.

Correll, S.J., Kelly, E.L., O'Connor, L.T. and Williams, J.C. (2014) Redesigning, redefining work. *Work and Occupations*, 41(1): 3–17.

Corwin, V., Lawrence, T. and Frost, P. (2001) Five strategies of successful part-time work. *Harvard Business Review*, 79 (7): 121–127.

Cory, G. and Alakeson, V. (2014) *Careers and carers: Childcare and maternal labour supply*. London: Resolution Foundation.

Costa Dias, M., Elming, W. and Joyce, R. (2016) *The gender wage gap: IFS briefing note BN186*. London: Institute for Fiscal Studies.

Cousins, C.R. and Tang, N. (2004) Working time and work and family conflict in the Netherlands, Sweden and the UK. *Work, Employment and Society*, 18(3): 531–49.

Craig, L. (2006) Does father care mean fathers share? A comparison of how mothers and fathers in intact families spend time with children. *Gender and Society*, 20(2): 259-281.

Craig, L. and Mullan, K. (2012) Lone and partnered mothers' childcare time within context in four countries. *European Sociological Review*, 28(4): 512–26.

Cresswell, J.W. (2013) *Qualitative inquiry and research design: Choosing among five approaches*. London: Sage.

Crittenden, A. (2001) *The price of motherhood: Why the most important job in the world is still the least valued*. New York: Metropolitan Books.

Crompton, R. (2002) Employment, flexible working and the family. *British Journal of Sociology*, 53(4): 537–58.

Crompton, R. and Harris, F. (1998) Explaining women's employment patterns: 'orientations to work' revisited. *British Journal of Sociology*, 49(1): 118–36.

Crompton, R. and Lyonette, C. (2007a) Occupational class, country and the domestic division of labour. In R. Crompton, S. Lewis and C. Lyonette (eds) *Women, men, work and family in Europe*. Houndmills: Palgrave Macmillan, pp 116–32.

Crompton, R. and Lyonette, C. (2007b) Reply to Hakim. *British Journal of Sociology*, 58(1): 133–4.

Crompton, R. and Lyonette, C. (2011) Women's career success and work–life adaptations in the accountancy and medical professions in Britain. *Gender, Work & Organization*, 18(2): 231–54.

Crompton, R., Lewis, S. and Lyonette, C. (2007a) Continuities, change and transformations. In R. Crompton, S. Lewis and C. Lyonette (eds) *Women, men, work and family in Europe*. Houndmills: Palgrave Macmillan, pp 230–44.

Crompton, R., Lewis, S. and Lyonette, C. (2007b) Introduction: the unravelling of the 'male breadwinner' model – and some of its consequences. In R. Crompton, S. Lewis and C. Lyonette (eds) *Women, men, work and family in Europe*. Houndmills: Palgrave Macmillan, pp 1–17.

Crompton, R., Lewis, S. and Lyonette, C. (2007c) *Women, men, work and family in Europe*. Houndmills: Palgrave Macmillan.

Cunningham, C.R. and Murray, S.S. (2005) Two executives, one career. *Harvard Business Review*, 83(2): 125–31.

Daniels, L. (2012) *Job sharing at senior level: Making it work*. London: Capability Jane. Available at: http://www.thejobshareproject. com/3434hjkv97fgb378fbv/jobsharefullreport.pdf.

Daverth, G., Cassell, C. and Hyde, P. (2016) The subjectivity of fairness: managerial discretion and work–life balance. *Gender, Work & Organization*, 23(2): 89–107.

Daycare Trust and Family Parenting Institute (2013) *Childcare costs survey 2013*. London: Daycare Trust and Family Parenting Institute.

Den Dulk, L., Peters, P. and Poutsma, E. (2012) Variations in adoption of workplace work–family arrangements in Europe: the influence of welfare-state regime and organizational characteristics. *International Journal of Human Resource Management*, 23(13): 2785–2802.

Den Dulk, L., Peper, A., Sadar, N.Č, Lewis, S., Smithson, J. and Van Doorne-Huiskes, J. (2011) Work, family and managerial attitudes and practices in the European workplace: comparing Dutch, British, and Slovenian financial sector managers. *Social Politics*, 18: 300–29.

Denzin, N.K. and Lincoln, Y.S. (2011) *The Sage handbook of qualitative research*. 4th edn. London: Sage.

Department for Business Innovation and Skills (2012) *Consultation on modern workplaces: Government response on flexible working impact assessment*. London: Department for Business Innovation and Skills.

Department for Business Innovation and Skills and Acas (2014) *Flexible working rights extended to more than 20 million*. Available at: www.gov.uk/government/news/flexible-working-rights-extended-to-more-than-20-million.

Dex, S. and Bukodi, E. (2012) The effects of part-time work on women's occupational mobility in Britain: evidence from the 1958 birth cohort study. *National Institute Economic Review*, 222(1): R20–R37.

Dey, I. (2007) Grounded theory. In C. Seale (ed.) *Qualitative research practice*. London: Sage, pp 80–93.

Dick, P. (2006) The psychological contract and the transition from full to part-time police work. *Journal of Organizational Behavior*, 27(1): 37–58.

Dick, P. (2010) The transition to motherhood and part-time working: mutuality and incongruence in the psychological contracts existing between managers and employees. *Work, Employment and Society*, 24(3): 508–25.

Dick, P. and Hyde, R. (2006) Consent as resistance, resistance as consent: re-reading part-time professionals' acceptance of their marginal positions. *Gender, Work & Organization*, 13(6): 543-560.

Doucet, A. (2006) *Do men mother? Fatherhood, care, and domestic responsibility*. Toronto: University of Toronto Press.

Duncan, S. and Edwards, R. (1999) *Lone mothers, paid work and gendered moral rationalities*. Basingstoke: Macmillan.

Duncan, S. and Irwin, S. (2004) The social patterning of values and rationalities: mothers' choices in combining caring and employment. *Social Policy Society*, 3(4): 391–399.

Dunne, M.I.A., Pryor, J. and Yates, P. (2005) *Becoming a researcher: A companion to the research process*. Maidenhead: Open University Press.

Durbin, S. and Fleetwood, S. (2010) Gender inequality in employment: editors' introduction. *Equality, Diversity and Inclusion: An International Journal*, 29(3): 221–238.

Durbin, S. and Tomlinson, J. (2010) Female part-time managers: networks and career mobility. *Work, Employment and Society*, 24(4): 621–40.

Durbin, S. and Tomlinson, J. (2014) Female part-time managers: careers, mentors and role models. *Gender, Work & Organization*, 21(4): 308–320.

Ely, R.J., Stone, P. and Ammerman, C. (2014) Rethink what you 'know' about high-achieving women. *Harvard Business Review*, 92(12): 100–9.

Emslie, C. and Hunt, K. (2009) 'Live to work' or 'work to live'? A qualitative study of gender and work–life balance among men and women in mid-life. *Gender, Work & Organization*, 16(1): 151-172.

Equal Opportunities Commission (2005) *Britain's hidden brain drain: Final report.* Manchester: Equal Opportunities Commission .

Equal Pay Act (1970) *The Equal Pay Act. Chapter 41.* London: The Stationery Office.

Erikson, R. (2011) Emotional carework, gender, and the division of household labour. In A.I. Garey and K.V. Hansen (eds) *At the heart of work and family: Engaging the ideas of Arlie Hochschild.* London: Rutgers University Press.

Evetts, J. (2000) Analysing change in women's careers: Culture, structure and action dimensions. *Gender, Work and Organization*, 7(1): 57–67.

Evetts, J. (2011) A new professionalism? Challenges and opportunities. *Current Sociology*, 59(4): 406–22.

Fagan, C. and Norman, H. (2012) Trends and social divisions in maternal employment patterns following maternity leave in the UK. *International Journal of Sociology and Social Policy*, 32(9): 544–60.

Fagan, C. and Rubery, J. (1996) The salience of the part-time divide in the European Union. *European Sociological Review*, 12(3): 227–50.

Fagan, C. and Walthery, P. (2011) Individual working-time adjustments between full-time and part-time working in European firms. *Social Politics*, 18(2): 269–99.

Family and Parenting Institute (2009) *Family trends: British families since the 1950s.* London: FPI.

Fawcett Society (2017) Gender pay gap briefing. Available at: https://www.fawcettsociety.org.uk/Handlers/Download.ashx?IDMF=2aea3562-bfd8-414d-99be-86f81161dffd

Fenwick, T. (2013) Understanding transitions in professional practice and learning: Towards new questions for research. *Journal of Workplace Learning*, 25(6): 352–67.

Flaherty, M.G. (2003) Time work: Customizing temporal experience. *Social Psychology Quarterly*, 66 (1): 17–33.

Flick, U. (2009) *An introduction to qualitative research*. 4th edn. London: Sage.

Foster, D. (2016) *Lean out*. London: Repeater Books.

Gabb, J. and Fink, J. (2015) *Couple relationships in the 21st century*. Houndmills: Palgrave Macmillan.

Gambles, R.L., Lewis, S. and Rapoport, R. (2006) *The myth of work–life balance*. Chichester: John Wiley and Sons.

Gangl, M. and Ziefle, A. (2009) Motherhood, labor force behavior, and women's careers: an empirical assessment of the wage penalty for motherhood in Britain, Germany, and the United States. *Demography*, 46(2): 341–69.

Garey, A.I. (1999) *Weaving work and motherhood*. Philadelphia, PA: Temple University Press.

Gascoigne, C. (2014) *Part-time working arrangements for managers and professionals: A process approach*. PhD thesis, Swindon: Cranfield University.

Gascoigne, C. and Kelliher, C. (2017) The transition to part-time: how professionals negotiate 'reduced time and workload' i-deals and craft their jobs. *Human Relations*, online, 9 October.

Gascoigne, C. and Young, Z. (2016) *Moving up in retail*. London: Timewise. Available at: https://timewise.co.uk/wp-content/uploads/2016/11/Moving_Up_In_Retail_Pilot.pdf.

Gascoigne, C., Parry, E. and Buchanan, D. (2016) Extreme work, gendered work? How extreme jobs and the discourse of 'personal choice' perpetuate gender inequality. *Organization*, 22(4): 457–475.

Gash, V. (2008) Preference or constraint? Part-time workers' transitions in Denmark, France and the United Kingdom. *Work, Employment and Society*, 22(4): 655–74.

Gatrell, C. (2005) *Hard labour: The sociology of parenthood*. Maidenhead: Open University Press.

Gatrell, C. (2007) Secrets and lies: breastfeeding and professional paid work. *Social Science & Medicine*, 65(2): 393–404.

Gatrell, C. (2008) *Embodying women's work*. Maidenhead: Open University Press.

Gatrell, C. (2013) Maternal body work: how women managers and professionals negotiate pregnancy and new motherhood at work. *Human Relations*, 66(5): 621–44.

Gatrell, C., Burnett, S.B., Cooper, C.L. and Sparrow, P. (2014) Parents, perceptions and belonging: exploring flexible working among UK fathers and mothers. *British Journal of Management*, 25 (3), pp 473–487.

Giddens, A. (1984) *The constitution of society.* Oxford: Blackwell.

Giddens, A. (1991) *Modernity and self-identity: Self and society in the late modern age.* Cambridge: Polity Press.

Giddens, A. (1992) *The transformation of intimacy: Sexuality, love and eroticism in modern societies.* Cambridge: Polity Press.

Gill, R. (2007) Postfeminist media culture: elements of a sensibility. *European Journal of Cultural Studies,* 10(2).

Gill, R. (2016) Post-postfeminism? New feminist visibilities in postfeminist times. *Feminist Media Studies,* 16(4): 610–630.

Gill, R. and Scharff, C. (2013) *New femininities: Postfeminism, neoliberalism, and subjectivity.* Houndmills: Palgrave Macmillan.

Ginn, J., Arber, S., Brannen, J., Dale, A., Dex, S., Elais, P. et al (1996) Feminist fallacies: a reply to Hakim on women's employment. *British Journal of Sociology,* 47(1): 167–74.

Glaser, B.G. and Straus, A.L. (1967) *The discovery of grounded theory: Strategies for qualitative research.* Chicago, IL: Aldine de Gruyter.

Golden, T.D., Veiga, J.F. and Simsek, Z. (2006) Telecommuting's differential impact on work–family conflict: is there no place like home? *Journal of Applied Psychology,* 91(6): 1340–50.

Greenhaus, J.H. and Powell, G.N. (2012) The family-relatedness of work decisions: a framework and agenda for theory and research. *Journal of Vocational Behavior,* 80(2): 246–55.

Greenwood, D. and Levin, M. (2006) *Introduction to action research: Social research for social change.* 2nd edn. London: Sage.

Hage, G. and Eckersley, R. (eds) (2012) *Responsibility.* Carlton, Vic.: Melbourne University Press.

Hakim, C. (1991) Grateful slaves and self-made women: fact and fantasy in women's work orientations. *European Sociological Review,* 7(2) 101–21.

Hakim, C. (1998) Developing a sociology for the twenty-first century: preference theory. *British Journal of Sociology,* 49(1): 137–43.

Hakim, C. (2000) *Work–lifestyle choices in the 21st century: Preference theory.* Oxford: Oxford University Press.

Hakim, C. (2002) Lifestyle preferences as determinants of women's differentiated labor market careers. *Work and Occupations,* 29(4): 428–59.

Hakim, C. (2006) Women, careers, and work–life preferences. *British Journal of Guidance and Counselling,* 34(3): 279–94.

Halrynjo, S. and Lyng, S.T. (2009) Preferences, constraints or schemas of devotion? Exploring Norwegian mothers' withdrawals from high-commitment careers 1. *British Journal of Sociology,* 60(2): 321–343.

Harkness, S. (2008) The household division of labour: changes in families' allocation of paid and unpaid work. In J. Scott, S. Dex and H. Joshi (eds) *Women and employment*. Cheltenham: Edward Elgar, pp 234–67.

Harkness, S.E. (2016) The effect of motherhood and lone motherhood on the employment and earnings of British women: a lifecycle approach. *European Sociological Review*, 32(6): 850-863.

Hatton, E. and Trautner, M.N. (2015) Images of powerful women in the age of 'choice feminism'. *Journal of Gender Studies*, 22(1): 65–78.

Haynes, K. (2008) Transforming identities: accounting professionals and the transition to motherhood. *Critical Perspectives on Accounting*, 19(5): 620–42.

Hays, S. (1996) *The cultural contradictions of motherhood*. New Haven, CT: Yale University Press.

Hegewisch, A. (2009) *Flexible working policies: A comparative review*. Manchester: Equality and Human Rights Commission.

Hegewisch, A. and Gornick, J.C. (2011) The impact of work–family policies on women's employment: a review of research from OECD countries. *Community, Work & Family*, 14(2): 119–38.

Hewlett, S.A. (2007) *Off-ramps and on-ramps:Keeping talented women on the road to success*. Cambridge, MA: Harvard Business School Press.

Hill, E.J., Erickson, J.J., Holmes, E.K. and Ferris, M. (2010) Workplace flexibility, work hours, and work–life conflict: finding an extra day or two. *Journal of Family Psychology*, 24(3): 349–58.

Hill, E.J., Grzywacz, J.G., Allen, S., Blanchard, V.L., Matz-Costa, C., Shulkin, S. et al. (2008) Defining and conceptualizing workplace flexibility. *Community, Work, and Family*, 11: 149–163.

Hill, R., Tranby, E., Kelly, E. and Moen, P. (2013) Relieving the time squeeze? Effects of a white-collar workplace change on parents. *Journal of Marriage and Family*, 75(4): 1014–29.

Himmelweit, S. (2007) The right to request flexible working: a 'very British' approach to gender (in)equality? *Australian Bulletin of Labour*, 33(2): 246–263.

Himmelweit, S. and Sigala, M. (2004) Choice and the relationship between identities and behaviour for mothers with pre-school children: some implications for policy from a UK study. *Journal of Social Policy*, 33(3): 455–478.

Hochschild, A.R. (1979) Emotion work, feeling rules, and social structure. *American Journal of Sociology*, 85(3): 551–575.

Hochschild, A.R. (1989) *The second shift: Working parents and the revolution at home*. Berkeley, CA: University of California Press.

Hochschild, A.R. (1997) *The time-bind: When work becomes home and home becomes work*. New York: Metropolitan Books.

Hochschild, A.R. (2008) Feeling in sociology and the world. *Sociologisk Forskning*, 45(2): 339–354.

Hochschild, A.R. (2012) *The managed heart: Commercialization of human feeling*, updated with a New Preface. Berkeley, CA: University of California Press.

Holloway, S.L. (1998) Local childcare cultures: moral geographies of mothering and the social organisation of pre-school education. *Gender, Place & Culture*, 5(1): 29–53.

Hollway, W. (2015) *Knowing mothers: Researching maternal identity change*. Houndmills: Palgrave Macmillan.

Hollway, W. and Jefferson, T. (2013) *Doing qualitative research differently: A psychosocial approach*. London: Sage.

Holt, H. and Lewis, S. (2011) 'You can stand on your head and still end up with lower pay': gliding segregation and gendered work practices in Danish 'family-friendly' workplaces. *Gender, Work & Organization*, 18(1): 202–21.

Hopkins, J.J., Sorensen, A. and Taylor, V. (2013) Same-sex couples, families, and marriage: embracing and resisting heteronormativity. *Sociology Compass*, 7(2): 97–110.

Hoque, K. and Kirkpatrick, I. (2003) Non-standard employment in the management and professional workforce: training, consultation and gender implications. *Work, Employment and Society*, 17(4): 667-689.

Hostetler, A.J., Sweet, S. and Moen, P. (2007) Gendered career paths: a life course perspective on returning to school. *Sex Roles*, 56(1–2): 85–103.

Houston, D.M. and Marks, G. (2003) The role of planning and workplace support in returning to work after maternity leave. *British Journal of Industrial Relations*, 41(2): 197–214.

Houston, D.M. and Waumsley, J. (2003) *Attitudes to flexible working and family life*. London: Resolution Foundation.

Hunt, S.A. (2009) Major demographic trends. In S.A. Hunt (ed.) *Family trends: British families since the 1950s*. London: Family and Parenting Institute.

Huskinson, T., Pye, J., Medien, K., Dobie, S., Ferguson, C., Gar Dner, C. et al (2011) *Childcare and early years survey of parents*. London: Department for Education.

Ibarra, H. (1999) Provisional selves: experimenting with image and identity in professional adaptation. *Administrative Science Quarterly*, 44(4): 764–791.

Institute of Leadership and Management (2013) *Flexible working: Goodbye nine to five.* http://www.i-l-m.com.

Jacobs, J. and Gerson, K. (2004) *The time divide: Work, family and gender inequality.* Cambridge, MA: Harvard University Press.

Janus, A.L. (2013) The gap between mothers' work–family orientations and employment trajectories in 18 OECD countries. *European Sociological Review,* 29(4): 752–66.

Johnston, D. and Swanson, D. (2007) Cognitive acrobatics in the construction of worker-mother identity. *Sex Roles: A Journal of Research,* 57(5): 447–59.

Joshi, H. (2008) Setting the scene. Paper presented at the Modern Motherhood Conference, Family and Parenting Institute, London.

Kanter, R.M. and Roessner, J. (1999, revised May 2003) Deloitte & Touche (A): a hole in the pipeline. Harvard Business School Case 300–112.

Kelan, E.K. (2010) Gender logic and (un)doing gender at work. *Gender, Work & Organization,* 17(2): 174–94.

Kelan, E. and Mah, A. (2014) Gendered identification: between idealization and admiration. *British Journal of Management,* 25 (1): 95–10.

Kelliher, C. and Anderson, D. (2010) Doing more with less? Flexible working practices and the intensification of work. *Human Relations,* 63(1): 83–106.

Kelly, E., Moen, P. and Tranby, E. (2011) Changing workplaces to reduce work–family conflict: schedule control in a white-collar organization. *American Sociological Review,* 76(2): 265–290.

Kelly, E., Moen, P., Oakes, J., Fan, W., Okechukwu, C., Davis, K. et al (2014) Changing work and work–family conflict: evidence from the Work, Family, and Health Network. *American Sociological Review,* 79(3): 485–516.

Kirchmeyer, C. (2006) The different effects of family on objective career success across gender: a test of alternative explanations. *Journal of Vocational Behavior,* 68(2): 323–46.

Klett-Davies, M. and Skaliotis, E. (2009) Mothers, childcare and the work–life balance. In S.A. Hunt (ed.) *Family trends: British families since the 1950s.* London: Family and Parenting Institute.

Kolb, D.M., and Porter, J.L. (2015) 'Office housework' gets in women's way. *Harvard Business Review,* (4). Available at: https://hbr.org/2015/04/office-housework-gets-in-womens-way

KPMG (2014) *Cracking the code.* London: KPMG.

Kvale, S. and Brickman, S. (2009) *Interviews: Learning the craft of qualitative research interviewing.* London: Sage.

Ladge, J.J. and Greenberg, D.N. (2015) Becoming a working mother: managing identity and efficacy uncertainties during resocialization. *Human Resource Management*, 54(6): 977–998.

Lambert, S.J., Haley-Lock, A. and Henly, J.R. (2012) Schedule flexibility in hourly jobs: unanticipated consequences and promising directions. *Community, Work and Family*, 15(3): 293–315.

Lanning, T., Gottfried, G., Darlington, R. and Bradley, L. (2013) *Great expectations: exploring the promises of gender equality.* London: IPPR.

Lawler, S. (2014) *Identity: Sociological perspectives.* 2nd edn. Cambridge: Polity.

Lawrence, T. (2008) Power, institutions and organizations. In R. Greenwood, C. Oliver, R. Suddaby and K. Sahlin-Andersson (eds) *The Sage handbook of organizational institutionalism.* Thousand Oaks, CA: Sage.

Leahy, M. and Doughney, J. (2006) Women, work and preference formation: a critique of Catherine Hakim's preference theory. *Journal of Business Systems Governance and Ethics*, 1(1): 37–48.

Levinson, D.J. (1986) A conception of adult development. *American Psychologist*, 41(1): 3–13.

Lewis, J. (2010) *Work–family balance, gender and policy.* Cheltenham: Edward Elgar.

Lewis, J. and Campbell, M. (2008) What's in a name? 'Work and family' or 'work and life' balance policies in the UK since 1997 and the implications for the pursuit of gender equality. *Social Policy and Administration*, 42(5): 524–41.

Lewis, J. and Giullari, S. (2005) The adult worker model family, gender equality and care: the search for new policy principles and the possibilities and problems of a capabilities approach. *Economy and Society*, 34(1): 76–104.

Lewis, P. and Simpson, R. (2017) Hakim revisited: preference, choice and the postfeminist gender regime. *Gender, Work & Organization*, 24(2): 115–33.

Lewis, S. and Humbert, A. (2010) Discourse or reality? 'Work–life balance', flexible working policies and the gendered organization. *Equality, Diversity and Inclusion: An International Journal*, 29(3): 239–254.

Lincoln, Y.S. and Guba, G.E. (1985) *Naturalistic enquiry.* Beverley Hills, CA: Sage.

Lovejoy, M. and Stone, P. (2012) Opting back in: the influence of time at home on professional women's career redirection after opting out. *Gender, Work & Organization*, 19(6): 631–53.

Lucey, H., Melody, J. and Walkerdine, V. (2003) Project 4:21. Transitions to womanhood: developing a psychosocial perspective in one longitudinal study. *International Journal of Social Research Methodology*, 6(3): 279–284.

Luhmann, N. (1971) 'Sinn als Grundbegriff der Soziologie'. In J. Habermas and N. Luhmann (eds) *In Theorie der Gesellschaft oder Sozialtechnologie—Was leistet die Systemforschung?* Frankfurt am Main: Suhrkamp, pp. 25-100. Translated in N. Luhmann (1990) *Essays on Self-Reference*. New York: Columbia University Press, pp. 21-79.

Lupton, D. and Schmied, V. (2002) 'The right way of doing it all': first-time Australian mothers' decisions about paid employment. *Women's Studies International Forum*, 25(1): 97–107.

Lupton, D. and Schmied, V. (2013) Splitting bodies/selves: women's concepts of embodiment at the moment of birth. *Sociology of Health & Illness*, 35(6): 828–841.

Lyonette, C. and Crompton, R. (2015) Sharing the load? Partners' relative earnings and the division of domestic labour. *Work, Employment and Society*, 29(1): 23–40.

Lyonette, C., Kaufman, G. and Crompton, R. (2011) 'We both need to work': maternal employment, childcare and health care in Britain and the USA. *Work Employment and Society*, 25(1): 34–50.

MacDonald, M., Phipps, S. and Lethbridge, L. (2005) Taking its toll: the influence of paid and unpaid work on women's well-being. *Feminist Economics*, 11(1): 63–94.

MacGill, F. (2014) Making sense of sustained part-time working through stories of mothering and paid work. PhD thesis, Bath: University of Bath.

Macrae, N. (1989) Workplace flexibility: past, present, and future. *Journal of Labor Research*, 10(1): 51–5.

Maher, J. (2013) Women's care/career changes as connection and resilience: challenging discourses of breakdown and conflict. *Gender, Work & Organization*, 20(2): 172–183.

Mainiero, L.A. and Sullivan, S.E. (2005) Kaleidoscope careers: an alternate explanation for the 'opt-out' revolution. *Academy of Management Executive*, 19(1): 106–23.

Manning, A. and Petrongolo, B. (2008) The part-time pay penalty for women in Britain. *Economic Journal*, 118(526): F28–F51.

Mason, J. (2002) *Qualitative researching.* 2nd edn. London: Sage.

Masuda, A.D., Poelmans, S.a.Y., Allen, T.D., Spector, P.E., Lapierre, L.M., Cooper, C.L. et al (2012) Flexible work arrangements availability and their relationship with work-to-family conflict, job satisfaction, and turnover intentions: a comparison of three country clusters. *Applied Psychology*, 61(1): 1–29.

Maushart, S. (2002) *Wifework: What marriage really means for women.* London: Bloomsbury.

McCarver, V. (2011) The rhetoric of choice and 21st-century feminism: online conversations about work, family, and Sarah Palin. *Women's Studies in Communication*, 34(1): 20–41.

McDowell, L., Ray, K., Perrons, D., Fagan, C. and Ward, K. (2005) Women's paid work and moral economies of care. *Social and Cultural Geography*, 6(2): 219–36.

McKie, L., Biese, I. and Jyrkinen, M. (2013) 'The best time is now!' The temporal and spatial dynamics of women opting in to self-employment. *Gender, Work & Organization*, 20(2): 184-196.

McKinsey & Company (2012) *Women matter: Making the breakthrough.* New York: McKinsey & Company. Available at: https://www.mckinsey.com/~/media/McKinsey/Business%20Functions/Organization/Our%20Insights/Women%20matter/Women_matter_mar2012_english%20(1).ashx

McKinsey & Company (2013) *Gender diversity in top management: Moving corporate culture moving boundaries.* New York: McKinsey & Company.

McLeod, J. (2015) Reframing responsibility in an era of responsibilisation: education, feminist ethics and an 'idiom of care'. *Discourse: Studies in the Cultural Politics of Education*, 1: 43–56.

McLeod, J. and Thomson, R. (2009) *Researching social change: Qualitative approaches.* London: Sage.

McRae, S. (2003) Constraints and choices in mothers' employment careers: a consideration of Hakim's preference theory. *British Journal of Sociology*, 54(3): 317–38.

McRobbie, A. (2009) *The aftermath of feminism: Gender, culture and social change.* Los Angeles: Sage.

Michielsens, E., Bingham, C. and Clarke, L. (2013) Managing diversity through flexible work arrangements: management perspectives. *Employee Relations*, 36(1): 49–69.

Miles, M.B. and Huberman, A.M. (1994) *Qualitative data analysis: An expanded sourcebook.* London: Sage.

Milkie, M.A., Kendig, S.M., Nomaguchi, K.M. and Denny, K.E. (2010) Time with children, children's well-being, and work–family balance among employed parents. *Journal of Marriage and Family*, 72(5): 1329-1343.

Miller, T. (2005) *Making sense of motherhood: A narrative approach.* Cambridge: Cambridge University Press.

Miller, T. (2011) *Making sense of fatherhood: Gender, caring and work.* Cambridge: Cambridge University Press.

Miller, T. (2012) Balancing caring and paid work in the UK: narrating 'choices' as first-time parents. *International Review of Sociology*, 22(1): 39–52.

Miller, T. (2015) Going back: 'stalking', talking and researcher responsibilities in qualitative longitudinal research. *International Journal of Social Research Methodology*, 18(3): 293–305.

Mills, M. and Täht, K. (2010) Nonstandard work schedules and partnership quality: quantitative and qualitative findings. *Journal of Marriage and Family*, 72(4): 860–75.

Moen, P., Kelly, E.L., Fan, W., Lee, S.-R., Almeida, D., Kossek, E.E. et al (2016) Does a flexibility/support organizational initiative improve high-tech employees' well-being? Evidence from the work, family, and health network. *American Sociological Review*, 81(1): 134–164.

Morgan, D.H.J. (2013) *Rethinking family practices.* Houndmills: Palgrave Macmillan.

Nanny Tax (2015) 2014 Wages survey. Available at: https://www. nannytax.co.uk/images/PDFs/NT-2014_WSAR_V1.pdf.

Neale, B. and Flowerdew, J. (2003) Time, texture and childhood: the contours of longitudinal qualitative research. *International Journal of Social Research Methodology, Theory and Practice*, 6(3): 189-199.

Neuburger, J., Joshi, H. and Dex, S. (2011) *Part-time working and pay amongst Millennium Cohort Study mothers: Working Paper 2011/2.* London: Institute of Education. Available at: http://www.cls.ioe. ac.uk/library-media%5Cdocuments%5CCLS_WP_2011_2.pdf?

Nilsen, A. (1994) Life lines: a methodological approach. In G. Bjeren and I. Elgqvist-Satltzman (eds) *Gender and education in a life perspective: Lessons from Scandinavia.* Avebury: Ashgate, pp 110–15.

Nilsen, A., Brannen, J. and Lewis, J. (2013) *Transitions to parenthood in Europe.* Bristol: Policy Press.

Nowak, M.J., Naude, M. and Thomas, G. (2013) Returning to work after maternity leave: childcare and workplace flexibility. *Journal of Industrial Relations*, 55(1): 118–35.

O'Neil, D. and Bilimoria, D. (2005) Women's career development phases: idealism, endurance, and reinvention. *Career Development International*, 10(3): 168–189.

O'Reilly, J. and Bothfeld, S. (2002) What happens after working part time? Integration, maintenance or exclusionary transitions in Britain and western Germany. *Cambridge Journal of Economics*, 26(4): 409–39.

Oakley, A. (1974) *Housewife: High value low cost.* Aylesbury, Bucks: Penguin Books.

Oakley, A. (1981) Interviewing women: A contradiction in terms. In H. Roberts (ed.) *Doing feminist research.* London: Routledge.

Oakley, A. (1998) Gender, methodology and peoples ways of knowing: some problems with feminism and the paradigm debate in social science. *Sociology,* 32(4): 707–31.

Oakley, A. (2016) Interviewing women again: power, time and the gift. *Sociology,* 50(1): 195–213.

OECD (2012) *Family database.* Paris. Available at: http://www.oecd.org/els/family/database.htm

ONS (Office for National Statistics) (2011) Hours worked in the labour market: 2011 (not seasonally adjusted). ONS and Eurostat. Available at: https://docs.google.com/spreadsheets/d/1UrIUNWCVnkzBVL nNo9R6LaWABlH2NZ9LvZmKSB98YIY/edit#gid=0.

ONS (2013) Women in the labour market. Available at: https://www.ons.gov.uk/employmentandlabourmarket/peopleinwork/employmentandemployeetypes/articles/womeninthelabourmarket/2013-09-25.

ONS (2014) *Statistical bulletin: Labour market statistics.* February. Available at: http://webarchive.nationalarchives.gov.uk/20160106225322/http://www.ons.gov.uk/ons/rel/lms/labour-market-statistics/february-2014/statistical-bulletin.html

ONS (2016a) User requested data: People in employment with a flexible working arrangement, by gender. Available at: https://www.ons.gov.uk/employmentandlabourmarket/peopleinwork/earningsandworkinghours/adhocs/005248peopleinemploymentwit haflexibleworkingpatternbygender

ONS (2016b) *SOC 2010.* Available at: https://www.ons.gov.uk/methodology/classificationsandstandards/standardoccupationalclassificationsoc/soc2010.

ONS (2016c) The gender pay gap: what it is and what affects it. Available at: http://visual.ons.gov.uk/the-gender-pay-gap-what-is-it-and-what-affects-it/

ONS (2017a) *Statistical bulletin: Births by parents' characteristics in England and Wales: 2016.* Available at: https://www.ons.gov.uk/peoplepopulationandcommunity/birthsdeathsandmarriages/livebirths/bulletins/birthsbyparentscharacteristicsinenglandandwales/2016.

ONS (2017b) *Statistical bulletin: UK labour market 2018*. Available at: https://www.ons.gov.uk/employmentandlabourmarket/peopleinwork/employmentandemployeetypes/bulletins/uklabourmarket/february2018.

ONS (2017c) *Families and the labour market*. Available at: https://www.ons.gov.uk/employmentandlabourmarket/peopleinwork/employmentandemployeetypes/articles/familiesandthelabourmarketengland/2017.

ONS (2017d) *Dataset: EMP04 Employment by occupation*. Available at: https://www.ons.gov.uk/employmentandlabourmarket/peopleinwork/employmentandemployeetypes/datasets/employmentbyoccupationemp04.

ONS (2017e) *Statistical bulletin: Annual Survey of Hours and Earnings: 2017 provisional and revised 2016 revised results*. Available at: https://www.ons.gov.uk/employmentandlabourmarket/peopleinwork/earningsandworkinghours/bulletins/annualsurveyofhoursandearnings/2017provisionaland2016revisedresults.

Opportunity Now (2014) *Project 28–40 Report*. London: Business in the Community (BiTC).

Pedulla, D. and Thébaud, S. (2015) Can we finish the revolution? Gender, work-family ideals, and institution constraint. *American Sociological Review*, 80 (1).

Perlow, L.A., Kelly, E.L., Correll, S.J. and Williams, J.C. (2014) Toward a model of work redesign for better work and better life. *Work and Occupations*, 41(1): 111–134.

Perrons, D. (2006) Squeezed between two agendas: Work and childcare in the flexible UK. In J. Lewis (ed.) *Children, changing families and welfare states*. Cheltenham: Edward Elgar, pp 243–66.

Perrons, D., Fagan, C., Mcdowell, L., Ray, K. and Ward, K. (2005) Work, life and time in the new economy: an introduction. *Time and Society*, 14(1): 51–64.

Pettinger, L., Parry, J., Taylor, R. and Glucksmann, M. (2005) *A new sociology of work?* Oxford: Blackwell.

Phillips, L. (2008) Flexibility puts women's careers on a knife edge. *People Management*, 24 July.

Phipps, A. (2014) *The politics of the body: Gender in a neoliberal and neoconservative age*. Hoboken: Wiley.

Phoenix, A. (1991) *Young mothers?* Cambridge: Polity Press.

Plantenga, J. and Remery, C. (2015) Provision of childcare services: A comparative review of EU Member States. CESifo DICE Report, 13 (1): 20–24.

Reay, D. (2005) Doing the dirty work of social class? Mothers' work in support of their children's schooling. In L. Pettinger, J. Parry, R. Taylor, M. Glucksmann (eds) *A new sociology of work*. Oxford: Blackwell Publishing.

Ribbens, J. and Edwards, R. (eds) (1998) *Feminist dilemmas in qualitative research*. London: Sage.

Ridgeway, C.L. and Correll, S.J. (2004) Motherhood as a status characteristic. *Journal of Social Issues*, 60(4): 683–700.

Riessman, C.K. (2008) *Narrative methods for the human sciences*. London: Sage.

Ritchie, J., Lewis, J., Mcnaughton Nicholls, C. and Ormston, R. (2014) *Qualitative research practice: A guide for social science students and researchers*. London: Sage.

Robson, C. (2011) *Real world research*. 3rd edn. Chichester: Wiley.

Roehling, P.V., Roehling, M.V. and Moen, P. (2001) The relationship between work–life policies and practices and employee loyalty: a life course perspective. *Journal of Family and Economic Issues*, 22(2): 141–70.

Rottenberg, C. (2013) The rise of neoliberal feminism. *Cultural Studies*, 28(3): 418–437.

Rottenberg, C. (2014) Happiness and the liberal imagination: how superwoman became balanced. *Feminist Studies*, 40(1): 144–68.

Rousseau, D.M., Tomprou, M. and Simosi, M. (2016) Negotiating flexible and fair idiosyncratic deals (i-deals). *Organizational Dynamics*, 45(3): 185–96.

Rubery, J. (2015) Regulating for gender equality: a policy framework to support the universal caregiver vision. *Social Politics*, 22(4): 513–38.

Rubery, J., Keizer, A. and Grimshaw, D. (2016) Flexibility bites back: the multiple and hidden costs of flexible employment policies. *Human Resource Management Journal*, 26(3): 235–51.

Sabelis, I. and Schilling, E. (2013) Editorial. Frayed careers: exploring rhythms of working lives. *Gender, Work & Organization*, 20(2): 127–132.

Saldana, J. (2003) *Longitudinal qualitative research*. Walnut Creek, California: Altamira Press.

Sandberg, S. (2013) *Lean in: Women, work, and the will to lead*. UK: WH Allen.

Schilling, E. (2015) 'Success is satisfaction with what you have': Biographical work-life balance of older female employees in public administration. *Gender, Work & Organization*, 22 (5): 474–494.

Sealy, R.H.V. and Singh, V. (2010) The importance of role models and demographic context for senior women's work identity development. *International Journal of Management Reviews*, 12(3): 284–300.

Sedikides, C. and Brewer, M.B. (2001) *Individual self, relational self, collective self.* Philadelphia, PA: Psychology Press.

Seery, B.L. and Crowley, M.S. (2000) Women's emotion work in the family: relationship management and the process of building father–child relationships. *Journal of Family Issues,* 21(1): 100–127.

Sen, A. (2000) *Development as freedom.* New York: First Anchor Books.

Sennett, R. (1998) *The corrosion of character: The personal consequences of work in the new capitalism.* New York: Norton.

Sheridan, A. (2004) Chronic presenteeism: men's absence from part-time work. *Gender, Work & Organisation,* 11(2): 207–225.

Shockley, K.M. and Allen, T.D. (2007) When flexibility helps: another look at the availability of flexible work arrangements and work–family conflict. *Journal of Vocational Behavior,* 71(3): 479–93.

Silverman, D. (2010) *Doing qualitative research.* London: Sage.

Singh, V., Vinnicome, S., James, K. (2006) Constructing a professional identity: how young female managers use role models. *Women in Management Review,* 21(1).

Slaughter, A.-M. (2012) Why women still can't have it all. *Atlantic Monthly* 85. Available at: https://www.theatlantic.com/magazine/archive/2012/07/why-women-still-cant-have-it-all/309020/

Slaughter, A.-M. (2015) *Unfinished business.* London: Oneworld.

Smith, J. and Gardner, D. (2007) Factors affecting employee use of work–life balance initiatives. *New Zealand Journal of Psychology,* 36(1): 3–12.

Smithson, J. and Stokoe, E.H. (2005) Discourses of work–life balance: negotiating 'genderblind' terms in organizations. *Gender, Work & Organization,* 12(2): 147–68.

Southerton, D. (2009) Re-ordering temporal rhythms: Co-ordinating daily practices in the UK in 1937 and 2000. In E. Shove, F. Trentmann and R. Wilk (eds) *Time, consumption and everyday life: Practice, materiality and culture.* Oxford: Berg.

Southerton, D. and Tomlinson, M. (2005) 'Pressed for time': the differential impacts of a 'time squeeze'. *Sociological Review,* 53(2): 215–239.

Stone, P. (2007) *Opting out? Why women really quit careers and head home.* London: University of California Press.

Stone, P. and Hernandez, L.A. (2013a) The all-or-nothing workplace: flexibility stigma and 'opting out' among professional-managerial women. *Journal of Social Issues,* 69(2): 235–56.

Stone, P. and Hernandez, L.A. (2013b) The all-or-nothing workplace: flexibility stigma and 'opting out' among professional-managerial women. *Journal of Social Issues,* 69(2): 235–256.

Strazdins, L., Clements, M.S., Korda, R.J., Broom, D.H. and D'Souza, R.M. (2006) Unsociable work? Nonstandard work schedules, family relationships, and children's well-being. *Journal of Marriage and Family*, 68(2): 394–410.

Strazdins, L., Griffin, A.L., Broom, D.H., Banwell, C., Korda, R., Dixon, J. et al (2011) Time scarcity: another health inequality? *Environment and Planning A*, 43(3): 545–59.

Strazdins, L., Korda, R.J., Lim, L.L.Y., Broom, D.H. and D'Souza, R.M. (2004) Around-the-clock: parent work schedules and children's well-being in a 24-h economy. *Social Science & Medicine*, 59(7): 1517–27.

Sullivan, O. (2001) *Cross-national changes in time-use: Some sociological (hi)stories re-examined.* Colchester: Institute for Social and Economic Research.

Sullivan, O. and Gershuny, J. (2011) Determinants of total household domestic work/care by household members and paid and unpaid help. Paper at the 33rd IATUR Conference on Time Use Research, 1–3 August, Oxford, UK.

Sullivan, O. and Gershuny, J. (2013) Domestic outsourcing and multitasking: how much do they really contribute? *Social Science Research*, 42(5): 1311–1324.

Sullivan, S.E. and Mainiero, L.A. (2007) The changing nature of gender roles, alpha/beta careers and work–life issues: theory-driven implications for human resource management. *Career Development International*, 12(3): 238–63.

Super, D.E. (1981) Approaches to occupational choice and career development. In A.G. Watts, D. Super and J.M. Kidd (eds) *Career development in Britain.* Cambridge: Hobson.

Sveningsson, S. and Alvesson, M. (2003) Managing managerial identities: organizational fragmentation, discourse and identity struggle. *Human Relations*, 56(10): 1163–1193.

Sweet, S. and Moen, P. (2007) Integrating educational careers in work and family. *Community, Work and Family*, 10(2): 231–50.

Taylor, M. (2017) *Good work: the Taylor Review of modern working practices.* Department for Business, Energy and Industrial Strategy. Available at: https://assets.publishing.service.gov.uk/government/uploads/system/uploads/attachment_data/file/627671/good-work-taylor-review-modern-working-practices-rg.pdf)

Thompson, S. and Ben-Galim, D. (2014) *Childmind the gap: Reforming childcare to support mothers into work.* London: Institute for Public Policy Research (IPPR).

Thomson, R. (2011) Making motherhood work. *Studies in the Maternal*, 3(2): 1–19.

Thomson, R. and Holland, J. (2003) Hindsight, foresight and insight: the challenges of longitudinal qualitative research. *International Journal of Social Research Methodology*, 6(3): 233–44.

Thomson, R., Kehily, M.J., Hadfield, L. and Sharpe, S. (2011) *Making modern mothers*. Bristol: Policy Press.

Timewise Foundation (2013) *The flexibility trap.* London: Timewise Foundation.

Timewise Foundation (2016) *The Timewise flexible jobs index 2016.* Available at: http://timewise.co.uk/wp-content/uploads/2016/05/Timewise_Flexible_Index_2016.pdf.

Timewise (2017) *Flexible working: The talent imperative.* Available at: https://timewise.co.uk/wp-content/uploads/2017/09/Flexible_working_Talent_-Imperative.pdf.

Tomlinson, J. (2004) Perceptions and negotiations of the 'business case' for flexible careers and the integration of part-time work. *Women in Management Review*, 19(8): 413–20.

Tomlinson, J. (2006a) Part-time occupational mobility in the service industries: regulation, work commitment and occupational closure. *Sociological Review*, 54(1): 66–86.

Tomlinson, J. (2006b) Women's work–life balance trajectories in the UK: reformulating choice and constraint in transitions through part-time work across the life course. *British Journal of Guidance and Counselling*, 34(3): 365–82.

Tomlinson, J., Olsen, W. and Purdam, K. (2009) Women returners and potential returners: employment profiles and labour market opportunities – a case study of the United Kingdom. *European Sociological Review*, 25(3): 349–63.

Torrington, D., Hall, L., Tayor, S. and Atkinson, C. (2011) *Human Resource Management*. 8th edn. Harlow: Pearson.

Traister, R. (2012) *Can modern women have it all?* Available at: http://www.salon.com/2012/06/21/can_modern_women_have_it_all/.

Tronto, J.C. (2013) *Caring democracy: Markets equality and justice.* New York: New York University Press.

Tuider, E. (2007) Discourse analysis and biographical research. About the how and why of subject positions. *Forum: Qualitative Social Research*, 8 (2). Available at: http://www.qualitative-research.net/index.php/fqs/article/view/249.

Tutchell, E. and Edmonds, J. (2015) *Man-made: Why so few women are in positions of power.* Farnham: Routledge.

Universities UK (2017) *Patterns and trends in UK higher education 2017.* Available at: http://www.universitiesuk.ac.uk/facts-and-stats/data-and-analysis/Documents/patterns-and-trends-2017.pdf.

Van Amsterdam, N. (2015) Othering the 'leaky body': an autoethnographic story about expressing breast milk in the workplace. *Culture and Organization,* 21(3): 269–287.

Van Daalen, G., Willemsen, T.M. and Sanders, K. (2006) Reducing work–family conflict through different sources of social support. *Journal of Vocational Behavior,* 69(3): 462–76.

Vincent, C., Ball, S.J. and Pietikainen, S. (2004) Metropolitan mothers: mothers, mothering and paid work. *Women's Studies International Forum,* 27(5): 571–587.

Vinnicombe, S., Sealy, R. and Humbert, A.L. (2017) *The female FTSE board report 2017.* UK: Cranfield University and University of Exeter Business School. Available at: file:///Users/zoeyoung/Downloads/Cranfield%20Female%20FTSE%20report%202017.pdf

Voydanoff, P. (2005a) Consequences of boundary-spanning demands and resources for work-to-family conflict and perceived stress. *Journal of Occupational Health Psychology,* 10(4): 491–503.

Voydanoff, P. (2005b) The effects of community demands, resources, and strategies on the nature and consequences of the work–family interface: an agenda for future research. *Family Relations,* 54(5): 583–95.

Voydanoff, P. (2005c) Work demands and work-to-family and family-to-work conflict: direct and indirect relationships. *Journal of Family Issues,* 26(6): 707–26.

Walby, S. (2011) *The future of feminism.* Cambridge: Polity.

Walker, M.U. (2008) *Moral understandings: A feminist study in ethics.* 2nd edn. Oxford: Oxford University Press.

Walkerdine, V., Lucey, H. and Melody, J. (2001) *Growing up girl: Psychosocial explorations of gender and class.* London: Palgrave Macmillan.

Walsh, I. (2008) *Flexible working: A review of how to extend the right to request flexible working to parents of older children.* London: Department for Business Enterprise & Regulatory Reform. Available at: http://webarchive.nationalarchives.gov.uk/20090609082429/http://www.berr.gov.uk/files/file46092.pdf

Walsh, J. (2007) Experiencing part-time work: temporal tensions, social relations and the work–family interface. *British Journal of Industrial Relations,* 45(1): 155–77.

Walters, S. (2005) Making the best of a bad job? Female part-timers' orientations and attitudes to work. *Gender, Work & Organization,* 12(3): 193–216.

Warren, T. (1999) Women in low status part-time jobs: a class and gender analysis. *Sociological Research Online*, 4(4): xvii–xviii.

Webb, J. (2001) Gender, work and transitions in the local state. *Work, Employment and Society*, 15(4): 825–44.

Wengraf, T. (2001) *Qualitative research interviewing: Biographic narrative and semi-structured method.* London: Sage.

West, C. and Zimmerman, D. H. (1987) Doing gender. *Gender and Society*, 1 (2).

Williams, J.C., Blair-Loy, M. and Berdahl, J.L. (2013) Cultural schemas, social class, and the flexibility stigma. *Journal of Social Issues*, 69(2): 209–34.

Wolf, A. (2013) *The XX factor.* London: Profile.

Women and Equalities Committee (2016) *Gender pay gap: Second report of session 2015–2016.* Available at: http://www.parliament.uk/womenandequalities.

Women's Business Council (2012) *Maximising women's contribution to future economic growth.* London: Department for Culture, Media and Sport. Available at: https://www.womensbusinesscouncil.co.uk/wp-content/uploads/2017/02/DCMS_WBC_Full_Report_v1.0-1.pdf.

Wood, A.J. (2016) Flexible scheduling, degradation of job quality and barriers to collective voice. *Human Relations*, 69(10): 1989–2010.

Working Families (2008) *Response to the consultation on implementing the recommendation of Imelda Walsh's independent review.* London: Working Families.

Wrzesniewski, A. and Dutton, J.E. (2001) Crafting a job: revisioning employees as active crafters of their work. *Academy of Management Review*, 26(2): 179–201.

Yin, R.K. (2012) *Application of case study research.* 3rd edn. Thousand Oaks, CA: Sage.

Zelizer, V.a.R. (2007) *The purchase of intimacy.* Princeton, NJ: Princeton University Press.

Zerubavel, E. (1989) *The seven day circle: the history and meaning of the week.* Chicago: University of Chicago Press.

Index